DEVOTIONS FOR CHILDREN

CHOSEN BY GOD

DENISE DE VOS

Copyright © 2024

Denise de Vos
denisedv73@gmail.com

ISBN 978-1-7637012-2-9

All Bible quotes are taken from the New King James version.
All illustrations by Denise de Vos ©

*To my beloved husband,
Bryant, whose unwavering
faith and godly example inspire
our children every day.*

ACKNOWLEDGEMENTS

In crafting these devotions, I am deeply grateful for the invaluable wisdom and insights of numerous ministers. Their sermons have served as the foundation upon which these devotions are built. I extend my heartfelt appreciation to the following ministers. (While some have inspired multiple devotions, others have contributed to a few, each lending their unique perspective and teachings to enrich this collection.)

Rev. A Aasman	Rev. R de Jonge	Rev T van Beek
Rev. D Agema	Rev. E Eikelboom	Rev. A van Delden (Snr)
Rev. H Alkema	Rev. P Feenstra	Rev. W van der Jagt
Rev. RD Anderson	Rev. P Holtvlüwer	Rev. J VanWoudenberg
Rev. C Bosch	Rev. J Moesker	Rev A Veldman
Rev. W Bosch	Rev. E Onderwater	Rev C Vermeulen
Rev. C Bouwman	Rev. A Pol	Rev. R Vermeulen
Dr. R Bredenhof	Rev. D Pol	Rev. I Wildeboer
Dr. W Bredenhof	Rev. D Poppe	Rev. G Visscher
Rev. J deGelder	Rev. J Poppe	Rev. J Visscher
Rev. K Dekker	Dr J Smith	Rev. D Wynia
Rev. W den Hollander	Rev. A Souman	
Rev. R den Hollander	Rev. S 't Hart	

I extend my heartfelt gratitude to Rev. Jopie van der Linde and Rev. Ryan Kampen for their meticulous checking of each devotion prior to its initial publication on the Christian Study Library. Their expertise and commitment to ensuring scriptural accuracy have been invaluable in shaping the content of this book.

I am equally thankful to Natalie van der Heide, and Shiana Holland for their dedicated efforts in reading through and editing the manuscript. Their attention to detail and invaluable input have contributed significantly to the refinement of this work.

Special thanks are extended to Marlene de Vos, Megan de Vos and Klaziena Vermeulen for graciously dedicating their time and effort to reviewing this manuscript prior to publication. I am also grateful to Edwin Visser for his exceptional work in designing and typesetting this book.

If there are still errors in this book, they are solely my responsibility.

PSALM 147:19

He declares His word to Jacob.

READ PSALM 147:12-20

How many copies of the Bible do you have in your house? One, two, twenty, or more than that? Do you ever hold the Bible in your hands and really stop to think about how special it is that you have your own copy of the Bible? In your hand, you are holding God's very own words. This is something very, very special.

Verse nineteen tells us that God chose to give His word to Jacob so that he could know God. You remember some of the stories about Jacob, don't you? He did some sinful things, like tricking his brother Esau into selling his birthright, and lying to his father, Isaac. Yet, God chose to give His special word to Jacob. He wanted Jacob as His child, and He wanted to have a covenant relationship of love with Jacob. He wanted Jacob to know all about Him and His love. That's why He gave Jacob His word.

God wants to have that special relationship with you too. You are God's child. Even though you sin all the time, God has chosen you to belong to Him. And God wants to speak to you, and He wants you to talk to Him. God speaks to you through the Bible. The Bible is God's special gift to you. When you hold the Bible in your hands, you are holding God's very own words to you. In the Bible God tells you all about His love for you, that He sent His Son, Jesus Christ, to die on the cross for you.

God wants you to respond to His word by praying to Him. He wants you to thank Him for His love and blessings. He wants you to tell Him about what is going on in your life.

REFLECTION

Do you remember to treat the Bible as God's special gift to you? What are some ways that you can show that it is God's special gift to you?

EXODUS 2:24

So God heard their groaning, and God remembered His covenant.

READ EXODUS 2:23-25

In the land of Egypt, a new king arose, but he was a horrible ruler. He continued to keep the children of Israel as slaves, treating them very cruelly. Things became so difficult for the Israelites that they cried out to God, begging Him to help. And God heard their groaning and remembered His covenant.

But what does it mean when we say that God remembered His covenant? It does not imply that God forgot about His covenant and suddenly remembered it. You see, God can never forget His covenant. Rather, it means that God listened to the prayers of the Israelites and is ready to take action. He is going to do something for the people of Israel because of the covenant—a special bond of love that exists between God and His chosen ones. Because of His deep love for the children of Israel, God is going to do something extraordinary for them.

What is God going to do for them? He is going to allow them to escape from this slavery—from this cruel king. The amazing thing is that God was already planning for the escape of the Israelites even before they cried out to Him. Eighty years earlier, God had caused little baby Moses to be born. God had given baby Moses special protection from the Nile River by making sure his mum, in faith, made a basket for him so that he didn't drown. And God had made sure that Pharaoh's daughter had come and rescued Moses and brought him up in the palace as her son. God did all this, eighty years earlier because He knew that He was going to use Moses to rescue the Israelites from slavery at this time. God was answering the prayers of the people, even before they had prayed them. Isn't that amazing?

What is even more amazing is that God already started working for your escape from sin—for your salvation—at the beginning of time. Throughout the whole Old Testament, God was working for the coming of Jesus so that He could die on the cross for you. You have salvation because God remembers His covenant of love with you.

REFLECTION

When you pray, do you remember to thank the Lord for your salvation?

EXODUS 3:7

And the Lord said: "I have surely seen the oppression of My people who are in Egypt."

READ EXODUS 3:7–12

Does it sometimes feel like God is far away? Do you wonder if He always hears you? The children of Israel were living in very difficult times. They were being punished and beaten while they were working as slaves, and in their suffering, they cried out to God and asked Him to deliver them.

Did God hear them, or did He ignore their cries? God never ignores the cries of His children, and so God heard and responded to the cries of the Israelites.

As Moses was walking in the desert one day, he saw something very strange. He saw a bush that was on fire, but the fire was not burning up the bush. While he was taking a closer look at the burning bush, God spoke to him. God told Moses that He had seen the suffering of His people, and He had heard their cry. For 400 years the Israelites had been in Egypt, and they had grown into a big nation. But now God was going to deliver them from their suffering and bring them to the Promised Land.

God called them "My people." They were His special children and so God heard them. He knew all their pain and anguish. And God was going to rescue them because of His covenant love and promises to them. Already in Genesis 15:13 and 14 God had said that the Israelites would become slaves in the land of Egypt and that after 400 years God would deliver them, and they would return to the land of Canaan. And God always keeps His promises. Whatever He says He will do, He does. And that is exactly what God tells Moses here. He was going to deliver the Israelites and bring them to the Promised Land.

You are God's child as well, and God hears all your cries too. He knows you very well, and He has given you great promises of love and forgiveness. So always pray to God and cry out to Him. For the sake of Christ, He will always hear you.

REFLECTION

Why does God always hear your prayers?

EXODUS 3:14

*And God said to Moses,
"I AM WHO I AM."*

READ EXODUS 3:13–17

The Lord had revealed Himself to Moses in the burning bush. The Lord told Moses that He was the God of Abraham, Isaac and Jacob. Moses certainly knew who God was. His mother and father had taught him about the Lord.

And yet in this passage, when Moses is instructed by the Lord to go to the people of Israel, he asks the Lord what His name is. He says to the Lord, "When the children of Israel ask what Your name is, what shall I tell them?" This might sound like an odd question because Moses already knew that He was talking to the Lord.

But in those days, names had a lot more meaning than they do today. A name described a person. For example, Eve was the mother of all living, and Abraham was a father of many nations. Moses wants to know what name he should use for God when he tells the people of Israel about Him. They haven't heard from the Lord for 400 years. So, Moses says, "When they say, 'Who is this God?' what shall I tell them?"

God tells Moses that His name is "I am who I am." God is saying that He is true to His word. Whatever He has promised, He will do. In this name God is saying, "I will be with you. I am who I said I am. I will be with My people." This is God's covenant name: Yahweh or Lord (note the capital letters). Whenever you see "Lord," remember that this God is your God. He will always carry out His promises. He is who He says He is.

Sometimes we might be a bit like Moses and want to know who God really is. Sometimes we too forget to trust Him and wonder if He is listening to our prayers. But here we are reminded that the Lord most certainly is who He says He is, and He will keep all His promises to us.

REFLECTION

What does it mean to you when you see the name "Lord"?

EXODUS 4:12

"Now therefore, go and I will be with your mouth and teach you what you shall say."

READ EXODUS 4:10-17

Excuses! We all make excuses! "I'm thirsty" or "I'm just about finished my book" sound like good excuses for not going to bed yet.

But sometimes we also make excuses to get out of doing good things we should be doing. Although you know what the right thing to do is, you are frightened and so you come up with an excuse for not doing it. You really should go and talk to that boy who is all on his own at church, but he might laugh at you when you don't know what to say, and so you make excuses for not doing it.

Moses also made excuses for not going to Pharaoh when God sent him to do so. He told the Lord that it just wouldn't work. "Pharaoh just won't listen to me, Lord." He also tried the excuse of not being able to talk properly: "Lord, I'm not an eloquent speaker." And he tried to get God to send someone else instead of him. He didn't want to do what God called him to do and so came up with many excuses.

But notice how God responded to Moses' excuses. God showed Moses that He is the almighty God. And if He wants something done, it doesn't matter how useless Moses is in himself or how much he feels that he can't do it, God will make it happen. God didn't need Moses to be great in himself, but God was going to work through Moses' weaknesses. God was going to give Moses everything that he needed to go to Pharaoh.

We also don't need to be great in ourselves. No, God will use weak people like us to make happen what He wants to happen. So, stop making excuses for not obeying the Lord. Instead trust in God and He will give you everything you need to obey Him. He will also help you to go to that boy who is all on his own. Trust God. Stop making excuses and obey His commands.

REFLECTION

Why shouldn't you be making excuses?

EXODUS 7:12

*But Aaron's rod swallowed
up their rods.*

READ EXODUS 7:8-12

Slithering snakes on the palace floor—what was going on? What is the Lord showing us in this passage?

Here we see the war between God and Satan. God was about to rescue His people from slavery in Egypt and bring them to the Promised Land. But when God is busy with His people, Satan always tries his hardest to stop God. And that's what we see happening in this passage as well.

Pharaoh demanded that Moses and Aaron produce a miracle to show that they were from God. They had to prove themselves. So they did exactly what God had told them to do. Aaron threw his staff onto the ground and it became a serpent or snake. But then Satan got busy as well and he made Pharaoh and his magicians do the same. Their staffs also became snakes. Satan always wants to make himself look as powerful as God. By doing this he wants us to think that God isn't that great and caring after all, and so Satan is trying to convince people to follow him instead.

Satan is still busy today trying to convince you to follow him. Sometimes we can easily see how Satan is trying to work. Maybe you hear someone blaspheme, or you see world leaders who think that they rule their countries instead of acknowledging that they are under God. At other times Satan can be very sly in how he tries to trick us. Maybe he makes you doubt if God is real or if you are really God's child. This is also Satan at work.

Satan goes around trying to make you follow him, but you must never worry that Satan is stronger than God and that he can take you away from God. You are God's child and God will not let you go.

In Pharaoh's palace God also showed His power over Satan. In a few quick gulps, Aaron's snake swallowed up the snakes of Pharaoh's men. God's kingdom always wins over Satan's kingdom. And so you may know that God will always hold onto you.

REFLECTION

Why did Aaron's snake swallow up the snakes of the magicians?

EXODUS 13:7

"Unleavened bread shall be eaten seven days. And no leavened bread shall be seen among you, nor shall leaven be seen among you in all your quarters."

READ EXODUS 13:3-10

Have you ever watched bread being made? What starts as a small amount of dough, grows bigger and bigger as it is left to rise. Yeast is added to the dough to make the bread rise. This little bit of yeast spreads throughout the whole lump of bread.

Every year, after the Passover, the Israelites in the Old Testament had to celebrate the feast of unleavened bread. Unleavened bread is bread that doesn't have leaven, which is like yeast, in it. For seven days they were only allowed to eat this bread without leaven.

What was God teaching the Israelites with this feast? What is He teaching us? One thing that it taught them was that sin had to be removed from their lives. Just like a little bit of leaven would spread through the whole loaf of bread, so a little bit of sin spreads through our whole life. In the New Testament, the Lord Jesus said that a little bit of sin left unchecked will spread throughout the whole church. Leaven was a picture of this sin spreading throughout everything.

And so, for seven days, they had to get rid of all the leaven from their houses. This showed that they had to get rid of sin completely from their lives. And this is what we must do too. Sin must be removed from our lives.

But while we still live on this earth, we are still sinful. And even though we want to remove sin from our lives, so often we say those nasty things again, or get angry or disobey.

This feast of unleavened bread pointed ahead to Jesus Christ. Even though the Lord Jesus Himself never sinned, He took all our sins on Himself, so that we can be forgiven. And even though we still struggle with sin today, Jesus Christ has removed the leaven, or sin, from our lives and filled us with his Spirit instead. And one day, on the new earth, this will be completely fulfilled. There will be no sin at all left in our lives.

REFLECTION

What does the feast of unleavened bread teach us?

EXODUS 14:22

So the children of Israel went into the midst of the sea on the dry ground.

READ EXODUS 14:21–26

The Israelites were trapped. In front of them was the Red Sea and behind them was the army of the Egyptians. What could they do? There was no way for them to escape. But then God moved the pillar of cloud that had been in front of the Israelites behind them. This showed that God went between the Israelites and the Egyptians. The Lord was not going to leave the Israelites alone but was going to fight the battle for them.

And that is exactly what God did. It was *God* who saved the Israelites. We know the miracle that God did. He made a pathway through the water of the Red Sea for the Israelites to pass through. He provided the light so the Israelites could see as they walked between the walls of water. And God was the one who broke the wheels of the chariots of the Egyptians as they tried crossing to catch the Israelites. God was the one who caused the water to fall back onto the Egyptians so that they all drowned in the Red Sea.

God saved the Israelites.

We are also trapped. No, not between the Red Sea and the Egyptian army, but we are trapped in our sins. Yes, we have been saved by Jesus Christ, but we are still so tempted by sin. So often we do the wrong things. We try so hard to stop sinning, but we do it again and again. We are trapped in our sin and cannot escape. We cannot save ourselves.

But God saves us, just like He saved the Israelites. He fights the battle for us. He rescues us from our sinfulness and makes us His children. Every time again He forgives our sins and helps us fight against them. He helps us love and serve Him. And one day, on the new earth, we will serve Him perfectly without any sin at all.

Let us praise God in our actions and our singing, just like the Israelites sang praises to God for saving them.

REFLECTION

What can we learn about God's love for us from this miracle at the Red Sea?

PSALM 1:2

But his delight is in the law of the Lord, and in His law he meditates day and night.

READ PSALM 1

What makes you happy? Chocolate? Sitting on the couch watching TV? Going on holidays or playing with your friends?

I'm sure a lot of these things make you happy. The Lord gives us many blessings in life that we are allowed to enjoy. But do you know what the Psalmist says makes him happy—very happy? He says that he delights in the law of the Lord. God's Word and commandments give him great delight.

What about you? Does God's Word make you happy? Do you enjoy reading your Bible? Often we can think that other things make us a lot happier than God's commandments. We'd prefer to be watching a movie than reading the Bible.

But God warns us in this Psalm to be very careful about the things that we learn from the world. We will be blessed if we *don't* walk in the way of the ungodly or stand in the path of sinners. This means that the world is trying to tell us how to spend our money, what food we should eat, where we should go on holidays and what clothes we should buy. But we shouldn't be learning these things from the world, but instead we should be learning these things from God Himself. True happiness can be found in obeying the Lord.

The problem is that we so often want to do what the world suggests rather than what God tells us. Sometimes we just want to think about ourselves even though God tells us to love others more than ourselves. Sometimes we just want to get angry at our parents even though God tells us to respect them. Even though we love the Lord, so often we still love sin so much.

The Lord knows how hard this is for us, so He reminds us in this Psalm to delight in His law—to obey Him. Enjoy reading the Bible and learning, not only about your sinfulness, but also about God's grace and love in sending Jesus, who never sinned, to be your Saviour.

REFLECTION

How can you make Bible reading something that makes you happy?

PSALM 2:1

Why do the nations rage, and the people plot a vain thing?

READ PSALM 2

Sometimes it seems that lots of bad things are happening in the world, doesn't it? Governments pass new laws that we know the Lord is not pleased with. We hear about fights and wars and other things. When you hear these things, do you get a little worried sometimes?

We know from the book of Acts that Psalm 2 was written by David. We don't know when, but there were many times when other kings and rulers planned different things to try to stop David from being king. And in this Psalm, David is asking why they were doing that? Why do the other rulers get together to try and stop the Lord's anointed from being king? Don't they know that they are fighting against the Lord, and no one can win against the Lord? The other rulers can do whatever they like, but God is the one in heaven who is in control of all things. He is the one who sits in heaven and laughs at them for trying to destroy His anointed king.

This Psalm doesn't speak only of David, but it also points ahead to Christ. Christ is the anointed King. He is the Ruler of the whole world. Satan tried everything he could throughout the whole Old Testament to stop Jesus from being born, but God laughed at his attempts and didn't let him win.

And today Satan is still trying hard to stop God's children from serving this King Jesus. But still today God won't let Satan win. You are God's covenant child. Jesus even prayed that you would be kept from the evil one, which we read in John 17.

So you do not need to worry if you see bad things happening in the world. Instead remember that the Lord is the mighty King of the whole world. People in this world today can only do as much as God allows them. Christ remains King. He remains in control of everything. And He holds you in His arms and carries you every day. He will not let Satan take you from Him.

REFLECTION

Why don't you need to worry when you see bad things happening in the world?

1 CORINTHIANS 1:4

I thank my God always concerning you for the grace of God which was given to you by Christ Jesus.

READ 1 CORINTHIANS 1:4-9

Are you a thankful person? More specifically, are you thankful for the church? Are you thankful that you can belong to the church? Maybe you are, or maybe you sometimes hear people say negative things about the church and you wonder if the church is really something to be thankful for.

The apostle Paul knew many bad things that were happening in the church at Corinth. In his letters to this church, he talks about many sins like arguing, getting drunk at the Lord's Supper, serving idols, and having sinful lifestyles. If you heard about these sins in your church, how would you pray for the church? We would probably tell the Lord about all these sins and ask the Lord to fix things. We probably wouldn't even think about thanking the Lord for such a church, would we?

But listen to how Paul prays for this sinful church at Corinth. He begins by thanking God for the grace He has given to them. He thanks the Lord that the people have heard and believed the good news about Jesus Christ.

This doesn't mean that Paul ignored their sins. In fact, he told them many times to turn away from their sins and focus on serving the Lord. But Paul can still thank the Lord for the church at Corinth because he knew that the church belonged to the Lord and that God was working in the people of the church.

Christ died on the cross for the people of the church at Corinth, just like He died on the cross for you and the people of your church. God loves the church, and it is made up of His special people who receive His grace. We all need God's grace just as much as everyone else in our church.

So remember, you can always be thankful for the church because it is a place where you can learn about God, be with other believers, and grow in your faith. Even when there are problems or sins in the church, we can still thank God for His love and grace towards His people.

REFLECTION

Why can you always thank the Lord for the church?

1 CORINTHIANS 10:31

Therefore, whether you eat or drink, or whatever you do, do all to the glory of God.

READ 1 CORINTHIANS 10:23-33

The world around us tells us to think about ourselves first. We need to do things that feel good for ourselves. We need to look after ourselves first. But is this what God teaches us? No! 1 Corinthians 10:31 tells us to do all things to God's glory. That is our purpose on earth: to praise and glorify God.

So how exactly can you glorify God? What does it mean to give God glory?

By having faith, we glorify God. When we believe in God, when we love Him, when we trust His promises to us, then we are giving God glory. God is praised in the faith that we have.

God also receives glory when we worship Him. Actually, this is probably the most important way to glorify God. Yes, God loves to hear us sing praises to Him, to worship Him in church and to thank Him for His blessings. He loves it when we take time to read His Word, and when we pray to Him. We can glorify God when we put time aside to worship Him.

God is also glorified when we obey Him in our everyday tasks. God is glorified in what we do and in how we do it.

In Corinth, some people were focused on their own glory instead of God's. Paul gives an example. Some people, knowing that idols weren't real anyway, wanted to eat meat that had been offered to idols. And Paul agrees with them that they are allowed to eat that meat. But Paul also tells them that if someone doesn't want them to eat the meat offered to idols, then out of love and kindness for the other person, they shouldn't eat it. By insisting on their own rights and saying, "I'm going to eat it anyway, just because I can," they were not showing glory to God. They were thinking of themselves.

So, as you do different things during the day, act in a selfless, kind and loving way. Instead of seeking praise for yourself, you should try to think about others, even if it means giving things up for them. Then you are bringing glory to God!

REFLECTION

How can you give God glory?

1 CORINTHIANS 15:57

But thanks be to God, who gives us the victory through our Lord Jesus Christ.

READ 1 CORINTHIANS 15:56-58

Have you ever been stung by a bee? Although a bee sting hurts, it's not dangerous for most people. But for people who are allergic to bees, the sting can make them very, very sick. Imagine that a scientist could make a bee that didn't have a sting. Then these bees without stings would no longer be dangerous. They would be disarmed bees.

Paul tells us that death has a sting. What does he mean by this?

The sting of death that Paul speaks about is sin. It is sin that gives death its power. It is because of sin that we die. If we had never sinned there would be no death. And how do we know about sin? From the law of the Lord. Our sin and the law are the two things that give death its power and sting.

But Christ has come to deal with these two things that give death its power and sting. The first is sin. Christ never sinned, but He paid for our sins. The other thing is God's law. Christ obeyed this law perfectly. So death has lost both its sting and power. Just like a bee without a sting would no longer be harmful, so death without its sting is no longer our enemy.

We do not need to fear death. Through the Lord Jesus Christ, we now have victory over death. Oh yes, unless Christ comes back earlier, we will still die one day, but our death will be the beginning of our eternal life with God.

Paul then tells us that because death is no longer our enemy, we need to continue to do our work for the Lord. This means that you need to be focused on the Lord as you do your activities throughout the day. If you are at school, at home, playing with friends, helping your parents, visiting your grandparents, or talking to your neighbours about the Lord, the work you are doing is not a waste of time but a way that you can serve the Lord.

REFLECTION

What does it mean to you that death has lost its sting?

EPHESIANS 1:1

To the saints who are in Ephesus, and faithful in Christ Jesus.

READ EPHESIANS 1:1-6

Paul was in prison when he wrote this letter to the people in Ephesus. He had not been sent to prison because he had stolen goods or killed or hurt anyone. No, he had been sent to prison because he was preaching about the Lord Jesus Christ. Satan was working hard to stop people from hearing about the Word of God. Satan did not want people to listen to Paul's preaching, and that is why he made someone arrest Paul and put him in prison.

But God is far more powerful than Satan, so God did not allow the fact that Paul was in prison to stop His Word from going out. Instead, Paul used the time he had in prison to write to the people in the churches that he had visited before. He was an apostle of Jesus Christ. This means that he had been sent by Jesus Christ to preach His Word. And so, Paul does that from his prison cell.

He calls the people in the church in Ephesus *saints*. To be a saint, means to be holy. To be holy does not mean that they did not sin, but that they were God's special possession. God loved them and they were His children. They were saved from Satan and belonged to God instead. These words are written for you as well. You are also a saint of the Lord Jesus. You belong to God. You are His special possession. You are His child. And so, you too belong to God and not to Satan.

And the greeting that Paul gives to the Ephesians from God is also the greeting He gives to you today. We are greeted with these words at the beginning of every worship service: Grace to you and peace from God our Father and the Lord Jesus Christ. The Lord gives us His grace. This means that the Lord loves us and, even though we are sinful, He continues to forgive us because of the work of Jesus Christ. And with the grace of the Lord, we also get peace, peace because we belong to the Lord.

REFLECTION

What do you find special in this opening of the letter to the Ephesians?

We love Him because He first loved us

1 JOHN 4:19

EPHESIANS 2:8

For by grace you have been saved through faith, and that not of yourselves; it is a gift of God.

READ EPHESIANS 2:1-10

What is the best gift you have ever been given? Maybe a new bike, a game, or a book? Or possibly a wonderful holiday with your family? We have all received some wonderful gifts in our life. In these verses, Paul tells us about a gift God gives us. God gives each of His children this wonderful gift. This gift is that we are saved through faith in Jesus Christ.

Why is our salvation such a great gift? Does it change anything in our lives? Yes, it certainly does! Without this gift from God, Paul says, we would all be dead in sin. If we didn't belong to God, we would hate God. We would want to do the opposite of what God tells us to do. Without this gift of salvation, we would want to listen to the devil, Satan, and do what he says. Satan would be happy because he's trying to get as many people as he can to serve him. He would be very happy if we all followed him. He would be happy to take us all to hell with him. And without God's gift, we would all be happy to follow Satan all the way to hell.

But God didn't want to leave His children in the hands of Satan. He didn't want us to stay dead in our sins, and so He sent His Son, His beloved Son, to die, to pay for our sins. All our sins were put to death with Christ on the cross. He suffered the eternal punishment instead of us. And He rose again, showing that God was happy with His payment for sin.

The Bible says that we too are raised and sit together in heavenly places with Jesus. This means that spiritually we have been raised and made alive. We no longer belong to Satan, but to Jesus Christ. Through Christ we now have power over sin. Yes, we do still sin, but we are also forgiven in Christ. God has given us the gift of salvation. We belong to Christ and not to Satan!

REFLECTION

What is the best gift you have ever been given?

EPHESIANS 2:22

In whom you also are being built together for a dwelling place of God in the Spirit.

READ EPHESIANS 2:19-22

Are you part of the church? The Lord wants us to belong to the church, to be part of the communion of saints. In these verses, he tells us how He wants the communion of saints to work.

Paul says that we were aliens or foreigners. By this he means that of ourselves we do not belong to God. Of ourselves we would not even want to be part of God's family or church. We would hate God. But Christ has come into our lives. He has paid for our sins. He has died for us and has made us part of God's church. We now belong to Him.

Paul gives us three pictures of what the church should look like. He says we are fellow citizens. A citizen is generally someone who lives in a certain country. If you live in Australia, you are probably a citizen of Australia. If you live in South Africa, you are probably a citizen of South Africa. You belong there together with the other people who live there.

Paul also says that we are of the same household. We, together with the others in the church, belong to the same family. Through Christ, God has been made our Father. And God had made everyone else in the church your brothers and sisters. In families we do things together. We eat and play games together. We laugh and cry together. Families are very close. We must have a close relationship with our brothers and sisters in the church too.

Paul also gives the picture of a building or temple. Jesus Christ is the first stone, and we are all built on Him. He gives us our strength. Together we are the temple of God. God the Holy Spirit actually lives in each of our hearts. He makes His home in us.

And so, God wants us to live with our brothers and sisters in the church. Together we must love each other and help each other serve the Lord. We are all heading to eternal life together.

REFLECTION

What does it mean to you that you belong to the church?

EPHESIANS 3:19

To know the love of Christ which passes knowledge.

READ EPHESIANS 3:14–21

Our life can be a little bit like a home renovation. We are broken and need to be changed. From ourselves we are completely broken and sinful, but God is busy changing us.

But this change can only happen if we have Christ dwelling or living in us. And we can only have Christ dwelling in us by prayer. That's why Paul is praying here for Christ to live in the people of Ephesus.

And Christ does live in you. As God's children you have the power of Christ in you. But do you feel that? Do you experience Christ's love in your life? Do you really know how much Christ loves you? That's the next thing Paul prays for, that the people will know Christ's love. Christ's love is so great that He can give us more than we even ask Him. Sometimes we wonder if God can help us when we keep getting tempted to sin. Or we wonder if Christ can bring our brother or sister who has turned away from the Lord back to Himself. Or we wonder if God can take away our sickness or anxiety. Paul prays for us, so that we may know that Christ is so great that He can give us whatever we ask. This doesn't mean that God will always give us what we ask. Sometimes it is better for us not to have these things, and because God loves us, He won't always give us these things. But that doesn't change how much love Christ has for us!

Paul prays for us to show the same love to others that we know from Christ; this should be our prayer also. It's so easy to love those who have the same interests as you, but you must pray that you can love all people. In this way we bring glory to God.

Yes, big renovations or changes need to happen in our lives. But that is only possible through prayer, prayer that the power of Christ will dwell in us and make us more like Him.

REFLECTION

How can you see the love of Christ in your life?

EPHESIANS 4:11

And He Himself gave some to be apostles, some prophets, some evangelists, and some pastors and teachers.

READ EPHESIANS 4:7-16

Have you ever received a gift on your birthday? Maybe a new book or a new toy? It's always nice to receive gifts, but did you know that the Lord has also given you gifts? And unlike some of the gifts you receive on your birthday, you need these gifts from the Lord! You need them to serve the Lord and to serve others.

Verse 11 speaks about some of the different gifts God gives to people. Some people are given the gift of being apostles, some teachers and some pastors. But even if you're too young to be a teacher or minister, you still have been given gifts by the Lord that you must use to serve Him. Maybe you're good at organising things or listening to your friends. Maybe you have the gift of cheering others up when they're sad or being a good leader. Or maybe you have a sensitive heart that helps you see when others are hurting, so you can ask them how they're doing.

Did you notice that verse 16 says, "By which each part does its share"? That means every single person in the church is needed! Think about your body. You have a nose, an ear, an eye, a foot, a heart, and lungs. Each body part is different, but each one is needed. If you didn't have your lungs, you couldn't breathe. If you didn't have your heart, you couldn't have blood pumping around your body. Every single body part is needed to make a complete body. In the same way, everybody in the church is different, but every single person is needed. Nobody can say that they aren't needed. God has put us all together, with our different gifts, to make one body, one church.

Christ has given us gifts to share with others. So use the gifts that God has given you to serve Him.

REFLECTION

What gifts do you have? If you aren't sure, ask your parents or friends to help you work out what they are.

EPHESIANS 4:14

That we should no longer be children, tossed to and fro and carried about with every wind of doctrine.

READ EPHESIANS 4:7–16

Do you think that you know a lot about the Bible? Maybe you think you are getting close to knowing most of what the Lord teaches you about Himself.

Well, the Lord tells you that you need to grow in your knowledge of Him. The apostle Paul tells the Ephesians that they are not to be like children any longer. Does this mean that God is not interested in children? No, not at all! There is nothing wrong with being a child. And you will remember that Jesus took the children into His arms and blessed them. He said that the kingdom of heaven belongs to children. Yes, children are precious to the Lord and certainly part of His covenant people. In other places in the Bible we are even told to be like babies. Just like a baby craves its mother's milk, so we must crave God's Word.

So what does Paul mean then when he says that we are no longer to be like children? Children sometimes believe whatever they are told. They can be told one thing, and they will believe that, and then told something else, which they will also believe. Children can easily be tricked.

And so, Paul means that when it comes to the truth of the Bible and to our faith in Jesus Christ, we must stand fast. We have to know the Bible, study it, and believe it—all of it! We must not be fooled into believing heresies and other false things. But we must believe the truth—the Bible—always.

And in this way, we can't remain like children in our faith. We need to grow in our knowledge of the Bible, in our love for Christ. You can do this because you are connected to Christ your head. He is leading you. He is guiding you. So listen to Him. Read His Word. Study the Bible. Pray, and pray some more. Ask God to help you to believe His Word always.

REFLECTION

Why is it important to grow in your knowledge of the Bible?

EPHESIANS 4:32

*And be kind to one another,
tenderhearted, forgiving one another,
even as God in Christ forgave you.*

READ EPHESIANS 4:25–32

Your brother has annoyed you again and so you get angry at him. Or someone at school has commented in a nasty way on your clothes and so you don't want to talk to her again. Or maybe you wish that your sibling will be punished harshly for the way they left you to clean up all the toys again. These feelings of anger, wrath and malice are so common for all of us. Yet God teaches us in these verses that we have to put all of these feelings far away from us. "Do not let the sun go down on your anger." Sometimes this can be so hard to do. Sometimes we actually *want* to be angry or annoyed at someone else because we think that they deserve it.

So, what should you do when you have these angry thoughts and feelings? You need to pray to the Lord. You need to ask the Lord to remove those feelings and help you to be loving and kind. Verse 32 says, "Be kind to one another, tenderhearted, forgiving one another, even as God in Christ forgave you." You won't be able to do this by yourself. It's a difficult thing to do and that's why you need the power of the Holy Spirit to help you in this. That's why you need to pray.

And the Lord will help you. Through the working of the Spirit, God will take away those feelings of anger and hatred. If you look at the words of King David in Psalm 4, you will see that David had many reasons to be angry at his enemies. And yet he prayed to the Lord and the Lord heard him. He put his trust in God and God took his anger away, so he could sleep in peace.

When we look at all our own sins and remember that Jesus Christ died for them, then we will also be willing to be kind and forgiving towards others.

REFLECTION

What should you do if you feel angry at someone else?

EPHESIANS 5:8

For you were once darkness, but now you are light in the Lord. Walk as children of light.

READ EPHESIANS 5:7-14

Do you know what darkness means in the Bible? It means things that are evil, bad or against God. Light, on the other hand, represents things that are good: truth, holiness, and righteousness. God Himself is light.

Here God says to us, "once you were darkness, but now you are light." How can God say that we are light? Does this mean that we do not sin anymore, but instead only show truth, holiness, and righteousness in our lives?

God calls us light because He lives with us. He has sent His Holy Spirit to live in our hearts. And because God Himself is light, then we too are people of the light. God promises that He will help us to overcome darkness through His Spirit.

Because we are children of the light, we must live in a way that shows this. Then we will shine to the world around us, and they will be able to see that we belong to God.

But how can you know how God wants you to live? By reading the Bible. The Bible has been given to us as a light that shows us the right path to take. It teaches us how to live as children of God, as children of the light. And then we must pray for the Holy Spirit to help us live as children of the light.

Sometimes there can be sins in our lives that no one knows about, or that we enjoy doing. Sometimes we do not want to give up on our sins. But God tells us here that even our secret sins are known to God. No sin is hidden from Him. The Bible shows us our sins. And we should want to know our sins so that we can confess them to God and ask for forgiveness. So, if you are struggling with something, speak to a parent or another older person and ask them to help you fight against your sins. Then you can pray together and ask God to forgive you (and He certainly will) and help you to live as a child of the light.

REFLECTION

What does it mean that you are light in the Lord?

EPHESIANS 5:15

See then that you walk circumspectly, not as fools but as wise.

READ EPHESIANS 5:15-21

A tightrope walker is someone who walks across a rope which is tied tightly, high above the ground. A lot of skill and years of practice are needed for someone to learn how to tightrope walk. A tightrope walker needs to walk very carefully, paying close attention every time he puts his foot on the rope. He also needs light to be able to see where he is going. He needs to be focused on where he is heading.

Paul tells us that we have to walk circumspectly. The word *circumspectly* is a word that is similar to the English word "acrobat" or "tightrope walker." So maybe Paul had this in mind when he said to walk circumspectly or carefully.

Paul is writing this to Christians. They lived in an evil time. They were being persecuted for serving the Lord, and wicked things were happening around them. And not only were bad things happening around them, but just like us, their hearts were sinful. Of themselves they wouldn't even want to serve the Lord. And yet the Lord had taken them out of the kingdom of Satan and brought them into His kingdom. He had made them His children. He has made us His children.

As children of God, we need to use every day that God gives us to serve Him. For an acrobat to learn to walk a tightrope, he needs to train hard and listen carefully to people who have done it before him. And so, as Christians we need to train hard and listen to those who teach us. We train by reading God's Word and listening to our minister, parents, teachers, and others who teach us how to serve God. We need to spend a lot of time learning what God's will is.

Just like the tightrope walker needs to be careful where he steps, we need to be careful what we do in life. We must do all things to the praise and glory of God. Of course, we can't do this ourselves, and that is why the Lord has filled us with His Spirit to help us walk carefully.

REFLECTION

What does Paul mean when he says we have to walk carefully?

EPHESIANS 5:19

...singing and making melody in your heart to the Lord.

READ EPHESIANS 5:19-21

Because we are God's children, He has filled each of us with the Holy Spirit. The Holy Spirit has been given to us by God to live in our hearts to help us serve God.

Being filled with the Spirit means that we want to worship God. One way that we can do this is by singing psalms or hymns. God is praised and worshipped by our singing. Paul says that we should make melody in our hearts to God. So, our singing should be from the heart. We should think about what we are singing.

Sometimes when we sing, we are also encouraging others to praise or trust God. Think of Psalm 150, where we encourage everyone to praise God. Singing is a wonderful way to worship God together with others.

The Spirit also teaches us to give thanks to God. Paul says to give thanks always. We cannot choose to be thankful sometimes and then not at other times, but we must give thanks always. Sometimes when things are hard, we do not feel like thanking God, but there is always something you can thank God for. You are God's child, and He loves and cares for you. He forgives your sins and promises you eternal life with Him. That is surely a reason to thank God. And that is why we are told to give thanks in all things. No matter what we are going through, we should always still thank God for His love and grace.

As God's children we are also told to submit to each other in fear of God. This means that we should always show love and kindness to others. You may think that someone else does not deserve your love or your kindness because they are not always kind to you. But God does not want you to be kind to others because they are worthy of this kindness, but for Christ's sake. Think of the love and kindness Christ showed you by dying on the cross when you did not deserve it. And so, for Christ's sake you must show love and kindness to others.

REFLECTION

How does the Spirit help you serve God?

EPHESIANS 6:18

*Praying always with all prayer
and supplication in the Spirit.*

READ EPHESIANS 6:10–18

Do you think about Satan often? Maybe you do, or maybe you don't. But know this well: Satan thinks about you often. He is thinking about you because he is trying hard to get you to listen to him instead of to God. He is attacking you every day.

Let me tell you some ways that Satan attacks you. Very often he uses lies. You might think that you don't really have to listen to your parents because they don't understand you anyway. That's a lie from Satan. If you tell your siblings that Mum said something she didn't, it is a lie from Satan.

Satan also uses temptations to cause you to sin. You might be tempted to greedily take the biggest piece of cake or to get angry at your brother or sister. These are temptations to make you sin.

At times, Satan uses persecution to try to make you forget about God or to stop praising Him. It might just be your friends calling you names for trying to obey the Lord. But that might be enough for you to stop praising God.

There are many other ways that Satan attacks you every day. So what should you do about it? You should pray! The Lord is majestic and powerful, and so you can ask Him to destroy the works of Satan. And He will certainly listen to you. That's why Jesus came to earth—to destroy the work of Satan. That's why He died on the cross, rose again and ascended into heaven. And He sends His Word and Spirit to you so that you too can fight against Satan. When you listen to God's Word and live by it, Satan is powerless. Through the power of the Holy Spirit, you can fight against the attacks of Satan.

REFLECTION

Do you remember to pray, asking the Lord to help you fight against Satan? Can you think of some ways in which Satan attacks you?

PSALM 27:4

One thing I have desired of the Lord, that will I seek. That I may dwell in the house of the Lord all the days of my life, to behold the beauty of the Lord.

READ PSALM 27:1-6

Do you ever stop and see the beauty around you? Do you admire the mother duck with her ducklings following close behind? Do you feel the softness of the petals on a flower? There is so much beauty in the world around us.

But even more beautiful than all these things, is the God who made them. The Lord God created all these things, but He Himself is even more beautiful. David in Psalm 27 talks about beholding or looking at the beauty of the Lord. What does David mean? David had never actually seen God, just like we cannot see God. And yet he speaks about seeing the beauty of the Lord.

Just before these words, David speaks about having one desire. There is one thing that he really wants more than anything else. This one thing is very important to him. The one thing that David wants is to dwell in the house of the Lord every single day.

In the temple was the altar, and on that altar, sacrifices were made to the Lord. David knew when he saw the altar and the sacrifices in the temple that God loved him, even though he was sinful. David was able to know of God's love for him, because one day Jesus would come and die for his sins. And that is the beauty of the Lord that David loves to see.

He loves to see God's loving kindness to sinful people, His care over His own, His Fatherly love, grace and forgiveness. That is the beauty of the Lord. That is the one thing that David wants to focus on every single day.

Is that also the one thing you want to focus on every day? Is that the most important thing for you? Is God and His love and grace to you more important to you than your toys or computer games or movies? Is God more important than your books or your holidays? Do you make time every single day to read God's Word and pray to Him?

REFLECTION

How can you take the time every day to think about the love and beauty of the Lord?

DEUTERONOMY 6:4

*Hear, O Israel: The L*ORD *our God, the L*ORD *is one!*

READ DEUTERONOMY 6:4-9

Do your parents ever ask you, "Did you hear me?" If they use an angry tone, it probably means that you have been asked to do something, but didn't listen. When they ask if you have heard them, they're not only asking if you have listened to their words, but also if you have obeyed them.

To "hear" in the Bible means more than just to listen to the words. It means to know and obey. What follows is very important and must be obeyed. "Hear, O Israel: The LORD our God, the LORD is one!" The Israelites, and all of us, must know that the LORD is one. This means that there is only one God. The gods of the nations are not gods at all. They can't do anything at all. God is the only one who must be worshipped.

The LORD, the covenant God, is also *one* in the sense that He has one purpose and direction. He doesn't change His mind or get moody. Not at all. The LORD is one, consistent, always the same. He is the same yesterday, today and tomorrow. He is a God who we can count on. We can believe in His promises.

It is this God that we are commanded to love with our whole heart, soul and strength. We can love Him with our whole being, in every part of our life. You can't just love the LORD on Sundays and forget about Him during the rest of the week. You must love the LORD while you are out and about, while you are at school, while you are at a party, when you are in your bedroom, or when you are on the computer. We must love God completely.

To love God in this way you must know Him and have a personal relationship with Him. You can't love someone that you don't know. So, take the time to read and study the Bible. Read it every day and pray to God, asking Him to help you to know Him better.

REFLECTION

What does it mean that the LORD is one?

DEUTERONOMY 11:10

For the land which you go to possess is not like the land of Egypt from which you have come.

READ DEUTERONOMY 11:8-12

The Israelites had been wandering in the desert for forty years and were standing at the entrance to the Promised Land. Before they entered, Moses gave a farewell speech.

After Moses reminded the Israelites of God's many blessings in the past, he told them that Canaan, the land they were going to enter was not like the land of Egypt where they had come from. Even though Egypt did not receive much rain, the food still grew very well. The people were able to use water from the Nile River, especially when it overflowed, to water their crops. They would dig valleys and trenches in the ground to direct the flood water to the places where the crops were growing. So even without the rain, they were able to have good vegetable gardens.

Canaan, however, would not be like that. In Canaan they would need to wait for rain from heaven for their vegetables to grow. They wouldn't be able to get water from a flooding river but would simply have to trust in the Lord to send the rain. But Canaan would still be better than Egypt, because they could be sure that the Lord would care for them. The Lord's eyes would be on His people every day of the year. He would care for them and give them everything they needed.

And so they didn't need to worry as they entered the Promised Land because they could trust the Lord their God. He would provide for them always.

And that is exactly what the Lord says to us too. The words that Moses spoke to the people of Israel are also for us. The eyes of the Lord our God are always on us, from the beginning of the year to the very end of the year. Isn't this wonderful? Because you are God's covenant child, you do not need to worry about the future, but you may know that God will be with you every day. And even when things do get hard for you, trust in the Lord. He is caring for you!

REFLECTION

How does God care for you?

The Lord's mercies are new every morning

LAMENTATIONS 3:23

JAMES 1:2

My brethren, count it all joy when you fall into various trials.

READ JAMES 1:2-8

Have you ever had something difficult happen in your life? Maybe you had a close friend or relative die, or you've been very sick yourself. Maybe you feel very lonely because no one wants to be your friend, or maybe you suffer from panic attacks.

These things are various trials that God puts in your life. In this verse we are told to count it all joy when we meet trials. Really? Do you really need to feel joy when you are going through difficult times?

The Lord doesn't mean that you can't feel sad and be struggling during these difficult times. Of course you can. What does God mean, then, when He says that we should count it all joy? He means that it is a joy for a Christian to know that God is busy in their life during these trials. He is busy growing your faith. He is using these difficult things to make you grow closer to Him. Often we pray more when things are hard. Trials often make us read the Bible more and trust in the Lord more. I'm sure you can remember crying out to God when that friend died, or when you were lonely. Yes, difficult times help us grow closer to the Lord.

And it is because we are growing closer to the Lord, reading His Word more and concentrating more while praying that we can find joy during trials. It is the fact that we are learning to trust the Lord more that gives us joy.

James says that when we learn to trust God more, something wonderful happens – we become steadfast. By this he means that the more we trust God, the more we learn to pray to Him. And then when the Lord puts new trials in our lives, we can keep trusting the Lord. So yes, you can struggle when you go through hard times, but let those struggles bring you closer to the Lord, and count it joy that the Lord is busy in your life.

REFLECTION

Can you think of a time that the Lord has been helping you learn to pray more?

JAMES 1:5

If any of you lacks wisdom, let him ask of God, who gives to all liberally and without reproach, and it will be given to him.

READ JAMES 1:5-8

Are you wise? Do you have a lot of wisdom or do you lack wisdom? Here we are told that if we lack wisdom, we must ask God for it and He will give it to us.

But what is wisdom? The Bible teaches us that the fear of the Lord is the beginning of wisdom. We know that to fear God means to know and believe in Him, to stand in awe of God, to love Him and to know the Bible. Wisdom, then, is to use those things that we know about God to help us make decisions about what we do every day. That sounds complicated, doesn't it? Simply put, to have wisdom means to know how to act in our everyday life in a way that will be pleasing to the Lord.

If you are struggling with your schoolwork, to have wisdom would mean to pray to God for help and then to be willing to ask the teacher to help you. Wisdom is trusting God when you are sick or lonely. Wisdom is joyfully obeying your parents when they ask you to clean your room. Wisdom is trusting that it is for the best if you cannot go to a friends party, even if you are upset. Wisdom is praying for trust in God when you are overly worried. Wisdom is having joy, even in hard times (v. 2)

Now do you think you are wise? We all act in unwise ways. We all lack wisdom. And that's why we are told to ask God for wisdom. And He has promised to give it to us generously. This means God, in love, is very happy to give us wisdom. But we need to ask Him for it. We need to pray for wisdom. So next time you need to do something, or next time you are struggling, ask God for wisdom before you act. He will help you make wise decisions. Never act before praying for wisdom. Then, yes, you will be praying many times during the day, but you can pray as you play and work, asking God to help you act in a way that is pleasing to Him.

REFLECTION

What must you do to get wisdom?

JAMES 4:15

Instead you ought to say, "If the Lord wills, we shall live and do this or that."

READ JAMES 4:13-17

So often you have to make plans for the rest of the day or the week or the next month. You might be planning to go fishing or shopping. You may be planning to go on holidays or to your brother's wedding. You probably have many plans for the times ahead of you. But do you realise that everything you plan only happens if the Lord wills it to happen? You can plan whatever you like, but it will only happen if the Lord allows it to happen.

That's what James teaches us in this passage. When you are planning something, always remember that the Lord could have different plans for you. This became very clear to everyone during the coronavirus pandemic. We had been going to church every Sunday for years, and suddenly we couldn't anymore. We had always been able to go to school, and suddenly we couldn't anymore. We had made many plans, but the Lord stopped them all. The Lord's plans were different than ours.

Always remember what James tells us. Remember that your life is like a vapour, or a mist. By this James reminds us that our life is so short. Compared to living forever, even a life of 80 or 90 years is short. So use this short life to serve the Lord. Live every day for the Lord.

Then you can plan to do activities. You can plan to go to church, to go to a wedding or to go on holidays, but when you plan, always remember that God is in control of your life. He may have different plans than you have. This is a great comfort because God's plans are always better than our plans. He is the creator of the whole universe, and He is your God. He loves you as His covenant child. You are His, so whatever His plans are for your life, they will be for your good. It may not always feel this way to us, but you can trust God. After all, He sent His Son to die for you, so He will also be with you in whatever plans He has for you.

REFLECTION

Why should you say, "The Lord willing," when you plan to do something?

JAMES 5:7

Therefore be patient, brethren, until the coming of the Lord.

READ JAMES 5:7-8

After a farmer plants seeds in the ground, he has to be very patient. He needs to wait for the rain to come early in the season to wet the seeds so that they can germinate. He also needs to wait for rain later in the season so that the crops can grow and mature. The farmer needs to wait patiently, relying on the Lord to send the rain. He can't do anything to make the rain come, so he must simply trust in the Lord. But that doesn't mean that the farmer does nothing while he waits. He spends his time fertilizing the crops and keeping out the weeds and other pests.

James tells his readers that they must wait patiently too, just like the farmer. Many of James' readers were suffering in different ways. Maybe they were being persecuted, suffering from sicknesses or from a lack of food and clothing. James tells them to be patient in all these troubles, no matter what they are. They need to be patient, knowing that the Lord will return one day. Just like the farmer needs to patiently trust in the Lord, so they need to trust in Him.

They can be patient in their troubles because they know what the end will be. After all their suffering and pain, the end will be the return of the Lord and eternal life with God. Knowing this end, they can be patient as they live their lives, also during their suffering. This doesn't mean their troubles will disappear, but they will be able to live patiently through them, trusting in the Lord.

And so we too must be patient. You might have things happen in your life that cause you trouble and sadness. But when these things happen, continue to be patient, trusting in the Lord, knowing the end for you also is eternal life with God. While you are waiting patiently for the Lord, don't just do nothing. Rather, like the farmer, keep busy, filling your mind with God's Word, praying and clinging to God. God's love will help you throughout your life.

REFLECTION

What does it mean to be patient?

JAMES 5:9

Do not grumble against one another, brethren, lest you be condemned.

READ JAMES 5:9-11

Do you ever grumble or complain? Do you think your parents ask you to do too much? Do you complain about the way your friends do things? Do you wish you had nicer clothes or a better soccer ball? How do you react when your brother or sister says something nasty to you? Do you get grumpy and angry? If you get sick and can't go to a party, does that make you angry?

James' readers were suffering many things and many of them started complaining and grumbling against each other. And that is exactly how we often behave too. We are quick to grumble and complain. This is because we are so often focused on ourselves and what we want.

But James tells us that, instead of responding in this way, we should be patient. Earlier in his letter he told us what it means to be patient. It means to be pure, peaceable, gentle, full of mercy and good fruit. That means we shouldn't be quick to get angry and argue, but we should be gentle and peaceable. Don't get angry at God. Remember that God is in control of everything that happens to you, and maybe He is using your sickness or annoying sister to teach you patience and gentleness.

Nor should you get angry at other people. Remember that you are just as sinful as others are. Just like you need forgiveness for your sins, so does your brother or friend who is annoying you. God's grace is for him just as much as it is for you.

What can you do to help you learn to be more patient? You should pray to the Lord. Ask God to help you set a guard over your mouth so that you don't get angry at others. Also pray for those people who make you angry. Ask the Lord to bless them as well. Look at them with the love of Christ. Show them forgiveness and mercy, just like God shows you.

REFLECTION

What should you do instead of grumbling and complaining?

PSALM 139:1

*O Lord, You have searched me
and known me.*

READ PSALM 139:1–12

Psalm 139 tells us that God searches us and knows us. God knows everything there is to know about you. He sees when you do kind things for others, but He also knows your thoughts—when you are angry at your brother or jealous of your friend's things.

How does that make you feel? Does that make you frightened? Well, if God was your enemy, then it would be a very scary thought.

But God is not your enemy. He is your loving Father. He cares for you. Knowing God is aware of your every thought can bring you great comfort, just like it did for David. Even though you sin and struggle with different things in your life, God *still* loves you and cares for you. He holds on to you.

In verse seven David asks, "Where can I flee from your presence?" David is not trying to hide from God, but he is comforted to know that God is with him wherever he is. God was with David when he fought Goliath, when he killed the lion, and when he had to flee from Saul. No matter where David went, God went with him and cared for him. And God cares for you in the same way. If you are in your bedroom, even if you are crying in there, God is with you. If you need to travel somewhere, God goes with you. You are never alone.

God sees you in the morning and in the evening. And while God is with you, He knows your every thought. He also knows your worries. Sometimes you can be so worried about something that it is even hard to pray. God knows that as well, and He will help you pray. And he will answer your prayer, even before you are able to pray. Verse 5 says that God lays His hand upon you. Just like a mother puts her arms around her newborn baby to love and protect them, so God loves and protects you!

REFLECTION

Does it make you happy to know that God knows all your thoughts?

PSALM 139:14

I will praise You, for I am fearfully and wonderfully made.

READ PSALM 139:13-16

Have you ever seen a newborn baby? Maybe you've even been able to hold a little baby in your arms. As you look at that baby, you have no idea what she is going to be like when she grows up, do you? You don't know if she will be tall or short. You don't know if she will be artistic or musical. In a way, this baby really is a mystery.

Yet, this baby is not a mystery to God. God is going to make that baby grow up to be the exact person He wants her to be. David sings, "For You formed my inward parts…. I will praise you for I am fearfully and wonderfully made." God made every one of us special in our own way. He knew what parents He'd give you, who your brothers and sisters would be, and what job you would do. In this way, He already made you special in your mother's womb.

Even more than that, God also planned every one of your days. David continues to sing, "And in Your book they all were written, the days fashioned for me." Isn't that a wonderful thought? Every single day that you have already lived, God planned beforehand. And in all the days that you will still live, God knows what will happen every hour, every minute and every second.

This is a great comfort. As your loving Father, God goes with you every day. Even when days are scary or lonely, God will go with you. If you have to go to the dentist, God has that planned and He will go with you. If you have to visit your sick aunty, God has that planned and He will go with you.

You do not need to be afraid. Your heavenly Father, who made you in exactly the way He wanted to in your mother's womb, has also planned every one of your days, and He will go with you each and every day.

REFLECTION

How does it comfort you to know that God has already planned what is going to happen today?

1 JOHN 1:5

*God is light and in Him
is no darkness at all.*

READ 1 JOHN 1:5-7

If you walk around in a dark room, you can't see where you are going, can you? But if you turn on the light you can see everything, and you can see where you are going. Light is the opposite of darkness. Light is good; it is pure.

John says that God is light. He is good, perfect, holy and pure. He is the opposite of darkness. There is nothing bad in Him. And John tells us that we must walk in the light just as God is in the light.

We cannot say that we know and love God, and then walk in the darkness. There were people in John's days who were doing exactly that. They said they loved God, but then they kept sinning. They didn't think their sins were too bad at all.

But John said that can't be the case. If you know God, God who is holy and full of light, then that will start to change you. If you know how good and perfect God is and if you love Him, then you will also want to live a holy life. You will want to flee from sin.

This is a warning for us as well. Often, we can think in the same way. Of course we love God. We want to serve Him and walk in the light. But then we think that our sins aren't that bad. We know that God wants us to obey our parents, but we still at times complain about them when they ask us to help around the house. God has commanded us not to kill, and we know that also means that we aren't allowed to hate others, but we still have horrible, angry thoughts about our sister, or peers at school.

God tells us that we must instead walk in the light as God is in the light. In this life we cannot be perfect, but we must desire to be holy. We must rely on Jesus and trust Him. If we do, then we are promised that Jesus will forgive us all our sins.

REFLECTION

What does it mean that God is light?

1 JOHN 1:9

If we confess our sins, He is faithful and just to forgive us our sins.

READ 1 JOHN 1:8-10

Some people in John's days believed that if they loved God enough and wanted to obey Him, eventually they would become nearly perfect. We can be tempted to think about ourselves this way too, even though we know we aren't perfect. Sometimes we think that our sins are not that bad.

What are some of the ways that we might be tempted to think that our sins are not too bad?

- Blame-shifting. We might say, "It is not my fault that I got angry—my brother stole my book from me. It is his fault."
- Blame-sharing. Often we think that our sins are not so bad because everyone does it. *Everyone bullies that kid at school, so it is not that bad when I do it.*
- We do not call it sin. Sometimes what God calls sin, we no longer call sin. For example, we know that when God tells us to obey our parents, He wants us to do it straight away. But we do not think it is wrong to wait ten seconds before obeying.
- Justify, or find "good" reasons for sinning. We might think, *I was not able to play on the computer the other night when I am normally allowed to, so it is ok to play on it now instead*, even though you know your parents would not allow you to.
- Ignore our sin. Sometimes we know we have sinned but just ignore it. For example, we know that we should ask someone else for forgiveness, but instead we go and read a book.

These are some examples of how we can think that we are pretty good people. But it is very dangerous to think that you are perfect. Because if you think that way, then you think that you do not need a Saviour. But there is no way to heaven other than through Jesus Christ. So confess your sins, and Jesus will certainly forgive them.

This does not mean that if you forget to confess a sin you will not be forgiven. If you know you are sinful and if you are asking God to help you fight your sins, God's grace also covers the sins you forget to confess. What a great God we have!

REFLECTION

Why is it dangerous to think you are a pretty good person?

1 KINGS 3:9

*Therefore give to Your servant
an understanding heart...*

READ 1 KINGS 3:5-9

What would you wish for if you could have whatever you liked? Imagine a genie in a bottle popped up and said you could have whatever you wished for... what would you choose? Would you ask to never be sick, to always be healthy? Would you ask for lots of money so you could buy whatever you liked? Maybe you would ask for that bike or other toy that you've wanted for a long time. Or maybe you would ask to be famous, or to be able to do your work easily at school and get good marks.

King Solomon was able to choose whatever he liked. And it was the Lord, the Almighty King, the one who is all powerful and who could give anything and everything, who offered Solomon whatever he liked. What should Solomon have asked for? God said he could have whatever he wanted, and God would give it to him.

Solomon had just become king of the people, so maybe he should have asked to win every battle, or maybe that the people would always love him, or maybe even for riches. But no, Solomon didn't ask for these things; rather, he asked the Lord for wisdom. He was beginning a new task and wanted to be able to rule wisely. He wanted to be able to know what was right and wrong. He wanted to do the Lord's will in his reign as king.

And this should be our wish as well. It should be our prayer. We should ask the Lord for wisdom daily, so we can know what is right and wrong when doing our tasks. We should ask the Lord to help us serve Him always.

The Lord gave Solomon the wisdom he asked for. Solomon pointed ahead to the Lord Jesus Christ who had perfect wisdom, and who always obeyed the Lord. He was perfectly obedient in our place. Because of His obedience and sacrifice, God hears our prayers for wisdom. Let us pray every day for this wisdom from the Lord!

REFLECTION

Why should you pray for wisdom every day?

1 KINGS 16:34

...according to the word of the Lord, which He had spoken through Joshua the son of Nun.

READ JOSHUA 6:26-27, 1 KINGS 16:34

When God speaks do you hear…really hear?

The verses we read today show us what happens when you stop listening to the word of the Lord. As the king, Ahab was supposed to know exactly what God had said in the first few books of the Bible. But King Ahab wasn't reading these books. He probably didn't even know where they were. Instead of hearing God's Word, he was worshiping idols.

So what happened? Was Ahab able to just ignore God's Word? Oh no, God will never let His Word be ignored. The Lord had said that if someone tried to rebuild Jericho, their oldest child would die when they started building the city and their youngest would die when they finished building it.

Why was it so important that Jericho wasn't rebuilt? On the people's journey into the Promised Land, Jericho was the first city that had to be destroyed. God Himself had made those walls of Jericho come tumbling down into a pile of stones. He was the one who opened the way so that the people could enter the Promised Land. So God wanted the people to keep that pile of stones to remind them of His love and grace in letting them enter the land. God wanted them to remember to serve Him alone.

But King Ahab wasn't serving the Lord anymore. And so God reminded them that His word can never be ignored. If the Lord says something will happen, it will happen. So when Ahab allows Hiel to rebuild Jericho, Hiel's oldest and youngest children died just like the Lord said.

And so also today we must keep reading God's Word as well. In His Word He tells us what will happen if we stop serving Him. He tells us of eternal punishment in hell. But the Bible also tells us about how God promises forgiveness of sins and eternal life. And those promises are just as true as His punishments. What the Lord says, will happen. As His forgiven children you will receive forgiveness of sins and eternal life.

REFLECTION

Why is it important to read the Bible every day?

JOB 19:25

*For I know that my
Redeemer lives.*

READ JOB 19:25–29

You probably know the story of Job well. God had allowed Satan to take everything away from Job. By doing this God was showing Satan that He would not allow Satan to stop His people from serving Him. But Satan continued to try and make Job turn away from the Lord. He used Job's three friends to try to convince Job to stop loving and serving the Lord.

In this chapter we read Job's answer to these three friends. Even though Job knew that he was a sinner, he knew that it was not because of these sins that everything had been taken away from him. Instead Job confessed that he had a Redeemer. A redeemer is someone who makes wrong things right. Jesus Christ has done that for us. He came to this earth to pay for our sins. Job wouldn't have known as much as we do about Jesus Christ, but he knew enough to confess that he had a Redeemer. Job believed that this Redeemer would save him.

And Job confessed this to his friends. He told them that he was not going to give up on serving the Lord, because he trusted that the Lord would sort everything out. Job had a Redeemer, a Saviour. Job belonged to this Redeemer and so he knew that one day he would have everlasting life. He confessed that he would see God after he died.

What a beautiful confession. Again, Job wouldn't have understood everything about the resurrection of the body, but he believed and confessed that when he died, he would go to be with the Lord. He would see the Lord.

And that is our confession too. We also have a Redeemer, a Saviour, the same Redeemer that Job had. And so, we too can confess that our Redeemer lives. Through His redeeming work, we have forgiveness of sins and eternal life. We too know that because of God's grace, we belong to Him, and no matter what happens to us in this life, we will not be taken away from the Lord.

REFLECTION

Why did Job confess that he had a Redeemer?

JOB 28:28

And to man He said, 'Behold, the fear of the Lord, that is wisdom, and to depart from evil is understanding.'

READ JOB 28:20-28

People have made some amazing things. Think about the International Space Station. Think about how much information a tiny computer or phone can store. That's a lot more information than you can remember in your whole life. Or think about a huge airplane that seems to glide effortlessly through the skies. People have to be very clever to build these things.

Yet, as clever as people are, they cannot give wisdom. Only God is able to give true wisdom. Only the Lord knows true wisdom. People can be very clever, but they cannot tell us why things happen. They cannot explain the things that happen in this world.

Job's three friends thought they were wise and gave Job many wrong explanations for why he had lost everything and got so sick. But God didn't allow them to have the last say. Instead God used Job to speak His words, so that we can all learn about true wisdom and where to find it.

We can't buy wisdom. We can't find wisdom by searching the seas or the forests. It is God alone that gives wisdom. God's wisdom tells us about who we are, how sinful we are, about God's love for us and the covenant God made with us. God's wisdom tells us about Jesus Christ and His love for us. It's this wisdom that we need in life. It's this wisdom that gives us peace to trust God when things don't go how we would like. It's this wisdom that gives us joy even in sad times.

And God gives us this wisdom. As His precious covenant children, He wants us to be wise in His ways. And that's why we have been given the Bible, God's words of wisdom to us. In there we can read all about God and how we can serve Him. Listen to God's Word and let it be the instruction of your life. Love the wisdom of the Lord. Love the Bible!

REFLECTION

Where can we find true wisdom?

JOB 38:4

"Where were you when I laid the foundations of the earth? Tell Me, if you have understanding?"

READ JOB 38:1-11

Job's world changed overnight. You can imagine him sitting down having breakfast when the first bit of devastating information came to him. His servants were dead. Then he was told about the fire that destroyed his sheep, the Chaldeans who stole his camels and that all his children died together in one house. How terrible it must have been for Job. Job wanted to understand why this all happened to him. He wanted answers.

You may wonder the same sometimes in your life. Why did God send COVID-19 to upset the whole world? Why did my grandparents have to leave the area? Why do I struggle so much with my schoolwork? Why hasn't the Lord given me any brothers or sisters? Why?

When Job was wondering why, the Lord came and spoke to him. The Lord asked Job a lot of questions. These questions are called rhetorical questions. Rhetorical questions are questions that have a very obvious answer. Everybody knows the answer, so they don't really need to be answered.

God asked Job, "Where were you when I laid the foundation of the earth? (38:4). "Were you there, Job? Do you know how I did it?" "Have you commanded the morning since your days began?" (38:12). In other words, "Job, is it you who makes the sun come up every morning?" The Lord asked Job many questions like this to show Job that God is God. He is the one who made the whole world, and He is the one who still has everything in His control.

So, when you are wondering why God allows certain things to happen, you too need to be reminded that God is God. He is in control of everything. Walk outside and see the sun shining. Who made it shine today? Listen to the birds singing. Who made them sing so beautifully? Look at worms digging in the garden? Who made these amazing creatures? Yes, God did! He is God, even when things are difficult for you.

Always remember that, and be at peace knowing that God is God!

REFLECTION

What are some other things in creation that show you that God is still God today?

Marvellous are Your works

PSALM 139:14B

LUKE 1:17

He will also go before Him in the spirit and power of Elijah... to make ready a people prepared for the Lord.

READ LUKE 1:5-17

In the days of the Old Testament, when a king was coming there was often a herald that went before him. This herald would announce to the people that the king was coming and at the same time would make sure the road was clear. They didn't have smooth roads like we have nowadays, but gravel roads and they could have bumps and holes in them. So, the herald had to clear these things away to make way for the coming of the king.

These verses tell us that John the Baptist was going to come to be a herald to the Lord Jesus. He was going to tell the people about the coming of the great King, Jesus Christ. He didn't have to make the roads clear for the Lord Jesus, but he did have to make the hearts of the people ready for Jesus.

The people of Israel weren't ready to receive Christ. They had hearts that were disobedient, and they weren't serving the Lord as they should have been. They had forgotten the things their parents had taught them. Their disobedience needed to be changed into obedience, and so the Lord was going to send John the Baptist to warn them to turn their disobedient hearts around, so they would be ready to receive Jesus Christ and listen to Him.

And Jesus Christ is coming again. Are you ready for His second coming? Is your heart ready to receive Him? To be ready for Christ's second coming, we must know how wicked and sinful we are. We must know that we sin daily, and it angers God. If your sins make you cry because you know that you have angered God again, that's good. Tell God that you are truly sorry for your sins and ask Him to forgive you. Ask the Lord to work His Spirit in your heart to help you to fight against your sins. Love the Lord with your whole heart and grow in your love by reading the Bible. Then you can truly look forward to Christ's second coming!

REFLECTION

How can you prepare for Christ's second coming?

LUKE 2:30

For my eyes have seen Your salvation.

READ LUKE 2:25-35

Do you wait excitedly for your birthday? A few days before your birthday you might wake up in the morning and remember that it is only three more days. Then the next day only two, then one, and then it is your birthday.

Simeon was also waiting eagerly for something. The Lord had told him that he would see the Lord Jesus before he died. Simeon believed the words of the Lord. He knew that the comfort of Israel was coming. You can imagine how he must have waited eagerly for this. He was probably waking up in the mornings wondering if this would be the day that he would see Jesus.

Then one day the Lord directed him, by the Spirit, to go to the temple. This was the day that Joseph and Mary brought the baby Jesus to the temple. Simeon took Jesus in his arms and then responded in praise. He had been eagerly waiting to see the Lord Jesus, and now he finally saw Him, and so he praises the Lord.

He says that he can now depart or die in peace, because he has seen salvation. He calls Jesus *salvation*. He knows that Jesus Christ has come to earth to bring salvation to all people. Anyone who believes in this Jesus will be saved. Simeon saw Jesus and knew that he had seen God's grace.

Have you seen Jesus?

Well, in a way we certainly have seen Jesus. We see Him when we read the Bible. We can see more and more of Him every day as we read more of the Bible.

But we will also see Jesus face to face one day. When Jesus returns on the clouds of heaven, we will see Him, not as a baby, but as the almighty King of kings and Lord of lords.

REFLECTION

As you struggle with sins in this life, or live with pain or hardships, do you eagerly wait for Christ to return? Do you look forward to the day when the struggle with sin will be ended and all suffering will be gone? Eagerly wait for Christ to return, and pray, "Come, Lord Jesus! Maranatha!"

LUKE 2:49

"Did you not know that I must be about My Father's business?"

READ LUKE 2:41-52

Do you think Jesus sounds a little disrespectful in this story? His parents hadn't been able to find Him for three days. You can imagine that they must have been panicking. Where was their son Jesus? And when they finally find Him after three days of looking, Jesus just tells them that He had to be in His Father's house. He doesn't say sorry or anything. To us it almost seems like Jesus was wrong. But we know that Jesus was perfect, so there is no way that He could have sinned. So what did Jesus mean?

When the Passover was celebrated, the people were, according to the law of the Lord, supposed to celebrate for seven days. But the leaders during those days had allowed the people who lived far away to go home early. This was the custom, which was different than God's law. Verse 42 says that Joseph and Mary went according to the custom. They didn't stay in Jerusalem for the full seven days. But Jesus did. He was obeying the law of the Lord. He was obedient to His Father's law. And so, when His parents came searching for Him, Jesus respectfully told them that He needed to be in His Father's house. He was obeying the law of the Lord.

After this, the Bible tells us that Jesus went with His parents back to their home. Again we see Christ obeying the law. He obeyed His parents as the Lord commanded Him to.

So, in this passage we see Christ's total obedience to God's law. He never sinned. Not once! And He was perfectly obedient for us. We sin all the time, every day again. But God, in love, forgives us because of Christ's perfect obedience.

Now, in thankfulness for God's love and forgiveness to you, live your life obeying God's laws. Always obey your parents. Show them the love and respect that God wants you to show them. Obey them, just like Jesus obeyed His parents.

REFLECTION

Why did Jesus have to stay in Jerusalem?

LUKE 5:8

When Simon Peter saw it, he fell down at Jesus' knees, saying, "Depart from me, for I am a sinful man, O Lord!"

READ LUKE 5:1-11

Simon Peter and his fellow fishermen had been fishing all night but caught nothing. They knew that nighttime was the best time to go fishing, so the next day, when Jesus told them to go out in their boats and put their nets down to catch some fish, they must have thought He was crazy. Why try fishing during the day?

But Simon said to Jesus, "Even though we haven't caught anything during the night, because You say so, we will put our nets out again." The fishermen obeyed the Lord, and when they pulled up their nets there were so many fish that they filled two boats, almost making them sink.

How did Simon respond to this amazing miracle? Did he say, "Wow, thank you Lord, you are just amazing. That's just great! We'll be able to sell lots of fish now. Wow!" No, he didn't say anything at all about the fish even though, being a fisherman, he would have known what a great miracle it was. Instead he bowed down at Jesus' feet, among all the fish, and worshipped Him. He realised that God was at work in this man Jesus. He may not yet have understood that Jesus was God Himself, but he sure knew that God was working in Him. And so, when Simon saw this great holiness of God, he realised how terribly sinful he was. God worked in Simon's heart so that he realised his own sinfulness. And so Simon said, "Depart from me for I am a sinful man, O Lord." He knew that because of his sinfulness, he couldn't stand before Jesus' holiness.

But Jesus told him not to be afraid. Yes, it is true that Simon Peter was terribly sinful, but Jesus' love for Simon was so great that He would die for Simon's sins, and so Simon Peter did not need to be afraid. Instead Simon had to go out into the world and tell other people about Jesus' great love for sinners. Jesus would use him, a fisherman, to work in His kingdom.

REFLECTION

When you read about God's holiness and greatness, how do you feel?

LUKE 5:13

Then He put out His hand and touched him, saying, "I am willing; be cleansed."

READ LUKE 5:12-16

Being a leper in the Bible times was very difficult. There was no cure for this terrible disease. The man in Luke 5 was full of leprosy. This means he would have had sores all over his body. He probably couldn't walk properly anymore, and he may have had toes and fingers falling off.

As a leper he would also have had to live by himself in isolation. He couldn't isolate with his family in a comfortable house like we could do during the corona virus. But he had to live on his own, outside the city. He couldn't go to the temple either. Again, during the corona virus we couldn't go to church for a while, but the leper couldn't go for the rest of his life! And there was no livestream for him to watch. Not being able to go to the temple meant that he couldn't make sacrifices and so he was separated from God as well.

God uses a leper to show His people what sin and death are like. By this picture, God wants to show us how wicked and sinful we all are. No, this leper hadn't sinned specifically to deserve this leprosy. Not at all. But God uses this picture to show us that because of our sins we deserve to be isolated or separated from God as well.

But, we read that when the leper went to Jesus and begged to be made clean, Jesus reached out and touched him. He touched the unclean leper and healed him! This is God's grace, His amazing love. And this is again a picture of what the Lord Jesus does for us. He touches us. He comes to sinners like you and me. He doesn't send us away, just like He didn't send the leper away. Instead He cleanses us too. He forgives us. What love and what grace! And so we can always go to Jesus with our sins. If we beg Him to forgive us, just like the leper begged to be made clean, Jesus will always forgive us. No sin is too big for Christ to forgive.

REFLECTION

What is the Lord teaching us about Himself by cleansing the leper?

LUKE 5:35

"But the days will come when the bridegroom will be taken away from them; then they will fast in those days."

READ LUKE 5:33-39

Have you ever tried drinking from an empty water bottle? You could put the water bottle to your lips, lift it up and even make the sucking and swallowing actions, but because that water bottle is empty it won't stop you from being thirsty, will it?

The fasting of the Pharisees was a bit like them trying to drink from an empty water bottle. They did all the actions, but their fasting was meaningless. In the Old Testament, the people of Israel were told to fast to show that they were sorry for their sins. But the Pharisees in Jesus' days weren't fasting because they were sorry for their sins, they were fasting because it made them look very religious. But their hearts weren't in their fasting. They thought that the act of fasting itself was enough to save them.

When Jesus was asked why His disciples didn't fast, He didn't answer by telling them how fasting should have been done. Instead Jesus gave them the gospel. The reason for fasting was to show sorrow for sins and their need for salvation. But Jesus was with them now. He is the way to salvation, so they didn't need to fast now. Just like a person wouldn't fast at a friend's wedding, so they shouldn't have been fasting when Jesus was with them. Instead of focusing on the actual act of fasting itself, they should have focused on what it meant. They should have listened to Jesus and His message of salvation. Jesus is the one who would make them right with God. He is the one who will give salvation. Fasting without listening to Jesus is a waste of time.

Are we sometimes a bit like the Pharisees? Do we sometimes go to church without listening to Jesus? Jesus warns us here not to try and earn our own salvation but instead to focus on Jesus and the salvation that He gives to us. So, yes, you must keep going to church and keep reading the Bible, but all the while also focusing on Christ and His love for you.

REFLECTION

Why didn't the people need to fast while Jesus was with them?

LUKE 6:5

And He said to them, "The Son of Man is also Lord of the Sabbath."

READ LUKE 6:1-5

The Sabbath day was a special day for the Israelites to celebrate God's love and the freedom they had from sin. That's why they had to make special sacrifices on the Sabbath. God wanted them to always focus on His love and forgiveness.

But the Pharisees had made many of their own rules for the Sabbath and so destroyed the real meaning of the Sabbath day. And so, when they saw the disciples of Jesus plucking grain on the Sabbath and eating it, they told them off for disobeying their man-made rules.

When Jesus heard them, He explained the true meaning of the Sabbath. It wasn't just about following lots of rules, but about understanding God's love for His people. Jesus told them about David, who was allowed to eat special bread meant only for priests when he was hungry. This bread was there to remind everyone of God's love. Just like bread keeps us alive, God takes care of us. So, when David was hungry, he was allowed to eat the special bread.

In this example, Jesus is telling the disciples not to replace the true meaning of the Sabbath with a false meaning. If they spent the whole day focusing on their man-made rules, they would not remember the day as a day to celebrate God's love and forgiveness.

And so today, we shouldn't spend Sunday focusing on rules about what we are and are not allowed to do. If we did that, we would forget about God's love for us and that we are saved because of Him and not because of our obedience. But we also can't just spend the Sunday doing whatever we please and focusing on ourselves. Then, too, we would be forgetting about God's love.

We must spend the Sunday going to church and focusing on God's love for us, how He has forgiven our sins, and how he is preparing us for eternal rest in heaven.

REFLECTION

Do you enjoy the Sunday? Why?

LUKE 9:29

As He prayed, the appearance of His face was altered, and His robe became white and glistening.

READ LUKE 9:28-36

Sometimes it can feel really hard to be a Christian, can't it? Of course you love the Lord, but you don't like it when people down the road tease you about your faith. Sometimes you might wish that you could do some of the things your unbelieving neighbours do on Sundays. Sometimes it is just so difficult to keep fighting against the same sins every day again.

It was also a struggle for the disciples of the Lord Jesus. They also had to give up so much to follow Jesus. On the Mount of Transfiguration, God the Father showed the glory of the Lord Jesus to reassure the disciples and us that following Jesus is worth all the struggles.

Moses and Elijah appeared on the mountain with the Lord Jesus. The disciples that went up with Jesus saw this. They saw that Jesus Christ's whole body was glowing and bright. The bright light wasn't just around the Lord Jesus but was shining out of Him. The Father was showing them that Jesus was so much greater than the prophets of the Old Testament. Jesus Christ is God Himself. The Father even came down in a cloud to the disciples to reassure them and to tell them that Jesus Christ was His only begotten Son.

The topic that Jesus, Moses, and Elijah talked about would also have reassured the disciples that they could believe in Jesus. They spoke about Jesus' death on the cross. They talked about Jesus saving us from our sins. They spoke about the great deliverance that was to come. Peter thought that they were talking about freedom from the Romans, and so he wanted to make tents for them to celebrate the feast of tabernacles. But Jesus told Peter not to do that because Jesus was talking about something else. He was talking about the deliverance from sin. Jesus still needed to go down to Jerusalem, He still needed to suffer and die, and He was willing to do that to give us salvation, to deliver us from sin and to give us a new relationship with the Father again.

REFLECTION

Why did Jesus shine with glory?

LUKE 12:32

"Do not fear, little flock, for it is your Father's good pleasure to give you the kingdom."

READ LUKE 12:22-34

Do you ever worry about things? Maybe you worry that your schoolwork will be too difficult or that you might not have enough food to eat. Maybe you worry that you will get sick or that your old pet dog will die soon. The Lord Jesus Christ knows you very well and He knows that as people we often worry. And that's why He tells us in verse 22 not to worry.

Let's have a closer look at what Jesus says in verses 31-32. He tells us to seek the kingdom of God. To seek is to really want something. It is to have a strong desire for something. It is God's kingdom we should be seeking.

You are a child of God's kingdom. You belong to God. Jesus tells us this in verse 32. "Don't worry about anything because you are already a child of the Lord, you are already part of His kingdom." So, because you are part of God's kingdom, seek it first. Think about God's kingdom. Focus all your thoughts on doing things to praise God.

Knowing you are part of God's kingdom means that you don't need to worry about other things, because God will give you what you need. Look at the ravens—they don't seem to do anything other than squawk and flap their wings. Yet your heavenly Father feeds them. Now if God feeds those birds, then He will certainly care for you, a child of His kingdom.

Little flock, don't worry or be fearful. Instead, focus on doing things in God's kingdom. Then many of your worries will be taken away. Then you will be focused *more* on how you can serve the Lord with your talents rather than focusing on getting good marks at school. Then you will focus more on doing things now to praise God than worrying about if you will be sick tomorrow or next week.

Leave your worries with the Lord and trust Him. Focus on using what the Lord gives you now to serve Him as a child in His kingdom!

REFLECTION

What does it mean to seek God's kingdom?

LUKE 14:16

Then He said to him, "A certain man gave a great supper and invited many."

READ LUKE 14:16-24

The Pharisees had invited Jesus to have dinner with them. The Pharisees were the rulers of the church at that time and they knew the Old Testament very well. 'Because they were the leaders of the church, descendants of Abraham, and obeyed hundreds of self-made rules, the Pharisees assumed they would be saved.'

Jesus had a lesson to tell these Pharisees and He does so with a parable. The parable talks about people who refused to come to a wedding feast because they had other things that they were busy with. One was busy with his land, another with his business and another with his wife. Buying land, owning a business or being married are all good things and are blessings from the Lord. But the problem was that these people acted as if these things were more important than the feast that they had been invited to. And that was wrong!

The great feast that the Lord Jesus is talking about is the great wedding feast on the last day, when Jesus returns a second time. When Jesus comes back on the clouds of heaven, all of His children will go with Him into heaven and from then on we will live without sin, with the Lord, on the new earth.

Jesus is telling the Pharisees that they are like the people in the parable because they think that their own things are more important than being with Jesus. They think they are good enough. They think they don't need forgiveness from Jesus because they obey all their rules. They think that because they are part of the church, they don't really need to live close to the Lord.

When we read this parable, the Lord is also warning us to make sure we always remember that we belong to the Lord. We need to remember that our eternal future is with God. Christ is coming back on the clouds of heaven and He must be our focus, and we must put Him first. We must think about that all the time and then we will remember to read His Word, ask Him for forgiveness, and pray to Him. Our relationship with the Lord is more important than anything else in life.

REFLECTION

How do you remember to put God first in your life?

LUKE 14:23

"Then the master said to the servant, "Go out into the highways and hedges, and compel them to come in, that my house may be filled."

READ LUKE 14:16-24

Although this parable teaches us that we must always put God first in our life, it also shows us God's great love and grace. When some people refused to come to the wedding feast because they had other things to do, the servant was told to go and gather the lame, the poor and the blind to come to the feast.

To be a part of God's great wedding feast, we must be poor and blind. This doesn't mean that we must actually be poor and blind, but rather that we must be poor spiritually. This means that we must realise that we can't save ourselves. We must be saddened because of our sins. We must go to Jesus, knowing that through Him we receive forgiveness of sins. It's only because of His death on the cross and His perfect obedience that we are allowed to go to the wedding feast of the Lord. We are allowed to belong to the Lord because of Jesus' love for us.

But, in this parable, even after the blind and poor had been gathered in to the feast, there was still room left. So the servant was told to go and convince many other people from the highways outside the city to come to the feast. This again points to God's grace and love, as He calls many people from every tribe and nation to belong to Him.

It also means that we must continue to share the good news about God's grace and love to many other people. You need to show God's love in the way you live. You need to live as a Christian. Show in the way you act that you are a forgiven child of the Lord. Be kind and loving to those around you. You must also share God's love with other people by telling them about the Lord. Also remember to pray for mission work where pastors go out and share this love of the Lord with people who have never read the Bible or heard of the Lord.

REFLECTION

How can you share God's love with people around you?

LUKE 15:24

"For this my son was dead and is alive again; he was lost and is found."

READ LUKE 15:11-32

This parable teaches us about the love of our heavenly Father.

Sometimes we can be like the younger son. No, you probably will not ask your dad for a lot of money and then run away from home and waste it all. But sometimes we want to ignore all the blessings that God gives us and go and do our own thing. The Lord has told us to stay far away from sin, but sometimes we actually want to sin, just like the younger son did. Do you ever want to ignore God? Maybe you want to disobey your parents, maybe you are nasty to your siblings, or maybe you look at wrong pictures.

But after the younger son had been gone for a while and was left with nothing at all, not even enough food, he realised how foolish he had been. And he remembered how loving his father was. And so, he returned home, ready to tell his dad how sorry he was because of his sins.

His dad welcomes him with tears of joy. He is so happy to see his son come home. And the Lord is like that to us. If we go to Him in humbleness, sorry for our sins, He will always welcome us. He will always forgive our sins. No sin is so great that God will not forgive it.

But, sometimes we can also be like the older son. The older son thought that he was good because he had obeyed all his dad's commands. He had stayed home and worked hard. We can be like that if we think that God should love us because we do good things.

But we see the father's love for him too. His dad did not send him away, but instead reminded him that he had always loved him. In the same way, God also shows us this same love, when we sometimes think we are good in and of ourselves.

Just like the dad in the story shows grace and love to both sons, so God shows grace and love to us!

REFLECTION

If you act like the older or the younger son, what should you do? How will God respond?

LUKE 17:10

"So likewise you, when you have done all those things which you are commanded, say, 'We are unprofitable servants. We have done what was our duty to do.'"

READ LUKE 17:5-10

When you first read these verses, they seem a bit harsh, don't they? Are these verses saying that we need to work nonstop, that we can never have a break? The servant in the parable works hard all day long, and then when he gets home at the end of the day, he isn't thanked for his work, but instead he is told to keep working by preparing a meal for his master and then still must keep working. Is this what we need to do as well?

Jesus is telling us that we are His servants every second of every day. There is not any time when we aren't His servants. We can never think, "Oh, I can forget about being God's servant now." No, we are God's servants all the time. This means that you have to do everything every day to the honour and glory of God. If you are at school, resting, playing with your friends, helping your mum, or relaxing with a good book, then all these things must be done to God's glory.

This doesn't mean that the things that you do will help you get into heaven or make you a better person. No, not at all. Actually, Jesus says in this parable that you must understand that all the things you do are unprofitable or unworthy. They cannot make you a better person or make you righteous before God. Even the best things that you do during the day are sinful, because you are a sinful person.

Yet God doesn't reject your works and say that they are useless. No, out of love and grace, He accepts the works that you do, even though they are sinful. He is pleased with them because of Christ's redeeming work. Because Christ has forgiven you, and because the Spirit is at work in your hearts, God loves all the works that you do out of love for Him.

Get rid of anything—pictures, books, movies, thoughts, hobbies—that stops you from serving the Lord. Instead, continue every day to praise God, to love Him, and to serve Him. Use every moment that the Lord gives you, in a way that is pleasing to Him.

REFLECTION

What does it mean to be a servant of the Lord?

LUKE 17:19

And He said to him, "Arise, go your way. Your faith has made you well."

READ LUKE 17:11–19

Do you praise God enough? Do you do it in the right way or in the right place? These might be questions that you are asking yourself after reading these verses. But that's not why Luke included these words. They're not there to make us feel guilty.

This story is in the Bible to teach us about Christ and His kingdom work. These verses tell us that Jesus is on His way to Jerusalem. Jerusalem is the centre of Christ's kingdom work. All the things that He is doing are working towards His kingdom, His reign.

These ten lepers were outcasts because of their skin disease. They were the lowly people. No one really cared about them. They weren't allowed to worship in the temple or have any contact with others. When these ten lepers see Jesus, they call out to Him from afar. They had heard all about Jesus and knew that He could heal them of their leprosy. They call out, begging the master to heal them. When Jesus tells them to show themselves to the priest, they know immediately that this means they are going to be healed, and so they head off to the priest.

On the way, they are all suddenly healed. All ten of them. Nine of them continue on to the priest, but one turns around and returns to Jesus to thank Him. Why does only one come back to thank Jesus? The Bible tells us that he saw that he was healed and then came back. The Holy Spirit opened his eyes to see what was really happening. By showing that He was able to heal them from their leprosy, Jesus was teaching them that He can save them from their sins. And this is what the one healed leper saw. He believed in the Lord Jesus. And that's why He goes back to Jesus to praise and worship Him.

Jesus is at work in your heart too. You too are part of His kingdom work. Fix your eyes on Jesus and praise and worship Him!

REFLECTION

What is Jesus showing by healing these lepers?

LUKE 19:10

"For the Son of Man has come to seek and to save that which was lost."

READ LUKE 19:1–10

While the Lord Jesus was walking through Jericho, there was one person who wanted to see Him. This man was a chief tax collector. The tax collectors in those days were not liked by the people because they often stole money. We know that this tax collector, named Zacchaeus, was not an honest man. He had stolen and cheated money off his own people.

Now Zacchaeus wanted to see Jesus, but there was a problem. He was a short man so he couldn't see over the people. But that didn't stop him. He climbed up a sycamore tree. And there he, a short chief tax collector, sat in a tree watching for Jesus.

When Jesus saw Zacchaeus, He commanded him to come down from the tree and to welcome Jesus into his home. Jesus didn't see this man by accident. No, Jesus went to Zacchaeus on purpose. He even knew his name. Zacchaeus was a sinner and an outcast. In and of himself, he would not have wanted Jesus, but Jesus chose to come to him, a lost sheep of Israel. Jesus wanted to come into his home and into his heart.

The people were angry when they heard Jesus telling Zacchaeus that He wanted to go to Zacchaeus' home. They didn't think Jesus should go to the home of a sinner. But Zacchaeus knew that he was a sinner and that he needed Jesus. So he came down from the tree and admitted that he had stolen from and cheated the people. Zacchaeus had now changed. By God's grace he was sorry for his sins, so he promised to give back what he stole.

Jesus had called Zacchaeus' name, and Zacchaeus had joyfully followed Jesus. Jesus also calls your name and commands you to follow Him. No matter what sins you have done, Jesus still comes to you in love, granting forgiveness. And so, you too must ask God to help you repent of your sins and to follow Jesus with your whole heart.

REFLECTION

Why did Jesus choose to go to the home of a tax collector?

LUKE 23:25

And he released to them the one they requested, who for rebellion and murder had been thrown into prison; but he delivered Jesus to their will.

READ LUKE 23:13-25

There were two people standing before Pilate: Barabbas and the Lord Jesus Christ. Barabbas, as you know, was a criminal. He was a guilty man. He was a murderer and deserved to be punished.

But Jesus Christ was also standing before Pilate, and He was innocent. Three times Pilate said that Jesus had done nothing wrong. He declared Jesus innocent. Jesus had done nothing at all that made Him deserve to be punished or put to death.

It had become a custom that every Passover one prisoner was allowed to go free. Pilate was hoping that if he asked the Jewish people who to set free, they would say Jesus and not Barabbas. After all Barabbas was a very wicked man, and Jesus Christ had done nothing wrong. But instead of calling out Barabbas, the people called out that Jesus should be crucified. "Crucify Him, crucify Him," they shouted. It wasn't the Romans who called this out, but the covenant people, Christ's covenant brothers and sisters.

No one stood up for Jesus. Peter had denied Him, all the disciples had fled, and the covenant people were calling out for Him to be crucified. The Son of God was made to be lower than the worst criminal.

Even though Jesus Christ was innocent, not guilty at all, He was still covered with sin. Not His own sins, but our sins. All of our sins were laid on Him. The sinful words we speak, our pride, our greed, our selfishness, our disrespect to our parents, our arguments …all of these sins are what made innocent Jesus covered in sins. He allowed Himself to be humiliated, to be made lower than the worst criminal, to have all of our sins laid on Him for our sakes. He allowed Himself to be punished as though He was full of sin because of His love for us.

Always remember this love of your Saviour. He became the Passover Lamb for you. He allowed Himself to be made guilty for you. Even more, He went to the cross for you!

REFLECTION

Why did Christ allow Himself to be punished even though He had done nothing wrong?

LUKE 24:31

Then their eyes were opened and they knew Him.

READ LUKE 24:28-35

You know the story well. Two of Jesus' disciples were walking home a few days after Jesus had died. They were sad because they were friends of Jesus, and they were discussing His death. Then suddenly Jesus appeared to them, but they didn't recognize Him.

Why didn't they recognize Him? They had been Jesus' disciples, and Jesus had only died a few days before. Verse 16 tells us that their eyes were closed so that they did not know Him. God kept them from recognizing Jesus because they didn't yet understand why He had to die. Until they understood why Jesus had to die, it would be impossible for them to really understand and recognize Jesus. These disciples had been expecting Jesus to be a Saviour who would save them from the Romans. To them a dead Saviour made no sense at all.

Before they would be able to really recognize Jesus, they would need to understand exactly who He was. That's why Jesus goes through the Old Testament with them, showing how the whole Old Testament points to our need for a Saviour. The whole Old Testament points to Jesus Christ. They needed to understand their sins and their need to be saved. Only when they had understood that, would they understand that Jesus didn't come to save them from their earthly enemies but to save them from their sins. It wasn't until after Jesus explained this to them that they suddenly recognized Jesus. God allowed them to recognize Jesus at that time, because then they saw Him as the one who came to save them from their sins, as the Saviour who had to die and rise again from the dead. They knew that Jesus couldn't stay in the grave. He had paid for sins with His death and was alive again. He was their living Saviour. Now they could rejoice in the death and resurrection of Jesus.

REFLECTION

What about you? Do you recognize Jesus? Do you understand that it is because of your sins that Jesus had to come? If you do, then you too can rejoice because Christ has died and risen!

PSALM 32:1

Blessed is he whose transgression is forgiven, whose sin is covered.

READ PSALM 32

Psalm 32 says that those whose sins are forgiven are blessed. Why is it so important that our sins are forgiven?

God created people because He wanted to have a relationship with us. He wanted us to praise and worship Him. In Paradise God walked in the garden with Adam and Eve and talked with them. And God still wants to live with His children today.

But, because of the fall into sin, this relationship with God is not the same anymore. God cannot have this close friendship with sinful people. God is a holy God, and we are sinful and wicked. Because God is holy, He is very angry with sin. And because God is a just God, He cannot ignore sins, but sin needs to be punished. And the only way to do that is by having the person who sinned go to hell forever. We deserve to go to hell forever.

But God is not only a just God; He is also a gracious God. And because God still wants to have a relationship with His children, He has made a way for us to escape this punishment of hell. He allowed someone else to be punished with hell instead of us.

In the Old Testament, before the people could come and worship in the temple, they first had to sacrifice an animal. In order to worship a holy God, their sins first needed to be taken away and forgiven. God could not allow sinful people into the temple to worship Him. And so, an animal was killed instead of the person. God accepted the person into the temple to worship because the animal was killed instead of them.

These sacrifices pointed to Jesus Christ. Today we can be forgiven and worship the Lord because Jesus Christ died on the cross instead of us. Yes, we are sinful, but Jesus Christ was punished and killed instead of us, just like the animal had to be sacrificed instead of the people in the Old Testament. And so, we may be God's beloved children!

REFLECTION

Why is it such a blessing to have our sins forgiven?

PSALM 37:4

Delight yourself also in the Lord, and He shall give you the desires of your heart.

READ PSALM 37:1–11

What is this verse saying? Is it saying that if you always delight in the Lord and do the things that He wants you to do, then the Lord will always give you what you want? It does sound a bit like that, doesn't it?

This Psalm teaches us how we should think about all the evil and bad things that are happening in the world around us. Often it looks like evil people are getting what they want and those who love the Lord are getting forgotten or persecuted.

But in this Psalm God reminds us that He is going to punish the evildoers. They will not be left unpunished. And the righteous, the children of the Lord, will not be forgotten either. God loves us and He has promised us eternal life with Him. This Psalm speaks many times of God looking after His children.

David says to the people who were suffering because of the evil people around them, "Delight yourself also in the Lord, and He shall give you the desires of your heart." David adds, "Even in all of your suffering make it your delight, your joy to love the Lord. Let it be the Lord who makes you glad and happy." Notice that David uses the name Lord with capital letters. This is the name of our covenant God. This is "I am who I am." This is the Lord who always keeps His promises. This is the Lord who loves His children and works everything for their salvation. It must be our joy to love this Lord!

We must not get angry and bitter at people who do evil in this world, but we must focus on the Lord of our salvation. It is He who gives us joy and happiness. Then our desire will be to serve the Lord more, to trust Him and to turn away from our sins. Our desire will be to be saved and to be happy in the Lord. It is these desires that the Lord gives to those who delight in Him.

REFLECTION

What does it mean to delight or have joy in the Lord?

1 PETER 1:1 & 2

To the pilgrims...elect according to the foreknowledge of God the Father.

READ 1 PETER 1:1-9

What is a pilgrim? It is not someone traveling around aimlessly, with no home; we call them nomads. It is not someone traveling to escape a country; we call them refugees. A pilgrim is someone who is traveling to a certain place. Pilgrims are focused on where they are heading. They look forward to getting there. Nothing along the way should take their focus off their destination.

Peter says that we as Christians, as God's children, are pilgrims. So where do you think we are heading? Where should all our attention be focused? Yes, we're heading toward eternal life. The new heaven and the new earth are our future so that is where our focus should be. Nothing should distract us from this focus.

This is such a beautiful thing to look forward to. God, in His grace, gives us such a rich future. We will one day live with Him forever. Peter calls this our inheritance. Many things in this life fade away. Actually, everything in this life disappears or will one day disappear. But our inheritance, our future with the Lord will never fade away. It will never disappear. It is forever. It is certain.

But how do you know that you will receive this amazing future? Verse 5 tells us that we are kept by the power of God — God's power! If it were up to us, we wouldn't be focused on this future. But God keeps us. We are His children and so He is not going to let us go. See, He tells us that here in this passage.

So as a pilgrim, as you travel through this life on the way to eternal life with God, stay focused on God and on heavenly things. Don't get caught up focusing on your toys, or your holidays or your games. Yes, you may certainly enjoy these things. But don't make them the most important thing in your life. While you are enjoying these things, remember to serve and love God in all that you do.

REFLECTION

Why does Peter call Christians "pilgrims"?

1 PETER 1:16

Because it is written, "Be holy, for I am holy."

READ 1 PETER 1:13-16

Do you fear God? What does it mean to fear God? The word *fear* can be used in a few different ways so it is important that we understand what it means to fear God. Adam and Eve were afraid of God after they had sinned in Paradise. They were scared because they had sinned, and they knew that God hated sin.

God still hates sin today. And because of our sins, God has every right to throw us into hell. That's what we deserve. But God already promised Adam and Eve a way out of this punishment of eternal death. God already told them that He was going to send His Son to pay this punishment for their sins. With His precious blood, Christ did come, and He has paid for our sins.

Knowing this amazing love and saving work of Christ for us, we should live our life in fear, Peter says. This means that we should have a deep respect, deep awe and deep love for the Lord. We know that God is going to judge our works, and we know that we deserve eternal punishment. But we also know that Christ's precious blood was shed on the cross because of our sins. And this can only leave us with a deep love and fear of the Lord.

Peter goes on to say that if we fear God, then we must also live a holy life. We must act in a way that shows that we have this deep respect and love for the Lord. We must aim to live a life that shows that we are Christians. By the clothes we wear, the music we listen to, the friends we have and the way we speak and act, we must show that we are children of this holy God.

Yes, we do remain sinful people. And yes, God continues to hate sin. But we also know that we are forgiven in Christ and so we must live a holy life.

REFLECTION

What does it mean to fear the Lord?

1 PETER 1:22

...love one another fervently with a pure heart.

READ 1 PETER 1:22-2:3

In church there are many people around you. How do you feel about them? Do you love them? God tells us, through the apostle Peter, that we must love them fervently. To love fervently means to really love them, to love them with your whole heart. It means a lot more than just being friendly to someone; it means to actually love that person.

How can you love others in this way? Through the Spirit sent by Jesus Christ. Christ Himself showed perfect love. He always loved fervently. Even when He was dying on the cross, He prayed for forgiveness for His enemies. And Jesus loves us too. He loved us even while we still hated Him. He died for us even though we didn't love Him. That's perfect love! Now we, by the power of the Holy Spirit, need to show the same love to others.

This love for others can be strengthened by the Word of God. If you don't read your Bible, then you can't expect to grow in love for others. Nothing in life is as important as the Bible. That's why Peter says that we must desire God's Word just like a newborn baby desires pure milk. A baby will never rest, never relax, never have peace and never grow without milk. Milk is *that* important to a baby. Without it the baby will die. So God's Word is *that* important for us. Without God's Word we would never rest, never have peace and never grow.

And we must grow. As Christians we must also grow in love for others. So read the Bible to learn about Christ's perfect love. When you see how much Christ has loved you, then you can also show this love to others. When someone makes you angry because of what they say to you, remember how much you have sinned against the Lord. Remember His forgiveness and love. If holy God has shown this much love to sinful you, how much more shouldn't you show this love to others?

REFLECTION

How can you grow in your love for others?

1 PETER 2:4

Coming to Him as to a living stone, rejected indeed by men, but chosen by God and precious.

READ 1 PETER 2:4-8

Have you ever climbed over a pile of rocks? It might have been near the beach or in the forest somewhere. It can be quite enjoyable jumping from rock to rock. Occasionally a rock might be loose and then as you put your foot on it, it moves and you have to be careful that you don't fall and hurt yourself.

Peter calls Jesus Christ a rock, or a stone. But Jesus is not a stone that wobbles and moves. No, He is a solid stone, one that is firm and strong and will not move. Christ will not change over time. He will not crumble or fall. Christ is a solid stone, which means that we can count on Him always.

Jesus Christ is the cornerstone. The cornerstone of the building is the first stone that is laid, on which all the other stones are built. If you don't have this cornerstone then the whole building will crumble and fall. This shows us how important Jesus is in our lives. Without Him, the church would not be able to stand. We need Him to carry us through each day.

Stones, as you know, are dead. They have no life in them at all. But Peter tells us that Jesus is a living stone. Our Saviour is alive. Yes, He did die, but He also arose from the dead and so He is very much alive today. He is in heaven working for us. He is there to help us, His children.

Christ Jesus is also described as a precious stone. If something is precious to you, that means it is important and you treat it with care and love. Remember that Jesus is your precious cornerstone. Treat Him as number one in your life. Keep going to Him in prayer. Keep trusting in Him to care for you and to give you strength. Trust Him to help you fight against Satan. Satan is like a wobbly rock that moves and makes us fall. Skip over him and trust in Christ, the precious living stone. With Him you are always safe.

REFLECTION

What does it mean to you that Christ is a precious living stone?

1 PETER 2:5

...you also, as living stones, are being built up a spiritual house, a holy priesthood, to offer up spiritual sacrifices acceptable to God through Jesus Christ.

READ 1 PETER 2:4-8

We know that Christ is the cornerstone, but what are we? We, too, must be living stones, just like Jesus. Christ has made us alive. He has made us living stones.

As living stones, we must remember that we are not on our own, and so we cannot just go about serving the Lord all on our own either. Peter says we are to be built together as a spiritual house. We can't just do our own thing and not think about other people in the church. We must all live together. Just as the stones in a building are joined to form the structure, we must work together with others in the church.

How can you do this? How can you be a living part of God's church? Firstly, you can get to know other people in your church. Talk to them and ask them about their life. Talk to people of different ages. If they share something that makes them happy, be happy with them. If they are sad about things, be sad with them. If someone does something wrong to you, show them forgiveness. Show kindness and love to the people around you. And then pray for them. Pray for those in your church who are sick, who are old, who have had a baby or who just got married. Ask the Lord to be with others in your church. In this way you are a living stone, a part of Christ's beautiful building.

Always remember that every stone of this building is precious. Every person in your church is specially made by God to be the person they are. God is working in their lives in just the same way that He is working in your life. Together you form this beautiful spiritual building.

You must offer your whole life as a sacrifice to God. No, you don't have to offer animals or bread or oil like they did in the Old Testament, but you must use your whole life to serve the Lord!

REFLECTION

What does it mean to be a living stone?

1 PETER 5:7

*...casting all your care upon
Him, for He cares for you.*

READ 1 PETER 5:5-10

Can you ever remember feeling very scared and being able to crawl up on your dad's knee? Dad wrapped his big, strong arms around you and that made you feel nice and safe. That thunder wasn't quite as frightening or that dog wasn't as scary with Dad's arms around you.

Peter uses a similar picture to tell us to trust completely in the Lord. He tells us to humble ourselves under the mighty hand of God. The Bible talks about God's mighty hand a number of times, and whenever it does, it shows us God's power and love. We know God created the whole world with His might and power. Psalm 102 speaks about this work of creation as the work of God's hands. Or think of the time that the Lord redeemed the people of Israel from the land of Egypt. God told Moses that He was going to stretch out His mighty hand to save Israel. God's mighty hand is something much, much stronger than your dad's strong arms around you. God's mighty hand is His power with which He created the world, and with which He is still in control of everything. It is also His power to save you from your sins, from everlasting hell. God's power is greater than anything else.

Of course, Peter isn't saying here that God has actual hands, but he wants us to see the power and might of our God. And then he tells us that when we have cares and struggles in this life, we must cast them on this almighty God.

Normally in life when you cast or throw something away, you don't go chasing after it again to get it back, do you? Peter tells us to do the same with our troubles. Cast or throw them before the Lord and then leave them there. Don't keep thinking about them, but trust God. Leave all of your troubles with Him. He is able to deal with your troubles. Hand your troubles over to the Lord and then trust Him to care for you.

REFLECTION

Are there troubles in your life that you can cast or throw to the Lord?

> *"I have inscribed you on the palms of My hands"*

ISAIAH 49:16

GENESIS 3:15

"And I will put enmity between you and the woman, and between your seed and her Seed; He shall bruise your head, and you shall bruise His heel."

READ GENESIS 3:9-15

Can you think about a time when you did something wrong? Maybe you said something very nasty to your sibling. Maybe you lied to your dad, even after he told you to tell the truth. You can probably clearly remember how you felt after sinning like this.

Sin makes us feel ashamed. We feel like everyone can see what we have done wrong, and we want to hide. Adam and Eve did exactly that. They were ashamed because of their sins and they hid.

Sin also makes us feel afraid. We're afraid of what will happen to us when Dad or Mum find out what we did wrong. We might even be afraid that the Lord will punish us for what we have done.

So often we try to blame others for the sin that we did. We might blame our sibling for being nasty. We might even blame our sinful nature by saying, "I can't help it if I get angry."

Sin also separates us from other people. Because we've lied, cheated or said something nasty, the loving relationship that we had with someone might be destroyed. Really, our sin is horrible. There's nothing good about sin at all.

But the Bible has good news for us. God could have destroyed Adam and Eve when they sinned, or chosen never to talk to them again. But God didn't. Oh no. Instead God came to them and, in great love, gently called out, "Where are you?" God took the time to speak to them and to give them a great promise.

God promised them that He would send Jesus Christ to come and crush sin and Satan. That's what verse 15 is speaking about when it talks about the Seed of the woman crushing the head of the serpent. And because Satan was totally crushed by Christ, we are forgiven today. That's the glorious news. Yes, sin is terrible, but when you ask God to forgive you, He will forgive you!

REFLECTION

How does sin make you feel? How does being forgiven by God make you feel?

GENESIS 4:7

"If you do well, will you not be accepted? And if you do not do well, sin lies at the door. And its desire is for you, but you should rule over it."

READ GENESIS 4:3-8

You know the story of Cain and Abel. Cain and Abel both made sacrifices to God. The Lord was pleased with Abel's sacrifice but not with Cain's. Cain knew that God was not happy with his sacrifice. We do not know how Cain knew that God was not happy. And Cain became very angry. He couldn't handle that God accepted Abel's sacrifice and not his.

But then we read that the Lord went to talk to Cain. What love and grace we see here. Cain sinned by having hateful anger, and when God saw this, he talked to Cain and showed him the right way to deal with his anger. The Lord told Cain that if he did well, then God would accept his sacrifice. Yes, there was sin in Cain's heart, but he had to rule over that sin. He had to fight that sin and not give in to his angry thoughts.

Do you know the same can be said of us today? We too have wicked hearts which are full of hatred and anger. Just think about it. I'm sure you can remember being angry at someone recently or thinking that something wasn't fair. Well God also says to you, "You need to change the attitude of your heart." It is your heart that is sinful. But you need to rule over that, and fight against sins.

You know the rest of the story. Cain didn't rule over his heart, and instead he gave in to his anger and murdered his brother Abel. How horrible! This was a terrible act of hatred, and Cain deserved to die for it.

But again God showed His love. Yes, Cain was certainly punished, but God still showed His love by putting a mark on Cain so that no one would kill him.

So, when you read this story of Cain murdering Abel, think about *your* heart. No, you may not have murdered anyone, but you have hated, you have been angry and you have been annoyed. Ask God to help you rule over your heart. Ask God to help you fight against that hatred, and instead have love and kindness in your heart.

REFLECTION

What can you do to rule over your sinful heart?

GENESIS 4:26

Then men began to call on the name of the Lord.

READ GENESIS 4:16-26

There are two paths in life: the path of the serpent's seed and the path of the woman's seed; the path of the children of the devil and the path of the children of the Lord.

In these verses we see both these paths. Cain follows the path of sin and Satan, while Seth follows the path of the Lord. Let's have a look at where these two paths lead.

God tells Cain that he is going to be a fugitive and vagabond. This means that he has to wander around all the time. But Cain doesn't want to listen to the Lord. He wants to do his own things. Instead of wandering around, he decides to build a city, to settle down. Disobeying the Lord leads to more and more sins. We read that Lamech, a great, great grandchild of Cain, takes two wives. The Lord clearly commanded that a man should only marry one wife, yet he decides to have two wives.

And we read of further sin. Lamech must have killed someone, because we read about him boasting to his wives about this killing. He's proud of the sins he has done.

We see so much of this in the world around us, as people follow the path of sin. Many people don't marry anymore. Men marry men. Women marry women. Babies are killed in their mothers' wombs by abortion. And people are happy and proud of their sins.

But then we also see the path of the children of the Lord. God gave Adam and Eve another child called Seth. And Seth also received children. These children were from the line of faith. These people lived differently. Oh yes, they also sinned, but they were sorry for their sins. They certainly didn't boast about their sins. These men called on the name of the Lord! They saw their failures and prayed to the Lord. We too must live on this path, the path of the Lord, and turn to Jesus Christ as our only hope and salvation.

REFLECTION

Which path will you follow—the path of Satan, or the path of the Lord?

GENESIS 6:18

But I will establish My covenant with you; and you shall go into the ark.

READ GENESIS 6:11-22

The people in Noah's days were living a completely evil life. They didn't love the Lord. They chose to ignore the commands of the Lord and to do their own things, living very wicked lives.

Holy God saw all this wickedness on earth, and He couldn't just ignore it. God can't just see all the evil and do nothing about it. God is a just God and He hates all evil. So, God was going to put an end to all the wickedness.

God chose Noah and told him the plan that He had. Noah walked with God. This doesn't mean that Noah never sinned, but it means that he loved the Lord, and he trusted the Lord. He had a close relationship with the Lord and all the people around him would have been able to see this.

God tells Noah that He is going to destroy all the people of the earth. This Bible story isn't really about Noah, but it is about God and His plan of salvation. God is going to make sure Noah is saved. Noah and his family are not going to be destroyed with the rest of the wicked people, but they are going to be saved. God makes a covenant with Noah. God wants to keep some people to have a relationship with. So, God promises Noah that he will be saved. Noah needs to trust the Lord and obey Him by building the ark.

Also today there is much wickedness in the world. Many people around us hate God and don't want to obey and trust Him. And God is going to destroy this evil world as well. God is not going to let the wickedness continue forever. He is going to get rid of it all. But we will not need to be destroyed with the rest of the world. God has made a way of salvation for us as well. That way is to believe and trust in Jesus Christ. We will be saved because of the work of Christ on the cross.

REFLECTION

Why did God save Noah from the flood?

GENESIS 7:16

So those that entered, male and female of all flesh, went in as God had commanded him; and the LORD shut him in.

READ GENESIS 7:11-16

Noah spent a long time building the ark. During this time, he preached to the people around him, warning them that God was going to judge all of their disobedience and wickedness. But the people didn't listen to the warning that Noah gave them and instead just kept on doing evil and wicked things.

We know what happened to all these people. Everybody who was on the earth, apart from Noah and his family, was destroyed by that flood. The flood was God's punishment and judgement against all their wickedness. Since the fall into sin, people were just becoming more and more wicked and it got to a point that God decided that all this wickedness needed to be destroyed.

And so, God's anger and punishment were poured out in this destructive flood. Not only did rain pour down from the skies, but God also opened up the earth so that water gushed forth from the ground as well. God's punishment was great.

During the flood that destroyed everything on earth, Noah and his family were not destroyed. Noah didn't think of this plan to build the ark and save himself. It was God's plan and He is the one who closed the door so that Noah and his family were safely in the ark.

Why did God choose Noah? Was he such a good person? We know that Noah was sinful as well. But God in grace chose to save Noah. God spoke to Noah, and Noah listened to the LORD. In faith he obeyed God. And so, God used the waters that destroyed everyone else to save Noah and his family.

The ark was the only way that Noah could be saved. There is no other way Noah could have been saved from the flood waters. This ark is a picture of our salvation from sin as well. When Christ returns, God will again destroy all the wickedness on Earth. And there is only one way that we can be saved: by God's grace alone. We are saved because of Christ's work for us.

REFLECTION

How is the ark a picture of our salvation?

GENESIS 12:2

I will make you a great nation; I will bless you and make your name great; and you shall be a blessing.

READ GENESIS 12:1-9

After the fall into sin, the Lord promised that there would be two groups of people: the seed of the serpent and the seed of the woman. There would be those who belonged to Satan and those who belonged to the Lord.

When God called Abram to get out of his country and follow Him, the Lord was working on these promises. This story is not about Abram but about what the Lord was doing for His people. That's why the Lord says, "I will do this, and I will do that." The Lord was at work. He called Abram and promised to bless him and make his name great, not just for Abram's sake but for the sake of all God's people. God was going to have a group of covenant people for Himself as He had promised.

Abram was quite settled in Ur, where he was living. But God told him to leave all his things behind and live the rest of his life wandering around in tents. Abram didn't know why he had to do it, but he simply had to live by faith and obey the Lord.

This wasn't always easy for Abram. He sometimes found it hard to believe God's promises when he didn't see them being fulfilled. And we can be exactly the same. God promises us many things, but we don't always trust the Lord. Sometimes Abram asked the Lord for something extra to know that God would fulfil His promises. But that's not the way of the Lord. What God promises, He does. He promised to make a great nation from Abram and send His Son to save His covenant people. Abram never saw this happen, but it did happen because God kept His promises. And so, we too can trust the Lord's promises to us. He has promised us that we are His special covenant children and that He will work all things in our life for our good, so that one day we can have eternal life with Him. And we need to believe this and trust the Lord.

REFLECTION

Why did the Lord call Abram out of Ur?

GENESIS 12:18

And Pharaoh called Abram and said, "What is this that you have done to me? Why did you not tell me that she was your wife?"

READ GENESIS 12:10–20

It seemed to start off so well. Abram was called by God to go to the land that God would show him. He trusted God, left his father's house, and obeyed the LORD. But then a famine came, and Abram was hungry. So what did he do? He did the wrong thing—he stopped trusting the LORD and went out of the Promised Land to Egypt.

Sometimes we can be like that too. Things go differently than we want, and we forget to trust in the LORD. But if we do that, we forget that the God who promised to look after us is greater than our troubles. He can help us in all things! And that's what Abram forgot as well.

When Abram went to Egypt, he told Sarai to lie. He told her to say she was his sister instead of his wife. Abram thought that if people thought Sarai was his sister, they would ask him first before wanting to marry her. He figured that because Sarai was so pretty, if someone liked her, they might talk to him first, and then they could leave quickly. We're not sure what Abram was thinking, but we know he wasn't trusting the LORD. It seemed that Abram's lie worked to save his life, but his wife was taken from him.

Where was God during this time? Had He forgotten His promises to Abram? No, God never forgets His promises. And that's why Abram should have trusted God instead of trusting his own plans. But when Abram got to the point where he was stuck (Sarai had been taken from him), God stepped in to remind Abram to trust Him. God sent a plague so that Pharaoh gave Sarai back to Abram. Abram made a sacrifice to God to show that he was sorry for his sins.

What about us? Sometimes we forget to trust God's promises too. God has promised to always be with us. This doesn't mean things will always be easy, but God will always be with us, forgive us, and give us eternal life with Him.

REFLECTION

What did Abram do wrong? Do we sometimes do the same?

GENESIS 14:20

"And blessed be God Most High, Who has delivered your enemies into your hand."

READ GENESIS 14:17-24

At the beginning of this chapter we read about some battles. At first they don't seem very important, until we read that Lot, Abram's brother, was taken captive. When Abram heard about this, he went out to fight and claim Lot back. And by the grace of God, Abram won the battle and rescued Lot and all the people and goods of Sodom.

When Abram returned from this battle, he was met by two kings. One was Melchizedek, the king of Salem, who was also a priest of God. He came out to bless Abram. He brought bread and wine and a blessing from the Lord.

But then along came the second king, the king of Sodom. The king of Sodom said Abram could keep all the riches and goods that he rescued if he just gave the people back to the king of Sodom.

It would have been very tempting for Abram to take all the riches and goods that he collected in the battle. After all, he had gone out and won them all back. But Abram knew that it was the LORD who helped him. And he knew everything belongs to the LORD. And that's what he told the king of Sodom.

He couldn't take the goods for himself. They belonged to the LORD. If Abram took them, he may have been tempted to trust in them instead of trusting the LORD. And so, Abram listened to the king of Salem, who was also a priest of God. He received the blessing from the LORD that Melchizedek gave him. But that also meant that Abram couldn't keep the goods for himself. He would trust in the LORD to look after him, not the king of Sodom.

What about us? Satan tries to tempt us to trust in *things* instead of trusting in the LORD. But, like Abram, we must always acknowledge that God owns everything and is in control of everything, and so we must always trust Him!

REFLECTION

How did Abram show his trust in the LORD?

GENESIS 15:5

Then He brought him outside and said, "Look now toward heaven, and count the stars if you are able to number them."

READ GENESIS 15:1–6

Promises are great, but sometimes they just don't seem to be enough. God promised us at our baptism that He would care for us, but sometimes we just wish He would care a bit more.

Abram had the same problem. God had promised him that he would have many children, and yet he was childless. He didn't even have one child. So, what good were God's promises if they didn't seem to happen? Abram was already eighty-five years old and he was struggling to understand God. So, God spoke to Abram and told him that He was his shield. God had always been faithful to Abram in the past, and He would continue to be faithful to him.

Then God took Abram outside and told him to look up at the stars. God told Abram to count the stars. Have you ever tried counting the stars? You can see the big ones that form the Saucepan or the Southern Cross, but what about all those tiny ones that form the Milky Way? And then those tiny little dots that flicker in the sky. Sometimes there are so many stars that they form a cloud. There is no way that we can count the stars. Yet God knows every single star. The number of stars is far beyond anything we can understand, yet God knows each star by name. That's how great our God is.

Abram needed to look beyond the stars to the great God who created them. God promised him that his descendants would be as many as the stars, and Abram needed to know that the God who created the stars could and would keep His promises. And Abram did indeed believe the Lord.

We too need to trust in the Lord to keep His promises to us. The Lord who promised at our baptism that He would always care for us, is the same God who made the stars and who still knows all their names. Next time you are tempted to doubt God's care for you, look up at the stars and remember the God who created them.

REFLECTION

Why did Abram have to try and count the stars?

GENESIS 15:18

On the same day the Lord made a covenant with Abram.

READ GENESIS 15:7–21

God told Abram to do something that sounds very odd to us. But it would have made sense to Abram. In Abram's day when two men wanted to make a promise about something, they would make a covenant. They would take some animals and cut them in two, laying each half opposite the other half to form a path through the middle. Then they would both walk through the middle of the animals and they would say, "We will do all that we have promised today. But if either of us breaks our promise, let us be cut in half like these animals." They both had to keep their promises. These promises could not be broken.

Abram did as the Lord said; he cut the animals in two and made a path between the two halves. But what then? Could sinful Abram walk between the animals with holy God? Absolutely not. There was no way that he could keep all his promises like God would.

While Abram waited for God to tell him what to do and looked at the animals he had prepared, he knew that they showed God would keep His promise and give the land to Abram's children and grandchildren.

When night came, Abram saw a burning torch go between the animals. This torch was God Himself. God walked between the animals. God made the covenant and promised to keep it. God could do this because He is almighty. He will always keep His promises.

But Abram could not walk in between the animals, because no person can walk with God to seal the covenant promises. God will keep His promises even though Abram could not keep his. Whatever happens, God will always keep His promises.

And God has made a covenant with us as well. We are His covenant children and so He will also keep all of His promises to us as well. Let us always trust God!

REFLECTION

Why did God (as a burning torch) walk between the dead animals?

GENESIS 16:13

Then she called the name of the Lord who spoke to her, You-Are-the-God-Who-Sees.

READ GENESIS 16:1-13

Does God really see you? Does God really care about what happens in your life? These are questions that Sarai and Hagar probably asked. And these are questions that we ask sometimes.

Sarai had been promised a child. Yet she had waited and waited for many years and she still didn't have a baby. She must have been wondering if she was ever going to have this promised child. She was getting older and older. What could she do? Sarai thought she had a good idea. She thought she knew how to solve the problem of not having a baby. She decided to give her servant Hagar to Abram and if they had a baby, that baby would be called Sarai's baby. This was something that was done more often in Bible times.

But Sarai's solution to the problem was not good at all. It only caused more problems. The real problem was that Sarai had stopped looking at God. She had taken her eyes off God and stopped trusting Him. She tried to sort things out without God.

Abram, by doing what Sarai said, had also taken his eyes off God and failed to trust in Him. And what about Hagar? She also wasn't focused on the Lord. Because Hagar was scared of Sarai, she ran away. But instead of doing this, she should have continued to trust God.

When Hagar was all alone in the desert, the Lord came to her in the form of an angel. The Lord spoke kindly to her, asking her what she was doing in the desert. The Lord told her to return to Sarai, and promised that He would be with Hagar and her son. Hagar realised that she was not alone but that God saw her wherever she was. And so, Hagar called Him, "You are a God of seeing." The Lord has seen and heard her. And this is what God is like. He sees every one of His children. He never forgets us, even in our pain and suffering. The Lord sees you and me wherever we are. He is the God who sees!

REFLECTION

Why does Hagar call God, "You are a God of seeing"?

GENESIS 17:15

Then God said to Abraham, "As for Sarai your wife, you shall not call her name Sarai, but Sarah shall be her name."

READ GENESIS 17:15-22

God came to Abraham with a great promise. It was a promise that didn't really make sense because it seemed impossible. God promised Abraham that his wife Sarai would have a son. Sarai was 99 years old which was far too old to have a baby. It was impossible. But with God all things are possible.

For the past thirteen years, Abraham may have thought that Ishmael was the promised son, but here God told him that his wife Sarai was going to have the promised son. Even though Sarai was old and hadn't had any children, God told Abraham that she would have a son.

Actually, Sarai wouldn't just have one son, but she would become the mother of many nations. She would have many grandchildren and great-grandchildren. Earlier in the chapter God had already changed Abram's name to Abraham; the name Abraham means 'father of many nations.' And now God changed Sarai's name to Sarah. Sarai means 'my princess', but Sarah means 'princess'. She would no longer just be Abraham's princess, but she would be a princess to many nations. Kings would come from her line. She would be a mother to many people. She would even be mother to the Messiah the Lord Jesus. Oh, what grace there is in this name change, in this promise to Abraham and Sarah.

God was going to work in amazing ways. What seemed impossible would happen. Sarah would have a son whose name would be Isaac. And we know that God did give Sarah this son a year later.

God has also done many other amazing things, many other things that seemed impossible. The most amazing thing He did was to send His Son, our Lord Jesus Christ, to become our Saviour. He paid for our sins, even though He never sinned Himself. And He has changed our sinful and wicked hearts to be ones that love and serve Him. Oh, what an amazing God.

REFLECTION

What did it mean that Sarai's name was changed to Sarah?

GENESIS 18:14

"Is anything too hard for the LORD?"

READ GENESIS 18:1-15

Three men appeared at Abraham's tent in the heat of the day. Even though Abraham did not realise it immediately, it was the LORD and two angels. The LORD had come with a message for Abraham. When Abraham saw these men, he asked them to stay for a little while and went and prepared some food for them. Sarah prepared some cakes and bread, and Abraham killed and cooked a calf. When the food was prepared, they brought it to the guests so that they could eat.

Once they had eaten, they asked Abraham where his wife Sarah was. They knew that Sarah was in the tent close by and would be able to hear this message. They told Abraham that Sarah would have a baby son within a year.

Sarah heard the words of the LORD, but she did not believe them at first. She thought she was too old to have children. How was this possible? The LORD knew what Sarah was thinking. He knew that she laughed within herself, and so He asked Abraham why Sarah laughed. And then the LORD said these amazing words to Abraham: "Is anything too hard for the LORD?" With God anything is possible. God can do all things.

Mary, the mother of Jesus, asked a very similar question when she was told by an angel that she was going to have a baby before she was married. She asked, "How can this be since I am not married?" And the angel's answer to her was, "For with God nothing will be impossible." We see the same words here. Nothing is impossible for God. He is able to do all things.

God was able to give Sarah a son when she was far too old to have a baby. He was able to give Mary a son when she was not married. But God did send that Son to Mary. And that Son was our LORD and Saviour, Jesus Christ. And through that Son, we now have salvation. And that is the great message of the Bible.

REFLECTION

What is the wonderful thing that God says in this passage?

GENESIS 27:19

Jacob said to his father, "I am Esau your firstborn."

READ GENESIS 27:18-29

This story about Jacob and Esau is very well known. I'm sure you remember how Jacob dressed in hairy goat's skin and his brother's clothes, and went to his father, Isaac, pretending to be Esau. Isaac asked Jacob very pointedly, "Are you really my son Esau?" In response to this, Jacob told a terrible lie, and said, "Yes I am." He was worried that Esau was going to receive the blessing that God had promised to him. Instead of trusting God to fulfil His promise, he lied and tricked Isaac into believing that he was Esau.

Was this right of Jacob? Of course not! He lied! He lied to get something that wasn't his. He stole from his brother.

Now, let's look at Jesus Christ. He acted in a completely different way than Jacob did. He too was asked if He really was who He said He was. Pilate asked Him if He was really the King, the Christ. If Jesus had lied, like Jacob, and said *no,* then He might have been released and then He would not have been sent to the cross. But Jesus told the truth, even though He knew that it would mean that He would have to go to the cross and suffer hellish agony. Christ gave up everything to suffer on the cross. Because of Jesus' suffering and death, we are now loved by the Father as His children. Jesus told the truth to give us these wonderful blessings.

Jacob *lied* to *steal* the blessing from his older brother, but Jesus told the truth to *give* blessings to us, who are His brothers and sisters.

We, like Jacob, often steal and lie. We might waste time in the bathroom so that we don't have to do the dishes. We might lie about whose turn it is in a game. Yet, because Jesus told the truth and never lied, we can now be forgiven and blessed by God.

REFLECTION

Do you remember to thank the LORD for the blessings you receive because Christ told the truth?

GENESIS 37:24

Then they took him and cast him into a pit.

READ GENESIS 37:23-28

Have you ever had someone treat you badly? Maybe they were very nasty and hurt you in some terrible way. You may wonder why the Lord allowed that to happen to you.

Joseph was treated terribly by his brothers. They were jealous of him, hated him and so they threw him in a pit and later sold him as a slave to some traders. Some of the brothers even wanted to kill him.

When we read about these brothers, the Lord is reminding us of how sinful we all can be. Sometimes we do terrible things that we later regret. Sometimes we do not obey God's good commandments and instead do the wrong thing. At times our sins can be a burden to us. We feel really bad because of our sins. It feels like a weight on our shoulders. We can almost feel sick because of the wrong things we have done.

The Lord wants us to feel this way about our sins so that we go to Him in repentance. If we just ignored our sins and did not care about them, then we would continue to do the wrong things and would not have a relationship with God. But we need to feel guilty because of our sins, so that we turn to God and ask Him to forgive us.

And the Lord will forgive us for Jesus' sake. Jesus Christ was also treated very badly by the people around Him who should have been His spiritual brothers. Like Joseph's brothers, these brothers were jealous of Jesus and rejected and hated Him. They not only *thought* about killing Jesus, they *did* kill Him. They crucified Him on the cross. But God used the plans of these wicked men to bring salvation to mankind. Because of Christ Jesus' death we can now be saved from our sins.

When other people treat us badly, then we should never doubt that God is still with us. We might not understand why the Lord allows things to happen, but just like God cared for Joseph, so you can know that He will care for you.

REFLECTION

How can you see the Lord's love for you in these verses?

"*My Presence will go with you, and I will give you rest*"

EXODUS 33:14

PSALM 145:3

Great is the Lord, and greatly to be praised.

READ PSALM 145

Can you think of a very important person? Maybe you think of the King or the Prime Minister. King David was one of those important rulers. He was the king of the people of Israel. And yet, in Psalm 145, David sings about someone who is much more important than he is. He sings about the Lord God, our heavenly Father.

David sings about God's mighty acts. Everything that God does is mighty, awesome, wonderful and great! Think about God's creation. Also think about the most wonderful act of sending His Son, Jesus Christ, to die on the cross for us. How awesome is that?

David sings of God's righteousness. God only ever does things that are right—that are good. He always keeps His promises. He never lets us down and so we can trust completely in Him.

David says that God's kingdom is an everlasting kingdom. Kings, or rulers on earth, will die and someone else will rule in their place. But that's not the case with God's kingdom. God will always be King. He will always be ruler. We never have to worry that God might stop being God. No, not at all. He will always be here, as the Father of His covenant people. We will even live forever with God in eternity. How exciting is that?

David also sings about God's care for His people: "He will hear their cry and save them." When you are sad, the Prime Minister or King doesn't know about it, do they? When you're sick, they don't write letters to help you. They don't even know what goes on in your life. Yet God, your Father, does. He knows when you cry. He knows when you hurt yourself. He knows when you are sick—and He cares! He cares, and He also helps you. He *can* help you because He is God, and He *will* help you because He is your Father.

How blessed we are to have this wonderful ruler as our Father!

REFLECTION

Can you find other things in this Psalm which show how much God loves you and cares for you?

PSALM 146:1

Praise the Lord! Praise the Lord, O my soul!

READ PSALM 146

Praise the Lord! This Psalm begins and ends with these words: praise the Lord! Do you always feel like praising the Lord? Do you feel like praising Him when your friends are being nasty to you or when your grandparent is sick and dying? Do you feel like praising the Lord when the party you were looking forward to has just been cancelled?

How can the psalmist tell us to praise the Lord all the time, with our whole being?

Let's just think about Jesus (who would have sung this psalm) for a moment. He did indeed praise the Lord always! Never once did He stop praising the Lord. Even when He suffered hunger, was mocked, was in pain, was sad or hurting, He praised the Lord. Oh yes, the Lord Jesus experienced all these sad and difficult moments, and yet He was able to praise the Lord all the time. What we are not able to do, He did perfectly.

Yet the Holy Spirit tells us in the Psalm that we are to praise the Lord always. We can do this when we praise Him for who He is and not for what He gives us. God is your Father because of Jesus Christ. Because of Jesus' perfect obedience, including His perfect praise, you are allowed to be God's child.

Verse 5 tells us that we are happy, or blessed, if we have this God as our helper. He is the one who created the heavens and the earth. He is the one who feeds the hungry and opens the eyes of the blind. He is the one who forgives your sins. It's because of who God is that you can praise Him. You can praise Him also when you are sad or hurting, when you are upset or lonely. You can praise Him because He is always with you. He never sleeps or goes on holidays. No, He cares for you always. He is always your God and Father. Praise the Lord. Hallelujah!

REFLECTION

Why can you praise God, even when you are hurting or sad?

1 SAMUEL 16:12

So he sent and brought him. Now he was ruddy, with bright eyes, and good-looking. And the Lord said, "Arise, anoint him; for this is the one!"

READ 1 SAMUEL 16:6-13

King Saul had turned away from the Lord, so the Lord is going to appoint a new king for the people of Israel. God is going to appoint a king who is loyal to Him, someone who loves Him.

God sends the prophet Samuel to go and anoint this king. Samuel is only told where he has to go, but not who will be the next king. He has to go and make a sacrifice to the Lord and invite Jesse and his sons to this sacrifice.

Samuel does as the Lord tells him, and when Jesse and his sons come before him, Samuel looks at the oldest son and thinks that he certainly looks like someone who could be a king. He thought God must certainly have chosen this son. But God tells Samuel that He doesn't look at how a person looks on the outside, but God looks at the heart. God is going to choose someone who can be a true king.

Now David had done nothing at all that would give God reason to choose him. His dad didn't even think it was worth having him go to the sacrifice. He was just the youngest son. He wasn't worthy to become the next king.

And that's just the point. God chooses people who in themselves are not worthy. And God gave David His Spirit. No, David was not worthy, but the Lord was with him and gave him what he needed to be king. And none of us are worthy to be chosen by God either. But God does choose us and makes us His children.

There was someone else who had no outward beauty, but He was worthy—worthy to be the true King. That's the Lord Jesus Christ. And He has died on the cross, risen and ascended into heaven as our great King. And as our great King, He makes us, sinful and unworthy people, to be people after God's heart. He works in each of us to make us love and serve the Lord.

REFLECTION

Why did God choose David to be king?

ACTS 1:11

"Men of Galilee, why do you stand gazing into heaven?"

READ ACTS 1:9-11

Has it ever happened that your mum told you to go and clean your room or set the table, but instead of going immediately, you just stood there looking at your mum? After a little while, your mum had to tell you to hurry up and go and do what she told you to do.

Well, the same type of thing happened to the disciples after Jesus ascended into heaven. The Lord Jesus had told them that they needed to go and tell the people throughout the whole world about His death and resurrection. They had to spread the gospel. After Jesus had told them these things, He ascended into heaven before their eyes. They watched as a cloud hid Him from their sight.

But then two angels came and told them not to stare into heaven, but to go and do the task that Jesus had told them to do. There was much work for them to do. Jesus wanted His kingdom on earth to continue to grow. The disciples needed to go and tell people about Jesus. They had to stop staring and get to work.

You need to be busy working for the Lord Jesus too. You need to tell your neighbours and others about the Lord also. But you also need to be busy yourself, growing in your love for the Lord. You need to take time to learn about the Lord and speak to Him in prayer. You also need to be busy learning at school, helping at home and playing with your brothers and sisters. As you do all these things, you need to be doing them for the Lord.

The angels also told the disciples that Jesus is coming back. So, as you do things throughout the day, do them for the Lord, looking to Christ, remembering that He will return on the clouds of heaven one day.

REFLECTION

Do you ever think about the fact that the Lord Jesus could come back at any time?

ACTS 4:12

Nor is there salvation in any other, for there is no other name under heaven given among men by which we must be saved.

READ ACTS 4:8-12

What has Jesus saved us from? We all know that Jesus is the only name by which we can be saved. But what does this mean? Does it just mean that we will have eternal life one day, or is it also helpful for today?

We have three enemies and Jesus saves us from all of them. He helps us to fight against all three enemies.

Our first enemy is Satan. Satan hates God and us, and he sends out his evil helpers to attack us. Satan wants us to take our eyes off Jesus and focus on ourselves. He wants us to think that we can save ourselves and that we don't need Jesus. Satan thought that he had won the battle when Jesus died on the cross, but Jesus rose from the dead and conquered Satan. And now Jesus gives us His Word and the Holy Spirit to fight Satan.

Our second enemy is the world. The world is anything that is against God. There are many things around us that tempt us to do the wrong thing. All these things want us to find happiness without Christ. Jesus saves us from these as well. He helps us to look to Him for true happiness. We can't really be happy without Christ.

Our last enemy is ourselves, our own sinful flesh. Deep inside ourselves we often love sin. Even though we love Jesus and know we shouldn't sin, we sometimes like to sin. Sometimes we just want to say something nasty back to others. Sometimes we just want to steal that lolly or be lazy. Our sinful nature still wants to sin. We also need saving from that.

Thankfully Jesus saves us from all three of these enemies. He has overcome Satan, the world, and our own sinful flesh. They do still attack us today and we do still sin, but Christ has already won the victory. None of these things will be able to separate us from our Saviour, Jesus Christ.

REFLECTION

What are our three enemies?

ACTS 16:34

...and he rejoiced, having believed in God with all his household.

READ ACTS 16:25-34

Do you think about the work of the Holy Spirit very often? Do you know exactly what He does? As part of the Trinity, the Holy Spirit is always working. He was already busy at creation and even today He creates new life.

But He is also busy in our hearts. He is the one who makes us serve and love the Lord. If it were not for the working of the Holy Spirit in our lives, we would not love the Lord at all.

In this Bible passage, we see some of the powerful working of the Holy Spirit. Paul and Silas were in prison. They were there because they had been preaching about the Lord Jesus, and the people who did not like their preaching sent them to prison.

And while they were in this horrible prison cell, instead of being sad and angry, Paul and Silas were praying and singing hymns to God. All the other prisoners were listening to them. Then suddenly God caused a great earthquake to shake the ground. This earthquake did not break down the walls of the prison, but it opened the doors and shook the chains off the arms of the prisoners. The prisoners, including Paul and Silas, could all have escaped.

When the jailer saw that all the doors had been opened, he assumed that the prisoners had all escaped and thought it was his fault. And so, he was about to kill himself. But Paul called out to him to let him know that no one had escaped, but that they were all still in prison.

When the jailer heard this, he was amazed. He fell at Paul and Silas' feet asking, "What must I do to be saved." And this is where we see the powerful working of the Holy Spirit. This jailer, who did not know the Lord at all, listened to the words of Paul and believed in the Lord Jesus. The Spirit changed his wicked heart to make him love the Lord. And in the same way the Spirit changes our wicked hearts to make us love the Lord as well.

REFLECTION

What does the Holy Spirit do in your life?

JONAH 1:1

Now the word of the L<small>ORD</small> came to Jonah.

READ JONAH 1:1-9

Imagine some men committed murder and, rather than being sorry for what they had done, they actually boasted about it. Then imagine that you had to go to these murderers and tell them about the Lord.

In a way, this is what Jonah had to do when he was told by the Lord to preach to the people of Nineveh. They were great enemies of the Israelites and had murdered many people and hurt their women and children. We can understand why Jonah didn't want to do this. But even though it was understandable, it was very wrong.

So what did Jonah do? He ran away, far away. He didn't even speak to the Lord and ask Him for help. Even Moses did that when he begged the Lord to send someone instead of him to Egypt. Jonah, however, didn't pray to the Lord but went on a boat to try and escape God. And even on the boat after the storm started, he didn't pray. When the sailors asked him about the storm, he said that he worshipped God, but he didn't show this in his actions. Jonah was part of God's special covenant people, and so God had promised to be with Jonah, but he was breaking the covenant. He wanted nothing to do with God.

Jonah's act of running away from God and the task God gave him to do, points us to our need of a saviour. Someone needed to come to this world, to preach to us sinners. And Jesus Christ is that person. He didn't run away when He was sent by His Father but came willingly. He came to die on the cross so that we can now be forgiven sinners. He came to teach us that He is the only way to salvation. Oh, what wonderful news.

Now we are all prophets of the Lord and can share this news of Christ's salvation. Let us not run away but always share the good news of God's love with those around us.

REFLECTION

How are the Ninevites a picture of us? Do we all need saving?

JONAH 1:10

"Why have you done this?"

READ JONAH 1:10-16

"What is this that you have done?" the sailors asked Jonah. They knew that this terrible storm was because of Jonah, so they wanted to know what he had done wrong.

God used the sailors' question to make Jonah aware of his sins. The Lord wanted Jonah to think about what he had done wrong and repent of his sins. The Lord used the storm and the sailors to bring Jonah to his knees. Jonah needed to know his sins.

When the sailors asked Jonah what they needed to do to calm the storm, Jonah told them to throw him into the sea and the storm would be calm. Jonah now realised his sins. He knew the storm was because of him. He deserved to be punished for his sins, so he told the sailors to throw him into the sea.

Instead, the sailors tried to save Jonah by rowing as hard as they could. Maybe they were trying to bring Jonah to Nineveh to obey God. But that didn't work. So they obeyed God's Word, by listening to His prophet Jonah, and threw Jonah overboard into the sea.

But before they threw Jonah overboard, they prayed to the Lord. They knew that this was the work of the Lord, so they asked God not to punish them for throwing Jonah overboard and into the raging sea.

The Lord immediately calmed the storm, saving the sailors. The sailors then praised God by offering a sacrifice. The Lord had made them and Jonah aware of their sins.

We too need to know how great our sins are. We too so often disobey the Lord. And just like Jonah's sins needed to be punished, so do our sins need to be punished. But Jonah couldn't pay for his own sins and neither can we. There is only one who can pay for our sins, and that is Jesus Christ. And He has come, and He has paid for our sins. Let us thank and praise God for His grace.

REFLECTION

What is God teaching Jonah in this passage?

JONAH 1:17

Now the Lord had prepared a great fish to swallow Jonah.

READ JONAH 1:17 AND MATTHEW 12:38–41

Jonah had tried to run away from the Lord. He didn't want to listen to God's command, so he ran to a ship hoping to hide from the Lord. But the Lord sees everything and caused a great storm at sea and made the sailors throw Jonah overboard, into the raging waters.

In the same way as the Lord had suddenly sent the storm, He now sent a very large fish to swallow Jonah alive. This verse says very clearly that it was the Lord who sent the fish. God was at work saving Jonah. Jonah did not deserve this. He really should have died, but God saved him out of grace and love! God rescued him!

In the New Testament, Jesus also talked about the sign of Jonah. The Lord saving Jonah through the fish, and Jonah being in the belly of the fish for three days and nights was a model of how God would bring salvation to us through the death, burial and resurrection of Christ.

The Pharisees asked for a sign from heaven, but they were given the sign of Jonah. Jesus didn't call down fire from heaven as a sign but pointed them to Jonah. Just like Jonah was saved from death by being in the belly of a fish for three days, so Jesus died and was buried in the earth for three days to save all of us, His children.

The Lord provided salvation to Jonah through a fish. He provides salvation to us also, not through a fish, but through Jesus Christ. Jesus Christ is much greater than Jonah. Jesus came, not to save us from death in the water, but from eternal death. He came to save us from hell. And He is the only way to be saved. By believing in Jesus who died, and who was in the belly of the earth for three days and then raised…by believing in Him and trusting in Him, we are saved from eternal death. We may look forward to living eternally with God!

REFLECTION

How does Jonah point to Christ?

JONAH 2:4

Then I said, "I have been cast out of Your sight; Yet I will look again toward Your holy temple."

READ JONAH 2:1-9

Jonah goes down, down, down into the depths of the sea. As he is going down, the seaweed gets tangled around his head. He can't find the surface of the water, he can't breathe but is carried down deeper into the water. He is drowning.

But then suddenly a large fish comes, and in one quick gulp swallows Jonah alive. Jonah is no longer in the water but in the belly of a fish. It is slimy and yucky and pitch dark in there.

What does Jonah do while he is in the belly of the fish? He is in there for a long time which means he has a long time to think. He knows why he is in the fish. He knows that God sent the raging storm and made him get thrown in the water. And Jonah feels the anger of God because of his sins. He feels hidden from God. It all feels hopeless to him there in the belly of the fish.

And so, Jonah prays to the Lord. In verse 4 Jonah says that even though he had been cast off by the Lord, he will again see the temple. God opens Jonah's eyes to the goodness of the Lord. Jonah is sorry for his sins. He wants to go to the temple, to the place where he can make a sacrifice for his sins. Jonah knows that the Lord will save him, and he will see the temple again. He remembers the Lord.

Sometimes we can feel as if God is far away from us as well. We might be suffering in some way. Maybe a family member has died or you just don't seem to have a lot of friends. Maybe you struggle in some other way. Even though your struggles may not be because of your sins like Jonah's were, you can look to God and remember His promises to you. You don't need to look to the temple but can look to Jesus Christ. He saves you, loves you and will always be with you.

REFLECTION

What did Jonah do in the belly of the fish?

JONAH 3:4

Then he cried out and said, "Yet forty days and Nineveh shall be overthrown."

READ JONAH 3

We get so used to going to church every Sunday that sometimes we don't pay a lot of attention to the preaching. We just go with the rest of the family. But listening to the preaching is very important.

Jonah also preached a message. "People of Nineveh, listen carefully. In forty days you are going to be destroyed. Repent, or you will be overthrown." If they didn't turn to the Lord, they would be destroyed. For a whole day, Jonah walked around preaching this warning to the people. He walked, stopped, called out the message, and then continued a bit further before doing the same again.

When the people heard this message, they responded. Verse 5 tells us that they believed God and put on sackcloth. The sackcloth showed that they were sorry and repented. When the king heard this message, he also responded. He said, "Who knows if the Lord will relent?" There was time, forty days, for the people to repent. He sent messengers out to all the people telling them to put on sackcloth and cry out to God. And the king did the same himself. He repented of his sins, and he told all the people to do the same: "Turn away from your evil ways."

And the people believed God, and they turned to Him in repentance. They listened to the preaching of God and believed. We too are called to listen to the preaching every Sunday again. We too must believe the Word of God.

When God saw that the people repented and believed Him, He relented. He decided not to destroy Nineveh anymore. God had mercy on the people who repented. And today also the Lord has mercy on all who come to Him in repentance and true faith. And that's why we need to hear the preaching every Sunday again. God calls us to believe in Him, repent from our sins, and turn to Him for forgiveness. And God will hear us. He will forgive us for the sake of Jesus Christ!

REFLECTION

Why is it important to listen to the preaching in church?

JONAH 4:4

Then the L<small>ORD</small> said, "Is it right for you to be angry?"

READ JONAH 4:1-4

After the people of Nineveh repented of their sins, the L<small>ORD</small> did not destroy the city. In a way it might have been nice if the book of Jonah finished there. But it does not. Chapter 4 tells us that Jonah got very angry with the L<small>ORD</small>. He was so angry that he even wanted to die.

He was angry because God did not destroy Nineveh. He did not want God to show grace and mercy to their enemies. He knew that God was gracious and forgiving. So, he knew that God would forgive the people of Nineveh if they repented, and Jonah did not like that. He wanted his enemies destroyed. He told the L<small>ORD</small>, that this was why he had run away to Tarshish in the first place. He did not want to see the grace of the L<small>ORD</small> to their enemies if they repented. He wanted God's grace and forgiveness for himself, but not for the unbelieving enemies.

Sometimes we can be a bit like Jonah. We want to decide what God can and cannot do. We are happy for God to show grace to us, we are happy for our sins to be forgiven, but we are not happy if God forgives our horrible neighbour or even the kid at school who refused to talk to us.

Sometimes we think that God's love should only be shown to people in the church. We are God's special people and so God's grace is for us only. But we have to remember that we do not deserve God's forgiveness and mercy any more than other people. We are not more worthy of God's love than others. If God works in that boy who used to say very nasty things about you, in such a way that he repents, then God can certainly show His grace to him as well.

Yes, we are God's special covenant people. But that does not mean that we are allowed to be proud and claim God's love only for ourselves. Instead, we should be humble. We must tell many others about God's grace and pray that many more people will come to know Jesus.

REFLECTION

Why was it wrong for Jonah to be angry that God did not destroy Nineveh?

Under His wings you shall take refuge

PSALM 91:4B

JOHN 6:51

*I am the living bread which
came down from heaven.*

READ JOHN 6:1-14, 51

While Jesus was on earth, He told us many things about Himself. He did this because He wanted to teach us who He really is, and why He came to earth. To teach us more about Himself, Jesus gives seven *I am* sayings. All these sayings are like pictures to help us understand a bit more about the Lord.

The first of these sayings is found in John 6. Jesus says, "*I am* the living bread" (v. 51). Bread was the main food the people ate in Jesus' day. If they weren't able to eat bread, they would die of hunger.

Jesus says that He is just like bread. Just like we need to have food to be able to live, so we need to have Jesus to live. Food keeps us alive physically. It gives us energy so that our hearts keep beating and our bodies keep breathing. Jesus keeps us alive spiritually. Jesus gave us the strength, wisdom, obedience and forgiveness we need so that we may continue to live as God's children. Just like bread becomes part of our bodies when we eat it, so Jesus must become part of who we are.

And just like we need to eat food every day to stay alive, so we need Jesus every day. You can't eat a piece of bread and say, "I don't need any more food for the rest of the week." So you can't read the Bible for five minutes and say, "I don't need to read it anymore this week." No, you need to make the Lord a part of your life every day.

Every day you need to get your strength and wisdom from the Lord Jesus. You need to read His Word, the Bible, to learn more about Him. You need to go to Him for forgiveness. You need to pray to Him, tell Him all about your life, and trust Him to help you through every day again.

REFLECTION

How can you make the Lord Jesus a part of your whole life?

JOHN 8:12

"I am the light of the world."

READ JOHN 8:1–12

I'm sure you remember the story of the Israelites wandering in the desert for forty years. Do you remember *how* they knew where they had to go? Yes, God led them with a cloud during the day and a pillar of fire at night. They didn't go anywhere without God. When the cloud moved, they moved; when the cloud stopped, they stopped. If they didn't follow the cloud, they would end up lost and would die. If they didn't have the cloud to protect them from the heat during the day, and the pillar of fire to keep them warm at night, they would die.

Jesus was talking to the Jewish leaders, who had just celebrated a feast that reminded them of the Lord leading the Israelites in the wilderness (John 7:2, 37), when he said, "*I am* the light of the world." Just like the Israelites needed to follow the light in the wilderness, so we need to follow Jesus. There is only one way to stay in the light, and that is by following Jesus. If we don't follow Him, we will be in darkness.

It was when the Pharisees brought a woman who had sinned to Him that Jesus said, "*I am* the light of the world." They wanted to use this woman's sins to try and trick Jesus. But Jesus didn't fall for their trick. Instead, He told the women that her sins were forgiven. And then Jesus said, "*I am* the light."

What Jesus meant is that He is able to forgive our sins. Sometimes we can feel like we are in darkness. Sometimes it may feel like we have sinned so badly that God might not forgive us. And yet the good news is that Jesus is the light. He will take away that darkness. As light, Jesus lifts away that darkness. He forgives us and takes away our sins.

Jesus is the true light. Let us always receive His forgiveness and follow Him!

REFLECTION

How is Jesus the light in your life?

JOHN 10:7

"I am the door of the sheep."

READ JOHN 10:7–10

In Bible times, a shepherd would keep his sheep in fenced-off areas. The sheep would be able to wander in and out of this area, but to do so they would have to walk through one opening, and the shepherd would place himself at the opening. So, if the sheep wanted to walk into this area, they would have to walk through this gate, or door, where the shepherd stood. So the shepherd acted like a door, opening and closing it to let his sheep in and out. The shepherd would even sleep in that opening at night, acting like a closed door to keep the sheep safe from robbers, lions, or other wild animals.

In these verses Jesus says that He is the door of the sheep: "If anyone enters by me, he will be saved." The only way that we, the sheep, can be saved is by entering through the door. And who is that door? It's Jesus Christ! He tells us that He is the door. So, if we want to be saved, then there is only one way—by believing in Jesus Christ.

Sometimes you might think that you really aren't good enough to be saved. You might wonder if your sins are so great that God might not save you. You might think that you don't love the Lord enough. You might be worried that because you don't always feel like going to church, you might not be saved. But Christ doesn't say, "Stop sinning and you will be saved," or, "Only when you always go to church joyfully will you be saved." No, Jesus says, "Enter by Me and you will be saved." Our good works will not save us. We are saved by grace, simply by believing in Jesus Christ. Jesus is the door and it's through Him that we are saved!

REFLECTION

What does it mean to you that Jesus is the door of the sheep?

JOHN 10:11

"I am the good shepherd."

READ JOHN 10:10-14

I'm sure you have seen sheep (or pictures of sheep) grazing in a paddock eating grass. When you see pictures of sheep in bible story books, you will often see that the sheep have a shepherd with them. This shepherd is looking after the sheep, leading them to places where there is enough food and water for them, and making sure that wild animals don't catch and eat the sheep.

Here in John 10 Jesus says, "*I am* the good shepherd." Why does Jesus call Himself the shepherd? What does He mean by that? Jesus uses these words as a type of picture to teach us some important things about Himself. We are the sheep and He is our shepherd!

Just like a shepherd will do anything for his sheep, Jesus will do anything necessary for us. In verse twelve, Jesus talks about hirelings. Hirelings are bad shepherds, who will run away if a wolf comes, and let the wolf eat the sheep. But Jesus isn't like that at all. He is the good shepherd. He loves us so much that He even gave His life for us. He came down from heaven to become a man so that He could die on the cross for our sins. He died so that we can be forgiven. He died so that we can live.

Jesus knows each of His sheep by name. He knows your name, whether it is Craig, Chantal, Rose, or whatever your name is. Jesus knows all the things that you are good at. He also knows all the things you struggle with, including your sins. He knows when you are happy and when you are sad. He knows you even better than you know yourself. And yet He still gave His life for you. You are His precious sheep, and He will always care for you.

REFLECTION

Is it comforting that Christ Jesus knows you so well, or does that sometimes make you scared?

JOHN 11:25

"I am the resurrection and the life."

READ JOHN 11:17-26

One day while Jesus was working, He heard about His friend Lazarus who was sick and dying. Lazarus' sisters, Mary and Martha, knew that if the Lord Jesus came quickly, He would be able to heal Lazarus before he died. So, they begged Him to come quickly to heal their brother.

When Jesus heard about Lazarus from Mary and Martha, He did something that seems very strange to us. Instead of rushing to heal Lazarus, as we would expect, He stayed two days longer in the place where He was. We would think that if He loved Mary, Martha and Lazarus (as the Bible says He did) He would have gone quickly to heal Lazarus.

But Jesus waited two more days before He went to Lazarus because He wanted to show His disciples something important about Himself. Jesus wanted Lazarus to die so that He could show His power and glory. Listen to how the Lord did this.

Jesus went to the grave of the dead man and called, "Lazarus, come out!" Immediately Lazarus came out of the grave. Jesus had raised him from the dead. Jesus had made the dead man alive again. Can you imagine that?

Jesus did this miracle because He wanted to show the people that He has great power over death. Just like Jesus could make someone who is dead alive again, so He can make us who are dead in our sins alive again. Of ourselves we would hate God and not obey Him at all. Without Jesus, we would be enemies of God. But Jesus has made us love God, and He has made us His children.

Jesus showed us how He can make us alive in Him, by raising a man from the dead. Jesus said, "*I am* the resurrection and the life. He who believes in me… he shall live."

REFLECTION

Do you believe in Jesus? How do you show in your life that you love God?

JOHN 14:6

"I am the way, the truth, and the life."

READ JOHN 14:1-6

Do you ever twist the truth a little? Do you ever exaggerate a story to make it sound a little bit better? I'm sure you do sometimes. It's something all of us have done.

But Jesus never did this. He always told the truth. In John 14:6 Jesus tells us, "*I am* the way and the truth and the life." What did Jesus mean when He said, "*I am the truth*"? What is truth? When we think about truth, we think about not lying. For example, if you were playing and broke a window, you should not lie when you tell your parents what happened. You must tell them exactly what happened. You need to tell the truth.

But *truth* is so much more than this. Truth means everything that is right and good. Truth means doing things the way God wants them done. And this is what the Lord Jesus means when He says that He is the truth. Every single word that Jesus spoke was true. Every single thing He did was true, good, and right! Jesus never did anything wrong.

When Jesus says that He alone is the truth, He means that nothing else is the truth. Many people today will tell you that you can believe whatever you want. But Jesus tells us that if we want to be saved, we must believe in Him. His words are the only truth. The Bible is the truth.

As God's child, you must also walk in the truth. We need to make the truth a part of our whole life. This means always telling the truth, but it also means doing what is good and right. This is very difficult to do, isn't it? But the good news is that God has sent His Spirit—the Spirit of truth—to help you do this. Have a look at verse seventeen where Jesus makes the promise that His Spirit of truth will dwell in you.

REFLECTION

What does it mean to walk in the truth?

JOHN 15:5

"I am the vine."

READ JOHN 15:1-8

Have you ever seen a vine? Maybe you have seen a grapevine or a passionfruit vine. A nice, healthy vine will have strong branches and leaves, and lots of juicy, ripe fruit.

Jesus says that He is the true vine. Of course Jesus doesn't mean that He is a plant and that He produces grapes or passionfruit. Instead, Jesus uses the vine as a picture of Himself. He produced perfect fruit throughout His life. Jesus is talking about the fruit of the Spirit like love, joy, peace, patience, kindness, goodness, faithfulness, gentleness, and self-control. As the *true* vine, Jesus was always perfectly loving, perfectly kind, perfectly patient and perfectly good. He always produced perfect fruit.

As covenant children of God, we are also part of this vine. We are the branches of this vine. This means that we are connected to Christ. Just like the branches of an actual vine will get water and food from the roots so that it can produce fruit, so we, as the branches of God's vine, must be connected to Christ and receive everything we need from Him to produce fruit. To be connected to Christ means that we must love Him, have faith in Him, believe in Him, and worship Him. How can you be connected to Christ? By reading His Word every day, praying to Him and trusting Him in all things.

The Spirit also connects you to Christ and so helps you produce good fruit in your life. He will help you to show patience to your annoying little sister, to show love when someone says something nasty to you, and to show joy when helping with the chores around the house. He will connect you to Christ and help you produce fruit.

REFLECTION

Are you taking time every day to listen to God's Word, to pray and to be connected to Christ? Are you producing good fruit in your life?

2 CHRONICLES 7:14

If My people who are called by My name will humble themselves, and pray and seek My face, and turn from their wicked ways, then I will hear from heaven, and will forgive their sin and heal their land.

READ 2 CHRONICLES 7:12-15

We read in these verses a promise from God to the people of Israel. If the land has no rain, or if it is plagued with a disease or locusts, God promises that if the people cry out to Him, telling the Lord that they are sorry for their sins, He will forgive them and He will heal the land.

What does this mean for us today? Does it mean that if we are going through a hard time, and if we then humble ourselves before God, He will then forgive us and take our troubles away?

No, it doesn't mean that God will remove our troubles, even though this was the promise to the people in the Old Testament. But it does mean that God will forgive our sins.

If we look at the chapter before this one, we see the prayer that Solomon prayed after he had built the temple for the Lord. This prayer shows how holy God is, and how sinful His people are. The people's sins kept getting in the way of them being able to have a loving relationship with the Lord. So Solomon prays that when the people receive hardship from the Lord and then turn to Him and repent from their sins, that God will forgive them.

The Holy of Holies in the temple showed that God is indeed a forgiving God and that He will forgive His people's sins when they ask Him. And that is still our promise today too. The Lord Jesus has come and has forgiven our sins. The Holy of Holies is no longer needed for the sacrifices as Christ has been sacrificed on the cross.

So, our promise today is much greater than the promise of having our troubles removed when we acknowledge our sins. We have forgiveness in Jesus Christ. And we have a place in the new Jerusalem waiting for us. God has promised us eternal life with Him on the new earth where there will never be any troubles again.

REFLECTION

What is the great promise that God gives to us?

2 CHRONICLES 33:10

And the L̇ord spoke to Manasseh and his people, but they would not listen.

READ 2 CHRONICLES 33:10-13

Have you heard about King Manasseh? He was one of the worst kings that ever ruled the people of Judah. He did so many wicked things. He brought idols into the temple of the Lord. He even sacrificed his children to the idols. It's hard to think of a more wicked thing to do.

The Lord sent prophets to warn Manasseh, but Manasseh didn't listen. Not at all. He just kept doing more and more evil.

So the Lord sent the Assyrians to capture Manasseh. Once they captured him, they treated him like an animal. They put a big hook in his nose and led him along with a rope from the hook, just like they would lead an ox or a cow.

The Lord allowed the Assyrians to do this because He wanted to get Manasseh's attention. Manasseh didn't listen to the prophets and so the Lord is going to get his attention this way. Do you know what happened? Manasseh repented! He was sorry for his sins. He told the Lord that he wanted to serve Him again. He told the Lord that he was sorry for all those wicked things he had done.

And the Lord, in grace and love, forgave Manasseh. He heard Manasseh's prayers of repentance and sorrow, and brought him back to Jerusalem. Because He loved Manasseh, God forgave him. Manasseh was His covenant child!

A wicked king is forgiven by his gracious Father. And God forgives you too. There is no sin that is so great that God will not forgive it. If you sin and are sorry, tell the Lord you are sorry. Tell Him that you hate your sin and that you want to fight against it. Tell God that you need His help and ask Him for it. Ask God to forgive you and make you clean again.

The Lord, in His covenant love, will certainly forgive you. He will continue to love you and hold on to you as His precious child.

REFLECTION

Why did the Lord forgive Manasseh?

2 CORINTHIANS 9:7

So let each one give as he purposes in his heart, not grudgingly or of necessity; for God loves a cheerful giver.

READ 2 CORINTHIANS 9:6-15

God loves a cheerful giver. Maybe you've heard this verse before and thought, "Well that's a good verse for my dad and mum, but I don't need to worry about it as I don't have any money to give away."

But do you know that even though Paul was talking about giving money here, this verse can refer to many other things as well? You have time and abilities that you can give. Maybe you can help others, play with lonely friends, clean for your mum, or let others read your books or play with your best toys. These are some ways that you can give. And if you do receive some money, then you can certainly give some of that too. You can add some to the collection at church.

Paul didn't tell the Corinthians exactly what to give, but *how* to give. He told them that they must give joyfully. We must be cheerful givers.

Why do you think it is important that you give cheerfully? If you think about all that the Lord has given you, then you should be overflowing with thankfulness, and want to share your many blessings with others. Think about the food you eat, the clothes you wear, the bed you sleep in. They all come from God. And what about the greatest gift of all? The indescribable gift of God's love in sending Jesus to earth so that He could save you. Jesus died for you. What greater gift than this could anyone give? And because God loves you in this way, He wants you to overflow with His love by sharing your things with others.

Naturally, this is not something that we want to do. Of ourselves we are selfish and prefer not to give. But with the help of the Holy Spirit, you can begin to learn to give and to do so joyfully. Ask the Lord to help you be a cheerful giver.

REFLECTION

In what ways can you give?

PSALM 46:10

Be still, and know that I am God.

READ PSALM 46

Be still. That sounds so easy, but when things are hard for you, is it easy to be still? If a loved one is sick or if you have a test that you are worried about or if you hear about a worldwide virus, can you just be still? Can you not worry?

In this Psalm, the Lord told His covenant children in the Old Testament that they didn't need to fear things because He was their help in trouble. Jerusalem didn't even have a river running through it, but only a very small stream. And yet verse 4 speaks about a river. This river talks about God's goodness and provision for His people. The Lord will provide everything that His people need. Not just a little of what they need, like a small stream, but everything that they need, like a large river. And so, the Israelites didn't need to be afraid. They could be still, knowing that God was their help and shelter.

The Lord gives this Psalm for us as well. We also can be still in God. This doesn't mean that difficult things will never come our way. Satan is still trying very hard to attack God's people. He tries every day to make us sin, and so every day we need to fight against sin. Sickness and death and hardships are still in the world today. We can't escape from these things, and they also happen to us as God's people.

But we don't need to fear. We don't need to be scared in these hard times. Why not? Because God will be with us and help us get through all these hard things. He has promised us that. And God has everything in His plan. If your tooth falls out, or your aunty gets sick, or a virus hits the whole world, it is all planned by God. But God also promises to be with you in these hard things. He will give you the strength you need, so simply be still and trust in the Lord.

REFLECTION

How can we "be still" in hard times?

PSALM 50:14

Offer to God thanksgiving.

READ PSALM 50:7-15

In Psalm 50 God called the Israelites together to listen to Him. God was not happy with the way they were bringing their sacrifices. They were acting as though God needed their sacrifices, as though He couldn't do without them. So God reminded them that He didn't need their offerings. Everything belonged to Him already. The cattle, the birds, the wild beasts, they were all the Lord's. Rather, the sacrifices were to teach the people about salvation through Jesus Christ. The sacrifices all pointed forward to Christ.

And so the people had to offer their sacrifices, not thinking that God needed them, but in thankfulness for God's love and forgiveness.

We can sometimes forget that everything belongs to the Lord, so we think that we can use our money and time for ourselves if we just put some money in the collection in church or just give some of our time to the Lord. But we need to remember that everything is the Lord's already: all our money, all our time, and all our things. Every second of every day belongs to the Lord and must be used to serve Him.

But this is so hard to do, isn't it? So often we make a big mess of our lives and spend a lot more time sinning than serving the Lord. And that's why it is also beautiful to read what the Lord tells the Israelites in verse 15: "Call upon me in the day of trouble; I will deliver you, and you shall glorify me." Trouble here means when we are sad because of our sins. When our sins trouble us, we must pray to God and then He will deliver us. This means He will forgive us. Christ has died on the cross, and when we call to God for forgiveness, He will certainly give it to us.

Then, with the help of the Holy Spirit, we can glorify God. We can use our days, our time and our money to serve the Lord.

REFLECTION

What does it mean to you that everything belongs to the Lord?

"Before I formed you in the womb I knew you"

JEREMIAH 1:5A

JOSHUA 1:2

Now therefore, arise, go over this Jordan, you and all this people, to the land which I am giving to them – the children of Israel.

READ JOSHUA 1:1-4

The book of Joshua begins with God's command to Joshua to lead the people over the Jordan River and into the Promised Land. You will remember that about 680 years before this, God had called Abraham and promised him this land of Canaan. And that's where Abraham, Isaac and Jacob lived as strangers until Jacob moved to Egypt. It was in Egypt that the people of Israel were slaves for 430 years. After this, God sent them Moses to be their leader and rescue them from Egypt. But when the people got to the Promised Land, ten of the twelve spies told the people that Canaan wasn't a good land. Therefore, God punished the Israelites for their lack of trust in Him, by sending them back into the wilderness for forty years.

A lot had happened and many years had passed since the Lord first promised this land to Abraham. But God is a faithful covenant Lord who never forgets His promises. He will make sure that whatever He has promised will happen.

At the beginning of the book of Joshua, the people were at the entrance of the land of Canaan. Even though Israel had sinned and was unfaithful to God, God always kept His love for them. Even when they complained about the food in the desert or worshipped a golden calf, God continued to love His unfaithful people. The fact that they were now again at the entrance of the land was proof of God's love and faithfulness.

The Lord even says in verse 3, "The land I have given you." God spoke as though what He had promised them—the land—had already been given to them. That's how faithful God is.

And so you too can always trust God's promises. Whatever He has promised, He will give to you. And even though you are sinful, just like the Israelites, and don't always show your love to the Lord, God's love for you will continue always. This is because He has sent His Son, the Lord Jesus, to pay for your sins.

REFLECTION

What does it mean that God is faithful?

JOSHUA 1:6

"Be strong and of good courage."

READ JOSHUA 1:5-9

When Joshua was about to start his task as leader of the people of Israel, God told him to "be strong and of good courage." When you think about someone or something strong, you might think of your dad who has big, strong muscles, or a thick rope that you can't break.

But God meant something entirely different here when He told Joshua to be strong and of good courage. God told Joshua to be strong in Him, in the Lord. Joshua had to be firm, confident, brave, and bold in obeying the Lord. He had to trust in the Lord in order to do all the tasks he needed to do. And he had enormous tasks to do. He needed to lead Israel into the Promised Land and fight against all the people of Canaan.

Joshua couldn't do any of these tasks on his own. No, he needed to do all these things by being brave and strong *in the Lord*. He had to listen to the Lord very closely to know what the Lord wanted him to do. He had to obey the Lord even when he was scared (and there were many times when he would have been scared). It also meant that he had to pray to the Lord all the time, asking God to help him as he did his tasks, asking the Lord to make him brave!

God had promised Joshua that He would be with him: "I will be with you. I will not leave you nor forsake you." And do you know that God gives you the same promises? He will always be with you too. He will never leave you either. And just like Joshua, you too need to be strong and of good courage. You can do this by listening to God's Word, by reading your Bible every day, and by always praying to God, asking Him to be with you and to make you strong to obey Him always.

REFLECTION

Do you remember to ask the Lord to help you be brave so that you can obey Him?

JOSHUA 2:11

"For the Lord your God, He is God in heaven above and on earth beneath."

READ JOSHUA 2:8–15

As Joshua began his task of leading the people into the Promised Land, he sent two spies to check out the city of Jericho. God led these spies to Rahab's house. Somehow the king of Jericho heard about the spies and sent men to Rahab's house to demand that she give the two spies over to the king. But Rahab had hidden the spies on the roof, so when the king's men came knocking on her door, she had her answer ready: "Two men did come, but they have already left out the gate." So the king's men headed off looking for the spies.

Rahab went up to the men on her roof and told them that she believed that the Lord had given the city of Jericho to the Israelites and that all the people of Jericho were scared because of the Israelites and their God. She also told them how they had heard what the Lord did for His people at the Red Sea after they came out of Egypt. Rahab believed in the Lord. God worked in her life and gave her the gift of faith. God changed her hard heart and caused her to believe in Him. God would one day send His Son, also for the sins of Rahab.

Rahab knew that her life and the life of her family was in danger. She knew that when Jericho was destroyed, she would be destroyed as well, and so she asked that her life be spared. The spies assured her that if she didn't tell anyone about them, she would not die when Jericho was destroyed.

Rahab then let the spies down through the window and advised them to hide for a few days.

After three days the spies returned to Joshua and told him everything that had happened. Hearing all this information about how the Lord worked faith in the heart of Rahab, and how the people of Jericho were trembling with fear, would have reassured Joshua that the Lord would keep His promise to bring the people into the Promised Land.

REFLECTION

What did God work in Rahab's heart?

JOSHUA 3:5

"Sanctify yourselves, for tomorrow the Lord will do wonders among you."

READ JOSHUA 3:1-6

The children of Israel were about to enter the Promised Land. But they had a big problem in front of them. How were they going to cross the Jordan River? This wasn't just a small stream that they could wade through, but it was a large river that was overflowing its banks. For three days they were camped on the banks of the river, waiting to see what would happen next. No doubt they would have spent a lot of this time wondering how they were going to get across that river.

But before they could move, they were first instructed by the Lord to sanctify, or consecrate, themselves. This meant that they had to make themselves ready to follow the Lord's instructions. They had to be holy. That's what the word "sanctify" means. It means "to make yourself holy." It means that they had to focus on the Lord and what He was doing. They had to prepare their hearts to listen to the Lord. They didn't know how they were going to cross the Jordan River, but that didn't matter. What did matter, was making their hearts ready to listen to and obey the Lord. They had to use their time to make sure they were ready to follow God. Only after their hearts were ready to listen to the Lord would the Lord give them the next instruction.

What about you? Do you ever have times in your life when you aren't sure how things are going to work out? How are you going to get through your schoolwork? How are you going to find new friends in a new area? How are you going to cope if you get sick? There will be many more "how" questions you may be struggling with.

But before you do anything to try and find the answers, consecrate your heart. Make sure you are ready to listen to the Lord. Focus on Him and what He wants you to do. Spend time reading your Bible and praying. Only then will you be able to obey the Lord.

REFLECTION

What did the children of Israel have to do before they could cross the Jordan River? Why?

JOSHUA 3:7

And the Lord said to Joshua, "This day I will begin to exalt you in the sight of all Israel."

READ JOSHUA 3:7-9

The children of Israel had been instructed to make their hearts holy. Only after they had made their hearts ready, would the Lord instruct them on how they would cross the Jordan River.

But then the Lord still said something else before they crossed through the river. He said that He would exalt Joshua. To exalt means to make great. Why would the Lord do that? What did it actually mean that Joshua would be made great? It didn't mean that Joshua would be able to walk around like a proud man because the Lord had made him someone very important; rather, it meant that the people could know that God was with Joshua, just like the Lord had been with Moses. The people had to know that Joshua was their new leader and that the Lord was using him to instruct the people. The people had to know that when Joshua spoke, it was God using him to tell them what to do. They had to know that they could follow him. When Joshua spoke it was God speaking to them.

Who do you follow in your life? Whose instructions do you listen to? Yes, it is Jesus Christ who you must follow. He has been exalted by the Lord. He has been made great. The exaltation of Joshua pointed to the exaltation of our Lord Jesus Christ.

So always look to Christ, the exalted one. Follow Him in everything that you do. He will always lead you in the way the Lord wants you to go. But how do you know what the Lord wants you to do? How do you follow Christ? By reading His Word, the Bible. Read it every day. Listen when it is explained to you. Don't try and do your own things, but always go to the Bible to see what God wants you to do.

The Lord has also given you parents, elders in church, and teachers who can help you understand the Bible. So listen to them as they explain it to you.

REFLECTION

Why did the Lord exalt Joshua?

JOSHUA 3:11

Behold, the ark of the covenant of the Lord of all of the earth is crossing over before you into the Jordan.

READ JOSHUA 3:9-13

After the children of Israel had prepared their hearts to listen to the Lord, and the Lord had shown them that they should listen to Joshua, the people were ready to see God perform a great miracle.

They saw the ark of the Lord going before them. This ark showed them that God was actually among them. It was God leading them into the Jordan River. All they had to do was follow the Lord. They didn't have to worry about that large raging river in front of them, they just had to follow and obey. The Israelites simply followed the ark towards the Jordan River. Verse 13 tells us that the soles of the feet of the priests got wet as they walked into the river.

That required amazing faith. They had no idea how they were going to cross that river, yet they still just followed the priests. But then the Lord showed the people His greatness and power. As the priests' feet touched the water of the river, the Lord stopped the flow way upstream and let the water downstream flow away. The Israelites could walk across the river on dry ground. They may have been wondering how they were going to get across the river, but God had prepared a mighty miracle.

God showed the Israelites His might and power. He was able to stop the raging river for them. If He was able to do that, then He was also powerful enough to help them with whatever would happen in the Promised Land.

And God is also powerful enough to perform an even greater miracle. Jesus Christ, the New Testament Joshua, was able to stop God's wrath and anger against our sins by His death on the cross. Just like the raging waters were stopped for the Israelites, God's great anger against us is stopped by Christ's death on the cross. Oh, what a great God we serve!

REFLECTION

What does this miracle teach you about God?

JOSHUA 4:7

And these stones shall be for a memorial to the children of Israel forever.

READ JOSHUA 4:1-7

If you were one of those boys or girls who crossed the Jordan River, do you think you would ever forget about such a great miracle? It was such an unforgettable event. The instant the feet of the priests who were carrying the ark entered the river, the waters of the river stood up in a heap and the path was dry. The moment all the people had crossed over to the other side, the water rushed back and overflowed the banks of the river.

But God knows how easily we can forget things and He knew how easily the Israelites could forget as well. However, they were not allowed to forget the Lord's care in bringing them across the Jordan River. So, one man from every tribe had to take a stone from the river and bring it to the place where they slept to make a memorial. This memorial would always remind them of the Lord's care over them and His grace in bringing them into the Promised Land.

There are things that we cannot forget either, things that we must always remember. We may never forget the goodness and grace of God, the love and care He shows in our lives. We must never forget the God who created us. We must never forget God's grace in sending His Son to earth to die for us, so that we can enter the eternal Promised Land. We must never forget the work of the Holy Spirit who changes us and helps us serve God.

Just like the Israelites, we might think that we wouldn't ever forget about the Lord's miracle of saving us. We'll always remember that Jesus died for us. But we can be forgetful as well, and that's why God gave us a memorial too. No, we don't have a pile of twelve stones to look at to remember the work of God, but we do have the Bible. The Bible records all the great deeds of our God and so we must look at, read and study the Bible every day!

REFLECTION

Why did God tell the Israelites to make the memorial?

JOSHUA 5:9

Then the Lord said to Joshua, "This day I have rolled away the reproach of Egypt from you."

READ JOSHUA 5:1–9

The children of Israel had come to the Promised Land for the second time. They had spent forty years in the desert and had crossed the Jordan River. The hearts of all the kings of the land had melted, so the children of Israel were ready to enter and take over the land of Canaan.

But God said, "Wait." Though the people thought that they were ready, God told them, "Not yet." First, God had to roll away the reproach of Egypt from them. This means that all their sins and shame from the past needed to be cleansed first. They couldn't enter the Promised Land while they still carried those sins on their shoulders. They first needed to be made right with God. They had to repent of their sins of the past and again commit themselves to serving the Lord alone.

God had given the children of Israel circumcision as a sign of the covenant, a sign that they were God's special people. They had a special relationship with the Lord. As part of this covenant, God had promised the Israelites that He would always care for them and always love them. He would forgive their sins when they repented. And the children of Israel had promised the Lord that they would always serve Him and make sacrifices to cover their sins.

But while the Israelites had been in the desert for forty years, they hadn't given their boys the sign of the covenant. So God said, "Before you go into the land of Canaan, we must renew the covenant." As part of this they had to circumcise all the males. This was a reminder that they were God's covenant people. They were going to serve the Lord alone.

These verses are very comforting for us as well. The Israelites were sinful, but so are we. But just like God rolled away their sins and gave them the sign of circumcision to remind them of His love and forgiveness, so He rolls away our sins and gives us the sign of baptism to remind us of His love and forgiveness.

REFLECTION

What does it mean that God rolled away the reproach of Egypt?

JOSHUA 5:13

Joshua...lifted his eyes and looked, and behold, a Man stood opposite him with His sword drawn in His hand.

READ JOSHUA 5:13-15

Joshua and the people of Israel had to fight the people of Canaan. But this battle was so much more than just people fighting each other. This war was a war of Satan against God and His people. It was a spiritual war. The devil was behind the heathen nations, but God and the heavenly hosts were behind Joshua and the Israelites.

Joshua needed to be reminded of this before the fighting started, so the Lord sent him a man with a sword drawn in his hand. This was no ordinary man, but a heavenly being. He was an angel.

When Joshua asked whose side the man was on, the man answered that he had come as the commander of God's army. He wasn't there to fight the physical battles. He wasn't going to be taking commands from Joshua, the leader of God's earthly army, but he was the commander of God's army.

In Exodus 23 God had already told the Israelites why they had to destroy all the enemies from the land of Canaan. If they didn't destroy all the enemies, then the Israelites would start serving the idols of the nations' instead of serving the Lord. That's why they had to win the physical battles and destroy all the enemies. And that's why the commander of God's army was there, to remind Joshua that the battles they were to fight were so important. Behind the actual battle was a hidden battle—a fight between the seed of Satan and the children of God. The angel reminded Joshua that God was there helping the Israelites in the battle against God's enemies.

There is a hidden battle happening in our lives as well. The devil is always trying to take us away from serving the Lord, but we don't need to worry. The commander of the Lord's army, the Lord Himself, is on our side and is helping us in our fight against Satan. We too must continue to serve and trust the Lord always, and He will be with us as well.

REFLECTION

Why did the angel come to Joshua?

JOSHUA 6:17

Only Rahab the harlot shall live, she and all who are with her in the house.

READ JOSHUA 6:15-18

The destruction of the city of Jericho is such a powerful story. We see God's might and power. Sometimes we may wonder if it was fair and just of the Lord to destroy the whole city. We wonder if God enjoyed killing all those people. Even the women and children were killed. We don't really like reading that.

So what can we learn about the Lord in this story? Firstly, we can see God's anger towards sin and judgement of it. God didn't destroy the whole city just for fun, or because He got pleasure out of it. Not at all. The city of Jericho was destroyed because it was full of wickedness. The city was so full of sin, and the people were so wicked, that God needed to destroy the whole city. God wanted His children, the people of Israel, to see His righteous anger at sin. The Lord has a holy hatred of sin. By destroying Jericho in this way, God showed how much He hates sin.

But God also showed more than His hatred of sin. One part of the wall stayed standing. The part where Rahab's house was didn't get destroyed when the rest of the wall and the city did. Here we see God's mercy and grace. Rahab was not destroyed with the rest of the people but was saved because she had faith. All the other people of Jericho rejected God, but Rahab and her household had faith instead. They trusted God.

Rahab was allowed to experience God's grace instead of His judgement. Rahab and all of us deserve to be totally destroyed by God's holy anger at sin. We all deserve the judgement that Jericho got. But instead we receive the grace that Rahab received. God worked faith in her heart so that she believed in Him. And God in His love and grace works that same faith in our hearts. We deserve to be punished by God's wrath, but instead Jesus Christ received that punishment in our place. He took all of God's anger at our sins on Himself, and so we, like Rahab, can escape this wrath and be saved.

REFLECTION

How can we see God's grace in this passage?

JOSHUA 23:3

"You have seen all that the Lord your God has done to all these nations because of you, for the Lord your God is He who has fought for you."

READ JOSHUA 23:1-8

You have heard the word "covenant" before, but what exactly does it mean? What does it mean to you that you are part of God's covenant?

In Joshua 23, Joshua gives a farewell speech to the children of Israel. And even though he doesn't use the word "covenant," he does remind the Israelites of what it means to be part of God's covenant.

They were God's special people. He chose them because He wanted to have a special relationship of love with them. He wanted to love them and to send Jesus to die on the cross for them. And so God had given the Israelites the land of Canaan. In verse 3, Joshua reminds the Israelites that the Lord had destroyed all the nations for their sake.

God has made a covenant with you as well. Because you were born to believing parents, you are part of that covenant. Isn't that wonderful? It's not because you are good or because He knew that you would serve Him. It's just because the Lord wants you to be His special child. He gave you parents who believe, and He made you part of this covenant. And so the Lord does many good things for you too, just like He did for the Israelites. He cares for you, He loves you, He gives you people in your life who can tell you about the Lord, and He forgives you. And He does all these things for you because you are His covenant child.

Joshua told the Israelites to make sure they always loved the Lord in return. They had to respond to God's gracious love by loving Him back. And that's the same for you as well. Because the Lord chose you, because the Lord loves you, and because you are part of His covenant, you must also love the Lord in return. And how can you show your love for the Lord? By obeying Him. When you think about all the loving things God does for you, then you will *want* to obey the Lord.

REFLECTION

What does it mean to be part of God's covenant?

The Lord is my strength and my shield

PSALM 28:7A

JUDGES 2:1

*Then the Angel of the L͏ord came
up from Gilgal to Bochim.*

READ JUDGES 2:1–5

Just imagine that you were one of the Israelites gathered for a feast at Bochim. While you are standing there chatting with your friends, you suddenly see the Angel of the L͏ord appear and start speaking. I'm sure you would stand up and listen carefully to what the Angel had to say, wouldn't you?

This Angel (who is the Lord Jesus, in the Old Testament) has come from Gilgal. This is important because Gilgal was the place where God had reminded the Israelites of His covenant when they first crossed the Jordan into the Promised Land. At Gilgal, God had reminded them that they were His special covenant people and that they had to serve Him. The people had celebrated the Passover there and had been circumcised there as they promised to obey the L͏ord.

The Angel comes from this place to Bochim, where the Israelites were not living in obedience to the L͏ord. Judges 1 tells us of all the times that the different tribes didn't destroy the Canaanites as they had been told to do. The people had disobeyed the L͏ord.

But because of His covenant love, God still comes to them and tells them of their sins. The Angel reminds them that the L͏ord has always loved them, but they have disobeyed the L͏ord. When the people hear this, they weep and mourn. When they are reminded of their disobedience, they weep because of their sins.

What about us? We too disobey God. We might put sport before Bible reading. We might spend more time in front of a screen than with our family. We disobey God every day!

Even though God told the Israelites that He would leave them in their sins, He continued to remind them to turn away from their sins because of His covenant love. Because of God's love for us in Jesus Christ, He will not turn away from us either. Instead, He continually comes to us in covenant love as well.

We can only say, "Oh, thank you, L͏ord, for your love!"

REFLECTION

Can you think of three things that take away from your love for the L͏ord?

JUDGES 2:9

And they buried him within the border of his inheritance at Timnath Heres, in the mountains of Ephraim.

READ JUDGES 2:7–10

Today we read a verse about where Joshua was buried. You may wonder why the Lord has included this verse in the Bible. Why is it important to know where Joshua was buried?

Well, this verse teaches us something about how great and loving our God is. It teaches us that God is always faithful and always keeps His promises. The important word here is *inheritance*. An inheritance was a piece of land that the Israelites received when they entered the Promised Land. All the tribes were given a piece of land—an inheritance. God, in His love, gave them this land. Even though the generation before them had been disobedient and died in the desert, the Lord continued to love Israel. Because of His love, the Lord gave the next generation of people an inheritance—some land in Canaan.

You will remember that Joshua was one of the two faithful people who spied out the Promised Land. Because Joshua obeyed the Lord and gave a good report, he didn't have to die in the desert but was allowed into the Promised Land. So the fact that Joshua was buried in his inheritance shows God's love and grace to Joshua.

Joshua's burial also points forward to something much greater. Let's think about Jesus. Jesus did not have His own burial place. Jesus was buried in someone else's land. But He didn't stay in the grave. The grave wasn't the Lord Jesus' final resting place. After three days He arose from the dead and now sits at the right hand of God in heavenly glory. And that's the eternal heavenly inheritance that Joshua's burial points forward to.

We as Christians today will also be buried when we die, but because of God's covenant love and faithfulness and because of Jesus' death, burial, and resurrection, our bodies will not stay in the grave forever. Our bodies too will rise when Christ returns, and we will then go to our Promised Land—the new heaven and earth—our eternal inheritance.

REFLECTION

What does Joshua's burial in the Promised Land teach us about God?

JUDGES 2:18

For the Lord was moved to pity by their groaning because of those who oppressed them and harassed them.

READ JUDGES 2:11-19

The Israelites had turned away from the Lord so He allowed the nations to make life hard for them as a punishment for their sins. The Lord wanted to teach the people to trust in Him. As a result, the Israelites groaned about these enemies.

Then amazingly we read that even though the people were disobeying the Lord and the Lord was punishing them for their disobedience, He still had compassion on them. The covenant Lord still loved His people and in His love He listened to their groaning and sent them a judge.

The Lord used the judges to teach the people of Israel to repent from their sins and turn back to Him. The Lord also used the judges to save them from their enemies. And while the judge lived, the people did have rest from their enemies. But as soon as the judge died, they went back to their old sinful ways.

We learn here how loving and gracious our Father is. Whenever the people of Israel turned away from the Lord, He called them back to Himself in love, through the judges. How does this make you feel? Does it give you comfort?

We are no different than the Israelites really. So often we do the wrong thing. So often we are stubborn and keep on doing the same sins. We don't always trust the Lord as much as we should. Even though we continue to fall into sin time and again, God comes to us in love and grace, and calls us to repent, just like He did to the Israelites. No, the Lord doesn't send us judges today, but He does use your parents, your elders, your pastors, your siblings, your grandparents and your friends to call you to repent.

So when you are told by someone that what you are doing is wrong, know that the Lord is coming to you in love and grace, calling you to repent. Listen to them as they teach you how the Lord wants you to serve Him, and thank the Lord for His love!

REFLECTION

How does the Lord teach you about your sins?

JUDGES 3:7

*So the children of Israel…
forgot the Lord their God.*

READ JUDGES 3:7–11

The children of Israel forgot the Lord their God. What does this mean? Does it mean that they just forgot to pray once or just didn't think about the Lord very much? It actually means a lot more than that. It means that they turned away from serving the Lord on purpose. They didn't really want to think about their relationship with the Lord as they did their everyday work.

It would be the same as if you went to steal some biscuits from your mum's pantry, knowing very well that the Lord has told you not to steal. You are sinning on purpose, and you may as well go to your Bible and rip out the commandment about stealing.

Sin makes the Lord angry—very angry. Verse 8 says that the anger of the Lord was hot. God was so angry that He sent the children of Israel to live under a heathen king for eight years.

After this time the children of Israel cried out to the Lord again. In His covenant love, God sent a judge named Othniel to save them from this king. The Spirit of the Lord came upon Othniel. God's Spirit was at work in Othniel so that he could save the people of Israel. It is only the work of God that can save the people.

We see God's compassion and love for His people again, even though they sinned against Him. By sending Othniel He gave the people peace again. But that peace didn't last forever—just forty years, after which the people turned away from the Lord again.

But we know that the Lord has also sent another person, our Lord Jesus Christ. He also saves. He saves us from *our* enemies—our sins—and gives us peace. The peace that He gives is a peace that lasts forever. Today we have to fight every day. Every day we are struggling with our sins. But one day we will have this everlasting peace. The battle will be over! Praise the Lord.

REFLECTION

What does it mean to forget the Lord?

JUDGES 4:1

*The children of Israel again did evil in the sight of the L*ORD*.*

READ JUDGES 4:1-3, 17-22

Jael killed Sisera by hitting a tent peg through his head while Sisera was sleeping. This is a story you probably won't forget in a hurry.

In verse 1 we read that the people had again done evil in the sight of the LORD. We read this many times in the book of Judges. And this was because the leaders of Israel were not leading the people as they should have been. The priests should have been asking God for direction on how to deal with the nations that were attacking them, but they weren't. Without godly leaders, the people were again straying away from serving the LORD.

This shows us how important it is for church leaders to guide the people of the church in the ways of the LORD. When the leaders go wrong, so often the whole church does too. Do you take the time to pray for your leaders so that they can receive wisdom from the LORD to guide you? Pray for your minister, elders, deacons, parents, teachers and any others who need to lead you.

This story teaches us more too. When the Israelites cried out to God to help them, God listened to them once again. Through Barak, they were able to destroy the army completely, including the escapee, Sisera. God gave a victory even though the people had done evil in His sight.

Does this mean that you can just keep on sinning and God will look after you anyway? Can you keep on doing the wrong thing and still expect to go to heaven? No, it doesn't mean this at all. If we look closely at the Bible passage, we see that even though at first Barak didn't want to go when Deborah sent him, God worked in Barak so that he repented and did end up doing what God commanded. You too need to repent and turn away from your sins. Ask God to help you put sin far away from you. And God in His love will indeed help you and save you.

REFLECTION

Which leaders in your church can you pray for?

JUDGES 6:1

So the Lord delivered them into the hand of Midian for seven years.

READ JUDGES 6:1–10

The children of Israel, living in the Promised Land at this time, were very frightened by the Midianites. Because they were so scared, the Israelites hid in the caves and dens in the mountains.

Why were they so frightened of the Midianites? Because the Midianites, together with other strong armies, came and destroyed the Israelites' crops and everything in the land. They left the Israelites with nothing—no wheat, barley, sheep, oxen or donkeys. They took or destroyed everything so that the Israelites had nothing left.

And they didn't just do this one year, but seven years in a row. For seven long years they raided the Israelites.

We may wonder why the Lord allowed this to happen to His children. Weren't they God's special people? Why didn't the Lord help?

Verse one tells us that it was the Lord who used the Midianites to raid the Israelites' camp. The Lord appointed this to happen for seven years. And that is because the Israelites did evil in the sight of the Lord. They had forgotten all about the love and care of the Lord and had stopped serving Him. They had stopped obeying the Lord and His commandments. So the Lord sent the Midianites to teach and remind them to serve the Lord again.

And it took seven years before the children of Israel finally cried out to the Lord for help. They were enjoying their sinful lifestyle too much. But when they finally called out to the Lord for help, He in His love and grace sent them a prophet. God wanted their hearts to change. He wanted them to live for Him again. So He sent them a prophet who reminded them of what the Lord had done for them in the past, and how they had not listened. He reminded them to obey the Lord.

The Lord loves us in the same way. He sent His Son to earth for us. Let us always remember the works of the Lord and love Him with our whole heart.

REFLECTION

Why did the Lord allow the Midianites to raid the Israelites?

JUDGES 6:12

And the Angel of the L&#xf;ord appeared to him, and said to him, "The L&#xf;ord is with you, you mighty man of valour!"

READ JUDGES 6:11–16

Gideon was busy crushing wheat in the wine press. He was in the wine press because he was hiding from the Midianites who had been stealing their wheat for the past seven years. While he was busy, suddenly the Angel of the Lord came to him and told him that the Lord was with him. Whatever task the Lord was going to give Gideon to do, the Lord would be with him.

But Gideon questions this. If the Lord was with him, why did the Lord let the Midianites steal from them for all these years? Gideon couldn't see that the Lord was with them. It sure didn't look like it to him.

And so he questions the Lord: "We hear about your miracles, but we haven't seen them. You said you were with us, but all we see is the Midianites attacking us. Where are you, Lord?"

Do you know that so often we ask the Lord the same thing? So often when we find it hard to obey the Lord, we say or think, "Lord, you said you would help me, but I keep on sinning. Why aren't you helping me?" Or, "I know that I am not supposed to use bad language but it's so hard not to when everyone around me does. Why don't you make it easier for me, Lord?"

But we cannot blame the Lord, just like Gideon should not have blamed the Lord. Instead Gideon should have looked at his own life and the life of the Israelites and seen how they had been disobedient. When we aren't obeying the Lord or reading the Bible, it can often feel as though God isn't helping us.

But how did God respond to Gideon? Did He get angry at him? No, instead God promised again to be with him. And that's God's promise to all of us. You are God's covenant child and so He will be with you! Don't blame God when you are struggling. Instead look closely at your life and see where you are disobedient, and ask God to help you in your struggles. He will be with you! He will go with you!

REFLECTION

What should you do if you feel like God isn't helping you?

JUDGES 6:23

Then the Lord said to him, "Peace be with you; do not fear, you shall not die."

READ JUDGES 6:17-24

"Peace be with you." We often hear these words in church. But what does it mean to have peace—peace with God? To have peace with God means that we have a loving relationship with the Lord. Of ourselves we are so very sinful that we wouldn't be able to stand before God. Just one little sin is enough to make God punish us with death—eternal death in hell. God should be very angry with us because of our sins.

In Judges 6 we read about Gideon being scared to stand before God. Once he realises that he has seen God Himself, he is scared that he is going to die. Gideon realises that he is very sinful. How can a sinful person like him stand before a holy, majestic and awesome God? No wonder Gideon was frightened. God is holy, God is awesome, God is sinless, God is perfect, God is all-powerful, and Gideon is totally sinful, dirty, and corrupt. Gideon would not have felt any peace.

And yet God's amazing words to Gideon are, "Peace be with you; do not fear, you shall not die." Oh yes, Gideon should have died, because someone so sinful cannot stand before such a holy God. But he doesn't die. Instead God was going to send His Son, Jesus Christ, to die as payment for Gideon's sins. Jesus Christ was going to take God's anger and punishment away so that Gideon could have peace with God.

Isn't that wonderful news? God offers us the same peace. Every Sunday again, God gives us His peace. He does so because Jesus Christ has come to earth. He *has* died on the cross. He *has* taken God's anger on Himself because of our sins. Now we don't have to live a life frightened and scared of God. No, we can have peace—true peace knowing that God loves us and accepts us as His children because of Jesus' sacrifice on the cross. What grace and love the Lord shows to us.

REFLECTION

Why was Gideon so frightened when he realised that the angel was God Himself?

JUDGES 6:25

Tear down the altar of Baal.

READ JUDGES 6:25-32

Gideon, obeying God's command, destroyed the altar to Baal and replaced it with an altar to God. In the morning when the people woke up and saw what Gideon had done, they were very angry. They were so angry that they told Joash, Gideon's father, to bring him out so that they could kill him.

Joash was the one who owned this altar to Baal. So we can assume that Joash would have worshipped Baal as well. So how does he respond to the altar being destroyed? Does he also get angry at Gideon like the people of the city do?

Amazingly, Joash must have realised that God is stronger than Baal. God worked in Joash's heart so that he saw that Baal was just a useless idol. He said to the people, "Are you trying to save Baal? If he is a god, why can't he save himself? You looked to this idol to help you and now he can't even help himself. If he is really a god let him save himself."

God is showing the people that Baal is no god at all. He is teaching them that He Himself is the only true God. He is the one the people should be looking to for help and salvation. He is also showing them that when there is a lie (Baal can help you) and the truth (God is the only true God), the truth will always win.

Many times today we hear lies. Even in our own hearts we know they are lies. Maybe the lie is that it doesn't matter if you say nasty things to your brother because he's always nasty to you. Maybe the lie is that sharing a bit of gossip won't hurt the other person.

Don't believe these lies. The people believed the lie that Baal could help them, but God's truth showed that Baal was nothing more than an idol. Never believe the lies, but always believe the true Word of God.

REFLECTION

What are some lies in your life?

JUDGES 6:40

And God did so that night. It was dry on the fleece only, but there was dew on all the ground.

READ JUDGES 6:36-40

Do you ever wish that you could ask for a sign from the Lord like Gideon did?

But was Gideon correct in asking for this sign? We read in the verses before this that Gideon knew exactly what the Lord wanted him to do. The Lord had told him that he was to fight the Midianites, and the Lord had promised that He would be with him. Gideon wasn't sure and asked God to eat a sacrifice with him. God reassured Gideon by doing this.

So Gideon knew what the Lord wanted him to do, and he also knew that the Lord had promised to be with him. Yet Gideon still didn't trust the Lord. So by asking the Lord for the sign of the fleece, he was sinning. And he knew that it was wrong because he even asked the Lord not to be angry with him.

Instead of asking for the sign, Gideon should have gone out in faith and obeyed the Lord. Yet God doesn't tell Gideon off, but patiently and lovingly gives the signs to Gideon. Because God is going to use Gideon, He reassures Gideon again.

What about you? Do you sometimes, like Gideon, know what the Lord wants you to do, but you don't want to obey? Maybe you know that you should talk to the person on the bus about the Lord when they ask why you go to church on Sundays, but you just don't want to. Maybe you know you should remind your friends to stop gossiping, but it is just too hard because they might laugh at you.

At times like this, you don't need to ask the Lord for a sign. The Lord has promised that He will be with you, so in faith obey the Lord. The Lord has already given us the signs of baptism and the Lord's Supper to remind us that He is indeed with us and He will indeed help us obey. Trust in the Lord.

REFLECTION

If God used doubting Gideon, do you think He can use you too? How?

JUDGES 7:7

Then the Lord said to Gideon, "By the three hundred men who lapped I will save you."

READ JUDGES 7:1-8

Gideon gathered together an army of 32,000 men. This wasn't nearly as many as the Midianites, who had 135,000 men. And yet the Lord told him that it was too many men. The Lord didn't want the people of Israel to think that they had won the battle because of their great numbers. The Lord wants to show them that He is the one who is going to give the victory. This battle is about something much more important than a physical war. God is showing them that He is the one who can save them, also from their sins.

Gideon told the people that whoever wanted to leave could go home. This left 10,000 men in the Israelite army. But that was still too many men. So Gideon took them to the water, and they all had a drink. The Lord made sure only 300 men drank the water a certain way because God was going to use just these 300 men in the battle. God told Gideon that with these 300 men, He would deliver the Midianites into the Israelites' hands.

Just 300 men. That's not many at all against 135,000 men. And yet the Lord led the battle in such a way that when the enemies heard all the trumpets and shouting, and when they saw the torches, they responded by attacking and killing each other. This story isn't about how clever or brave these 300 men were, but about the Lord and how He won the battle. All Gideon had to do was trust and obey the Lord, and God gave the victory.

And that is what we need to do in our lives too. We need to trust the Lord. Even when things look too hard for us or when temptations look too great, we must trust the Lord. He has already promised us that we will win the battles as well. We know that Christ has already won over Satan. We have been promised forgiveness of sins and eternal life. Now we have to believe these promises and in faith obey the Lord.

REFLECTION

What can we learn from this story?

JUDGES 8:1

Now the men of Ephraim said to him, "Why have you done this to us by not calling us when you went to fight with the Midianites?"

READ JUDGES 7:22-8:3

What a victory! With only 300 men, Gideon was able to destroy the Midianite army of 135,000 men.

During this battle, Gideon had included men from his tribe, Manasseh, but also men from the tribes of Asher, Zebulun, and Naphtali. There weren't any men from the tribe of Ephraim fighting in the main battle, yet Gideon had sent some of the men of Ephraim to catch the last escaping Midianites as they were fleeing.

Then we read that the men of Ephraim got angry at Gideon. They were annoyed because Gideon hadn't called them to fight in the main battle. They were jealous. They wanted to share in the victory. They wanted to be seen as heroes. How could Gideon not have asked them to fight? Just catching the escaping Midianites wasn't good enough for them.

By being jealous and angry, the men of Ephraim were forgetting to thank the Lord for the victory He gave against the Midianites. They weren't even seeing God's grace in allowing this amazing victory. They weren't even thankful that they were allowed to catch the escaping Midianites. Their jealousy made them blind to God's love in their own lives.

Do you sometimes become jealous of other people in your life? Someone at school may do much better than you. Maybe she is able to work out the math problems in no time, but it takes you a lot of hard work. Maybe someone else is a much more confident person than you and gives great answers during class. Someone else may find memorising Bible verses much easier than you do. At times like this you can become jealous: Why can't I find learning easier? Why didn't the Lord give me those talents?

But when you become jealous like this, you forget to see the Lord's blessings in your own life, not only in the talents He has given you, but also in His love and grace in saving you through Jesus Christ. So instead of being jealous, thank the Lord for the blessings He has given you.

REFLECTION

Can you think of examples when your jealousy causes you to be blind to the Lord's blessings in your life?

JUDGES 8:3

Then their anger toward him subsided when he said that.

READ JUDGES 7:22–8:3

After the amazing victory that God gave against the Midianites, the men of Ephraim were jealous that they had not been called to fight in the main battle and so they got angry at Gideon. How did Gideon respond?

Gideon didn't respond in anger. Instead he gave a soft answer. Proverbs 15:1 says, "A soft answer turns away wrath," and we can see that happening in this story. Gideon said to the men of Ephraim, "Even the leftover bits and pieces after your harvesters have been through, are better than all the grapes of Abiezer." With this saying, Gideon was telling the men not to be jealous and angry at what God had done in their life, but instead to focus on the blessings that God had given them. God had allowed them to capture the escaping princes of Midian.

Gideon didn't take the praise and glory for the wonderful victory. He acknowledged that it was God who gave the victory. God is the one who should receive all praise and glory. After this amazing victory, Gideon, by the grace of God, remained humble.

This makes us think of Christ Jesus. He is the one who humbled Himself the most. He humbled Himself so much that He left the glorious place He had in heaven and came down to earth to become a person like us. He humbled Himself so much that He was willing to die on the cross. He did this so that we could receive salvation. We may be God's children because of Christ's willingness to be humble.

It's this humility that we need to show in our own lives. How can we as Christians be anything but humble? Every day we see the wonderful work of God in our lives. We see His love and grace. But we also see the talents that He gives us. Let us not boast and brag about our talents, but let us humbly acknowledge the grace God shows by giving us these gifts. Let us praise and thank the Lord for the blessings in our lives.

REFLECTION

How should you respond if someone praises you for your amazing drawing or cricket skills?

"Fear not, for I am with you"

ISAIAH 43:5A

PSALM 63:1

*O God, You are my God; Early will
I seek You. My soul thirsts for You.*

READ PSALM 63:1–8

Are you ever lonely, frustrated, angry, hurting, or just plain sad? Do you ever feel like you want to receive comfort and joy? Hopefully you have parents, friends or others you can go to when you feel like this. But even though they can comfort you a bit, they can't take away your pain, they can't remove your hurt, they can't fill your emptiness.

But God can help, and God wants to help! God wants you to go to Him with all your troubles. When David wrote Psalm 63, he was in the wilderness. He may very well have been fleeing from Absalom. You can imagine that he might have been very scared, lonely, and sad in the wilderness. His own son was trying to kill him.

It's while David is feeling like this that he sings, "Oh Lord, You are my God. I thirst for You, I long for You." Imagine a man in the desert who is really thirsty. All he wants is water to quench his thirst. David is really sad, and all he wants is for God to comfort him. David wants to drink from God's love.

And David knows that God *will* comfort him, that God *will* satisfy his needs, that God *will* be with him. In verse 3 he says that God's love is better than life itself. God's love is bigger, greater, and stronger than anything and everything else in life. God's love covers all things for His covenant children. God's love is so great that He gives us Jesus Christ as our Saviour. God's love is so great that He gives us His Spirit to be part of us, to live in us.

And so God will help you when you are lonely, frustrated, angry, or sad. Pray to Him and ask Him to fill you with His love and comfort. Ask Him to help you in your hurt. Remember, His love is bigger than life itself. As God's special child you will receive comfort and help from God. God will carry you through difficult times.

REFLECTION

Do you remember to go to God in prayer when you need comfort?

ROMANS 4:24

It shall be imputed to us who believe in Him who raised up Jesus our Lord from the dead.

READ ROMANS 4:22-25

We all have a problem with sin. We can't save ourselves. Our sins need to be paid for somehow, but we can't do it. We can't make ourselves right before God. Instead we just keep sinning more and more every day, increasing our pile of sins.

The good news is that God, in His love and grace, has given us the gift of justification through Jesus Christ. Justification, or to be justified, means that God, as our Judge, doesn't see us as sinful anymore. He sees us as without sin. Isn't that amazing? Even though we sin every day again, God says that we are justified, that we are without sin.

How is this possible? There is only one way, and it is God Himself who made that way possible. In love He sent His Son, Jesus Christ, to take care of our problem with sin. We can't save ourselves and so God sent His Son to save us. With His death on the cross, Christ paid the debt that we should have paid for our sins. He stilled God's wrath and anger at sin.

But Christ didn't remain dead. He was also raised from the dead by God. God was the one who made Jesus' heart pump again, His eyes open again and His lungs fill with air again. By raising Jesus from the dead, God told the whole world that He was happy with Christ's sacrifice on the cross. Christ's death made full payment for our sins. If Jesus had remained dead, death would have had the final power. It would have shown that God wasn't happy with Christ's sacrifice.

But Jesus didn't stay dead. He arose because God was satisfied with the payment Jesus made. This means that we, as God's children, are now justified. When we stand before God as Judge, He will declare that we are without sin. Our sins have been paid in full! We are justified!

REFLECTION

What does it mean that we are justified?

ROMANS 6:3

Or do you not know that as many of us as were baptised into Christ Jesus were baptised into His death?

READ ROMANS 6:1-11

We all sin many times a day. We all break the commandments of God. But what do you do with your sins? Romans 6 teaches us that our sins have been buried with Christ, by baptism. You are connected to Christ by your baptism. This means that your baptism is a sign that your sins have been buried with Christ. When Christ died, your sins died with Him. So when you ask for your sins to be forgiven, they are indeed forgiven. They are remembered no more.

But Christ also rose from the dead. He didn't stay dead. This is shown in baptism too. Sometimes when a person is baptised, they are immersed or lowered under the water, (instead of being sprinkled with water). This is a sign that their sins are forgiven, gone, and buried with Christ. But then they rise out of the water again. This is a sign that just as Christ rose from the dead, so a baptised person rises up again too. When we have been raised with Christ, we are made clean, washed, and purified. You are a new person.

But how then must you act? What does your baptism mean to you? It means that you should not see yourself as a sinner anymore. Oh yes, you still struggle with sins. You still sin every day. But you also have a new name, a new identity. You are a forgiven sinner. And so you have to live as a forgiven sinner. You have to walk in the newness of life.

You have the power of Christ to live a new life. The Holy Spirit is at work in your life. Sin should no longer control you and should no longer have a hold of you. Instead, you will hate sin and want to obey God's laws.

Yes, it is very hard not to sin. And yes, you will sin every day. But remember that the power of Christ's resurrection is even stronger than the power of sin. Ask God to help you to live as a new person, as a forgiven sinner. And thank God for His forgiveness when you do sin.

REFLECTION

What does it mean to you that you are baptised?

ROMANS 5:19

So also by one Man's obedience many will be made righteous.

READ ROMANS 5:19-21, 6:23

"The wages of sin is death." Do you know what that means? It means that the only wages we can ever earn is death. We sin all the time and so God ought to punish us all with eternal death—death in hell.

But God doesn't do that. Instead He sent us the gift of His only Son, Christ Jesus. Yes, Jesus came to pay the punishment that we deserve. He died on the cross for our sins. He took away God's anger at our sins and the curse of our sins.

But Jesus did a lot more than just die on the cross. Jesus' death on the cross makes us innocent, but it doesn't make us righteous. Think of this example. There are bank accounts where you can go into overdraft. This means that you can spend more than you have got in your account and then you owe the money back to the bank. Say you had an account like this and you spent $100 more than you had. You would owe the bank $100. If you paid this $100 back to the bank, then your account would still be empty. Your debt would be paid, but you wouldn't have any money.

In the same way Christ has paid the debt for our sins, but that by itself doesn't make us righteous. Our sins have been paid for, but we still don't have any good works. And that is the other thing that Jesus did for us. He was also perfectly obedient in our place. He obeyed every single commandment perfectly, and God says that by Christ's obedience we are made righteous.

Jesus has poured all His perfect obedience and good works into our bank account, and so when God sees us, He no longer sees our sins, but through Christ He sees our works as perfect. We are now righteous before God.

Instead of death in hell, we receive Christ's perfect obedience. Where you don't obey your parents, Christ obeyed His perfectly in your place. Where you don't speak lovingly to your friends, Christ did that perfectly for you. Isn't that wonderful news?

REFLECTION

What two things has Christ done for you?

ROMANS 7:25

I thank God – through Jesus Christ our Lord!

READ ROMANS 7:14-25

Can you think of times in your life when you sinned, asked the Lord for forgiveness, and were determined never to do that sin again? But then a few days later you were doing the same thing again? Maybe you said that you were never going to get angry at your sister again. Or maybe you said you were never going to laugh at dirty jokes again. And yet so often you find yourself doing the same wrong things over and over again.

This can make you really sad and frustrated. You can even get angry at yourself and wonder if you are really a child of the Lord. You really do love the Lord and you really do want to serve Him, but at the same time you just keep doing the wrong thing. It's this fight going on inside you.

Do you ever feel that way? Actually, all Christians know this fight very well. The apostle Paul certainly knew it too. He says, "The good things that I want to do, I don't do, but the bad things that I don't want to do, they are the things I actually do." And so Paul cries out, "Oh wretched or broken man that I am, who will help me?" Paul sees this fight in his own life and hates that it happens, hates that he keeps on sinning. But he also knows that he is forgiven in Jesus Christ and that Christ will deliver him from this fight against sin. That's why after he asks, "Who will deliver me?" he immediately adds, "I thank God—through Jesus Christ our Lord!"

Yes, Paul needed to keep fighting against sin in his life, but he knew that God would forgive him, help him, and continue to love him, because of Jesus' death on the cross.

So in your fight against sin, don't give up. Keep on fighting, keep on praying for forgiveness and keep on asking God to help you. Because you are His covenant child, He will continue to love you, and one day you will be in eternal glory and you will never have to fight against sin again!

REFLECTION

What can you do to help yourself fight against your sins?

ROMANS 8:18

For I consider that the sufferings of this present time are not worthy to be compared with the glory which shall be revealed in us.

READ ROMANS 8:18-27

Isn't it wonderful to know that we are safe with Jesus Christ? In verse 1 of this chapter, Paul says that there is no condemnation for us because we belong to Jesus. This means that we are saved because we belong to Christ. Our sins are forgiven, God loves us and we have an eternal future with God to look forward to. Isn't this wonderful?

Does this mean that we as Christians are never sad or unhappy? Does this mean that nothing hard or horrible ever happens to us? I think you know that it can't mean this, because so often we do have hard things happen to us. We do struggle, cry, and hurt because of things in this life.

Paul explains this suffering as groaning as we wait for the glorious future that God has promised us. Sometimes things can be so hard that we can't even pray anymore, and our prayers become just a groan. Verse 26 tells us that at times like this, the Spirit groans for us. He makes our prayers perfect before the Father. The Spirit makes intercession for us, with groaning, as we wait for Christ's return together.

Paul tells us that creation also groans. We see this in earthquakes, fires, floods, and droughts. These are examples of the creation groaning. Creation too is suffering as it is waiting to be made new again.

Together with creation we do suffer and groan in this life. But as people that belong to Christ we know that this earth isn't our final home. No, it's just our home for a number of years. It's our home for as long as we live. One day God will make a new heaven and a new earth. This new life will be more glorious than we can imagine. Paul says that its glory hasn't been revealed to us. This means that it will be so wonderful that we can't even describe it. And we can look forward to this future! Yes, we will suffer in this life, but one day we will live a glorious life with God Himself.

REFLECTION

Do you look forward to living eternally with God?

ROMANS 13:11

And do this, knowing the time, that now it is high time to awake out of sleep.

READ ROMANS 13:11-14

Do you sometimes find it hard to wake up in the morning? Maybe your mum has to shake you a few times and say, "Wake up, wake up." The apostle Paul tells his readers to wake up as well. Here Paul is speaking about something different than waking up like you need to do every morning. Paul is telling the readers that they need to wake up spiritually. They can't keep living a sinful life like they had been in the past. And this is important, this is urgent. They need to wake up now. They need to look at their lives and change the way that they are living now.

When you wake up in the morning, you take off your pyjamas and put on your nice clean clothes. In the same way, we have to put off our works of darkness. This means you have to stop saying nasty things, stop being selfish, stop lying, stop cheating, stop disobeying, stop gossiping…and you can finish the list. These are the works of darkness that we have to cast off, to get rid of.

Paul also tells us to put on the armour of light, or put on the Lord Jesus Christ. This means we have to show works of obedience, love, care, honesty, and kindness in our life. These are works of light.

Because Christ died for us, we can put on these works of light, through the Spirit. We must go to Him with our daily struggle against sin. We must go to Him for forgiveness. Because of God's great love for us, He reaches out to us and says, "Yes my son, my daughter, you are broken and sinful and you have broken all my commandments and done many works of darkness, but I have put your sins on my Son, Jesus Christ. I poured all of my anger at your sins on Him. He has paid for your sins so that you can be forgiven. Now go in my power, and live as children of the light."

REFLECTION

What does Paul mean when he tells the readers to "wake up"?

PSALM 73:3

For I was envious of the boastful, when I saw the prosperity of the wicked.

READ PSALM 73:1-17

Do you sometimes feel like other people have so much more than you? Are you jealous of others, especially unbelievers? They can seem to have all the latest toys and gadgets, while you don't because your parents think it is better that you don't have these things. They can do what they like, while you have to visit your aging grandparents. Sometimes it can just seem so unfair. Those unbelievers can seem so happy and have so many good things and they don't even love the Lord. Yet, while you love the Lord and serve Him, you have difficult things happening in your life.

That feeling of jealousy isn't something that only you feel. Many Christians over the years have had jealous feelings. Asaph, the author of this Psalm was also jealous. He starts this Psalm by confessing that the Lord is good. He knows that the Lord is good, and he does serve the Lord. But then something happens. He feels himself slipping in his faith. He starts becoming jealous of all the good things the unbelievers have and how good their lives seem. And he feels himself slipping away from the Lord.

The same can happen to you. Of course you love the Lord and want to serve Him, but then you see the good lives of unbelievers and you start getting a bit angry and jealous. Why do they have it so good while you don't? You don't want to feel jealous; you really want to be happy in the things the Lord has given you. But somehow that jealous feeling still creeps in, just like it did for Asaph.

So what did Asaph do? He went to the temple and worshipped the Lord. He knew that he needed to focus on the Lord and not on the unbelievers. He looked to God and then everything changed for him. When he focused on the Lord and on worshipping Him, his jealous feelings could fall away. And that is exactly what you need to do when you feel jealous too. Worship the Lord and focus on Him.

REFLECTION

What was Asaph so jealous about?

PSALM 73:25

Whom have I in heaven but You? And there is none upon earth that I desire besides You.

READ PSALM 73:18-28

In the beginning of this Psalm, Asaph was jealous of all the good things that the unbelievers had. But then he turned to worshipping the Lord in the temple. Once he focused on the Lord, everything changed for him. This is because he was now looking the right way. Instead of looking at the people around him, he was looking to heaven, he was looking towards the Lord.

When you are jealous of others, that jealousy can disappear for you too when you focus on the Lord. Although it may seem like unbelievers can do whatever they want and that they have so many good things, this doesn't do them any good because they don't serve the Lord. Their good things can seem like blessings, but they are not. They will do them no good when they die or when the Lord Jesus returns. The end for the unbelievers is eternal hell, eternal destruction. They can have as many good things as they like in this life, but for eternity they will be suffering in hell. So, would you really want to be one of them? Would you really want all their good things without serving the Lord? Would you really want to do whatever you wanted today, if it means that you will spend eternity in hell?

Of course you wouldn't. And that is what Asaph realises as well. He says that he was a fool for being jealous of the unbelievers. He even says that by being jealous he was acting like an animal. Instead of being jealous, he should have been focusing on the Lord and the blessings the Lord was giving him.

The Lord is always with us and guiding us. Even when things may not seem that good to us, God is caring for us, and in His love and grace He still loves us as His children. When we are weak, God is strong. The Lord is all that we need. We don't need the newest toys and gadgets. We need the Lord and the Lord alone. He is enough for us.

REFLECTION

Why don't we need to be jealous of the things unbelievers have?

1 THESSALONIANS 1:1

To the church of the Thessalonians in God the Father and the Lord Jesus Christ.

READ 1 THESSALONIANS 1:1-4

Do you sometimes wonder if you are good enough to be a member of God's church? You do want to serve the Lord, but so often you sin. You get angry when you shouldn't. You think about yourself more than others. You might even hate somebody else, and so you feel like you really don't deserve to belong to God's church.

Let's have a look at what Paul says to the Thessalonians. Paul knew that there were sinful people in the church there. He had heard about some of their problems and sins, so he wrote them a letter to talk about these things.

But Paul didn't start the letter with a harsh criticism. He didn't start by telling them off. No, he started by calling them the church of the Lord Jesus Christ. Even though they had their sins and shortcomings, they could still be called the church of Jesus Christ because of the grace of God. God loved them and forgave them even though they were sinful; He did so simply because they belonged to Jesus Christ.

You too belong to the church of God. Yes, you are sinful, but because of God's grace and love in Jesus Christ, you too are forgiven and can belong to God's church. You aren't part of God's church because of anything good in yourself, but you are part of God's church simply because God loves you and wants you to be His. He sent Jesus Christ for your sins.

We see in this letter that Paul also gave thanks for them all. He thanked God for every single member of that church. He didn't just give thanks for the church in general, but for every single member. No matter what their sins of the past were, God in His love and grace forgave them when they repented. Never can your sins be too great that God's grace can't save you. Never can your sins be too big to stop you from being a member of God's church.

REFLECTION

How should it show in your life that you are part of God's church?

1 THESSALONIANS 1:6

And you became followers of us and of the Lord, having received the word in much affliction, with joy of the Holy Spirit.

READ 1 THESSALONIANS 1:2-6

The people in Thessalonica had difficult things happening in their lives. Since they had become Christians, some of them may have lost their friends and even lost their jobs. And yet Paul says that they had joy! Isn't that amazing to be able to have joy in these hard circumstances?

How were they able to be joyful while living in a difficult time? Verse 5 tells us that they received joy through the Word of God and the Holy Spirit. To have joy is different than being happy. Sometimes when things are hard, you may not feel very happy, but do you know you can still have joy, even when you are not happy?

To have joy means to know that you are God's precious child. As God's child you know and believe with absolute certainty that the Lord Jesus Christ is your Saviour. You know that God is always caring for you. Then, if you are feeling scared, you can have joy in knowing that God will be with you. If you are sad, you can still have joy knowing that God is working in your life and keeping you close to Him.

How do you get this joy? You get it in the same way as the Thessalonians received it. You must read and study God's Word. It's in there that you learn about God's love, grace and forgiveness. We read about God's care for His people. We also read about how holy God is, and that because of His holiness, He sent Jesus to pay for our sins so that we can be His beloved children.

This Word of God gives us joy when the Holy Spirit uses it to work in our hearts. The Holy Spirit reminds us of God's Word and helps us to believe that Jesus died for us. He reminds us that we are God's children.

So read the Bible every day. Think about what you are reading and ask the Lord to work with the Holy Spirit in you, so that you receive this joy!

REFLECTION

How can you have joy, even when things are difficult for you?

1 TIMOTHY 6:6

Now godliness with contentment is great gain.

READ 1 TIMOTHY 6:1-10

What makes you happy? What gives you the greatest joy? Is it when your mum gives you a little bit of money and takes you to the shop to buy something for yourself? Is it the latest book you have received, or the holiday you are looking forward to? I'm sure these things will make you happy, and that's okay. You are allowed to be thankful for the blessings you receive from the Lord.

But do these things really make you happy? Can you still be happy without them? Or are you always wanting more, thinking that if you could just have a few more books, a few more clothes or some new games you would be truly happy?

The false preachers in Timothy's day taught the people different things than Jesus Christ taught them. They were often proud and more interested in the money they may have received for their preaching than making sure they actually preached about Jesus Christ. But the gospel is not about money or how earthly things can make you happy. That is why we are warned here that we shouldn't be focusing on money or earthly things to make us happy.

Contentment or being happy can only come when we focus on godliness. To focus on godliness means to think about God and not ourselves or the things we want. It means to focus on the blessings of God's love and grace and forgiveness. It means to think about the eternal life with God that we look forward to.

This doesn't mean that you are not allowed to enjoy the money or the earthly blessings that the Lord gives you. Verse 10 doesn't say that money is the root of all evil, but that the *love* of money is the root of all evil. The Bible says you are a fool if you think that having lots of money can make you happy.

True happiness comes from learning more about the Lord, singing praises to Him, reading the Bible and thanking God for His love for you. That's what can really make you happy.

REFLECTION

What things make you truly happy?

LAMENTATIONS 5:19

You, O Lord, remain forever; Your throne from generation to generation.

READ LAMENTATIONS 5:15-22

The people of Israel were God's special people. God had crowned them with His special love and grace. But here in verse 16 the people said that the crown had fallen from their heads. Things had gone very badly for them as a nation because they had turned away from the Lord. And even though they had repented of their sins, things were still bad. But the people knew that they had hope in the Lord. They knew that God would always be King and so He would hear their cry and restore their crown according to His promises.

In these verses, the people describe how bad things had become for them because of their sins. They had become poor and needed to turn to their enemies for food. There was no one to deliver them from their enemies. All their singing and dancing had stopped. The joy had gone out of their lives. Their crown had fallen. They had been God's royal people, but now they were nothing.

But they could rejoice in knowing that God's throne would be forever. Even though they didn't amount to much on earth, God still ruled in heaven.

In those days many of the nations around them believed in many different gods. We know that there is only one God, but they believed that every nation had its own god. So, they thought that if there was a battle on earth, there was also one happening among the gods. And if a nation lost on earth, then the god of that nation lost in heaven. But the children of Israel knew that this wasn't true. They knew that there was only one God. They knew that even though they had lost on earth and been taken by their enemies, God still ruled in heaven. He is the only God and He will be God forever and ever. "You, O Lord, remain forever," they said. God would fulfil His promises and restore their crown!

REFLECTION

Why is it good that God is God forever?

LAMENTATIONS 5:21

*Turn us back to You, O LORD,
and we will be restored.*

READ LAMENTATIONS 5:15-22

The children of Israel had repented of their sins and were waiting for the LORD to restore their crown. In these verses they were asking the LORD why it was taking so long for them to be restored as God's people. They knew that God reigned forever. They knew that His promises would always stand. And so they knew that God would restore them, but why did it take so long?

When they said, "Turn us back to you, O LORD," they were not asking that they would repent of their sins. They had already done that. They were asking that the LORD would let them return to Jerusalem. They didn't want to be in exile anymore, but they wanted to be back in the city God had chosen for them and back as God's special people. They wanted to see God's grace in their lives.

But God didn't restore them in the way that they wanted, because He was going to restore them in a much greater way. God had much greater promises for the children of Israel. God was not only going to live with them in Jerusalem, but God was going to live in them with His Holy Spirit. God was going to send His Son, the Lord Jesus Christ. So even though the children of Israel thought that God was taking far too long to restore their crown, God was busy working for them.

Through the coming of the Lord Jesus Christ, they would not just return from exile, but they would be crowned with glory and honour. Jesus Christ had a crown of thorns put on His head so that they could have the crown of glory. And He has done that for us also.

We are not unimportant people wandering around on this earth, but we are God's chosen children. We are His covenant people. Because of Christ's work for us and the Holy Spirit in us, we already have this crown of glory. We are kings and queens of our great King, the LORD God Almighty.

REFLECTION

What was the great promise that God had for the children of Israel?

LEVITICUS 1:9

And the priest shall burn all on the altar as a burnt sacrifice, an offering made by fire, a sweet aroma to the Lord.

READ LEVITICUS 1:3-9

Can you imagine what it must have been like for the Israelites when they made a burnt offering? They had to take one of their best animals and offer it on an altar in the tabernacle or temple. The Bible says it had to be without blemish. This means it wasn't allowed to have a misshaped ear or crooked leg. They had to bring this bull to the priest who would kill it. Then he would take some of the blood of the animal and sprinkle it on and around the altar. Next the animal would be cut into smaller pieces and placed on the fire that was on the altar and the animal would have to be burnt completely. To us, all this blood and awful smell of burning animals seems so gross, but the Bible says that it was a sweet aroma (smell) to the Lord.

What did this sacrifice mean? It was teaching the Israelites how sinful they were. God hates sin. God is very angry with all our sins. And the Bible says that sin must be punished with death.

But we don't want to die, do we? We don't want our sins to stop us from having a relationship with God. The good news is that God has made a way possible for us to live with Him. He has made a way for someone else to die instead of us. That person is Jesus Christ our Lord. He died instead of us. God's anger at our sins means we should be killed or sent to eternal hell, but instead, Jesus died for us and now we can continue to live with God.

That's what the burnt offering pointed to. Jesus hadn't come yet in the Old Testament so they had to offer an animal to pay for their sins. The animal was burnt to show that it really should have been the people who were burnt because of their sins. They deserved death, but God lovingly said that an animal could die instead of them.

What a loving God we have, a God who sent Jesus to die instead of us.

REFLECTION

Why did the animal on the burnt offering have to be burnt completely?

"Whoever drinks of the water that I shall give him will never thirst"

JOHN 14:4A

PSALM 57:1

Be merciful to me, O God, be merciful to me! For my soul trusts in You.

READ PSALM 57

You remember the stories of David fleeing from Saul, don't you? The Bible tells us a number of times that David was very frightened while he was fleeing. You can imagine that he would have been shaking with fear. He would just have had to sneeze or cough, and Saul could have discovered him in the cave and killed him.

David writes Psalm 57 while he is in a cave fleeing from Saul. In this Psalm, David uses pictures of lions, fire, and teeth to show how much danger he is in.

Are you ever frightened? Are there times when you are scared? Now it most likely won't be because someone is trying to kill you, but you could be frightened of thunder, or scared because your parents need to travel far away for a while, or you may be frightened because you're worried about something your classmate says to you. There could be many reasons why you feel frightened and afraid.

When David is frightened, he doesn't spend all his time praying for God to tell him what is going to happen next, or for God to take Saul away. Instead, he asks God to be merciful to him, and then he sings about God's greatness. He sings of how he can trust in this great God. He knows that God is most powerful and can do all things. He knows that God has everything in His control. And it is this knowledge of God's greatness that he sings about. Because David knows that God is looking after him and is in control of his life, he is able to sing praises to God.

So, when you are frightened, you should also go to God, confessing how great He is and asking Him to help you to trust in Him. Read God's Word so that you can learn how great and mighty God really is. Trust God to look after you. Know that you are God's precious child and that He will certainly care for you.

REFLECTION

What should you pray when you are frightened?

PSALM 116:1

I love the Lord, because He has heard my voice and my supplication.

READ PSALM 116:1–14

You may have sung this Psalm very often. It is usually one of the first psalms that you learn as a little child: "I love the Lord." And these are beautiful words to sing.

The author of this Psalm had been going through some very difficult things. He says that the pains of death surrounded him. But during his troubles he called out to the Lord. He prayed and the Lord heard him and helped him.

The good news for us is that the Lord hears and answers us too. When you cry out to Him in your trouble, He will hear you. He will listen to your prayers and He will give you all you need. This doesn't mean that your troubles will always go away. But God will always help you through your hard times. He will carry you and give you what you need.

And it also means that God will help you with your biggest need. Your biggest trouble is your sins. They are so great that God cannot love you because of them. And yet God does love you. He loves you because He has chosen you to be His child and because Christ has died on the cross for you. He loves you for Christ's sake.

Because of God's grace to you, you can ask, just like the psalmist does, "What shall I render to the Lord for all His benefits towards me?" How can I thank the Lord for His blessings to me?

And just like the psalmist, you can thank the Lord for His love for you by accepting His gift of salvation to you. Thank Him for His forgiveness and love, and promise to always serve the Lord. With the psalmist you can say, "I will pay my vows to the Lord." To vow means to promise. Together with all other believers, you can thank and praise the Lord for His goodness.

REFLECTION

How can you thank the Lord for His blessings to you?

2 PETER 3:7

But the heavens and the earth which are now preserved by the same word, are reserved for fire until the day of judgement and perdition of ungodly men.

READ 2 PETER 3:1-9

Have you ever stood around a big bonfire? You can enjoy the warmth while you watch all the twigs and branches being burnt up. But, if there are some rocks or pieces of precious metal like gold or silver in the fire, they will not burn—they will not disappear.

2 Peter chapter 3 speaks about the day of Judgement, when Christ will return, and tells us that the earth will be refined with fire on that day. This means that *everything* wicked and sinful from this life will be burnt - totally destroyed, just like the branches in the bonfire. But God's refining fire will not destroy everything. Our faith and belief in Jesus Christ will not be destroyed by fire. God is going to renew the earth, destroy everything sinful and make all things new.

So what should we be doing today while we are waiting for Christ to return? Should we just keep on doing our daily activities? Yes, we must certainly continue with the things God has given us to do. You need to keep going to school, keep playing board games, keep helping at home and keep playing with your friends. But as you do these things, you must ask yourself if you are doing these things to God's glory. Would you be happy for Christ to return while you are doing your activities? Would you be happy for Christ to see what you are doing?

Are you looking forward to Christ's return, when there will be a new heaven and earth? Just think about it: on the new earth you will never sin again; you will never even have to struggle with sin. You will never displease God again with any of your thoughts or words. Everything you do will be perfect and without sin. It will not need to be destroyed with fire because it will be sinless. Oh, what a great future we have to look forward to!

REFLECTION

Do you remember to pray for Christ to return?

2 SAMUEL 9:7

So David said to him, "Do not fear, for I will surely show you kindness for Jonathan your father's sake…"

READ 2 SAMUEL 9:1-13

When Mephibosheth was a young boy of five years old, he had become lame in his legs. His nurse had been fleeing with him when he fell. He hurt his legs so badly that he was never able to walk again. Mephibosheth was the son of Jonathan. You will remember that Jonathan and King David had been very good friends. David had promised that he would always look after Jonathan's family and treat them with kindness.

In 2 Samuel 9, David wants to know if there are any children of Jonathan alive still so that he can show this kindness to them. When he is told about Mephibosheth, he asks for Mephibosheth. He wants to talk to him.

Mephibosheth lived in a barren place, probably far away from other people. Because he could not walk, he couldn't work and couldn't do anything to help himself. When he comes before the king, he is frightened that he is going to be killed. He realises he is totally useless. He even calls himself a "dead dog."

Mephibosheth is a picture of what we are all like spiritually. Just like he couldn't do anything to make his life better, we can't do anything to improve ourselves either. Just like Mephibosheth was not worthy to come before the king, so we are not worthy to go before God.

But King David showed great kindness to Mephibosheth. He did so because of his promises to Jonathan, Mephibosheth's father. In the same way, God shows great kindness to us. Even though our sins are so great, He still loves us. And He does so because of His covenant promises. He has promised in the Bible that He will always love and forgive those who come to Him through Jesus Christ.

King David was not able to heal Mephibosheth. He could show him kindness, but he could not heal him. But the LORD, our great King, can and does heal us. He forgives all our sins today, and one day He will remove them completely and we will be perfect. We will live a perfect, sinless life.

REFLECTION

How is Mephibosheth a picture of what we are like?

2 SAMUEL 18:9

The mule went under the thick boughs of a great terebinth tree, and his head caught in the terebinth; so he was left hanging between heaven and earth.

READ 2 SAMUEL 18:9-15

Absalom had done many things wrong in his life. There were many sins that he never repented from. In this chapter he is in a battle against his father. You probably remember the story well. Absalom had long hair. We can read in a previous chapter that he had a haircut once a year, and every time he cut off about 2.3kg of hair. That is a lot of hair. You can imagine how long his hair must have been. In those days, hair like that made a man look handsome. The Bible tells us that Absalom was a very handsome man.

Yet these good looks of Absalom meant nothing when he got caught in a tree. As he was trying to escape, his head was caught in the tree and his mule kept running, so Absalom was left hanging from a tree. He had done this to himself because of his sins. He was stuck. There was no way that he could escape.

We know that a person hanging from a tree was cursed by God. Absalom's own sin and folly put him under God's judgement and curse. We too, because of our many sins, should be cursed by God. Sometimes we even get trapped in our sins. We keep doing the same sins time and again. Sometimes it feels like we are stuck in our sins, just like Absalom was stuck in the tree.

But the good news is that God has made a way for us to be made free. We don't need to be stuck in our sins. There is an escape. We can be free and forgiven from our sins because Jesus Christ was hung on the tree - the cross - for us. He received the full curse of God and took the full anger and wrath of God for us. Even though Christ hadn't sinned, our sins were put on Him so that He could be cursed by God, in order that we could be forgiven. What a wonderful Saviour we have!

REFLECTION

Why did Jesus hang on the cross?

2 SAMUEL 23:15

And David said with longing, "Oh, that someone would give me a drink of water from the well of Bethlehem, which is by the gate!"

READ 2 SAMUEL 23:13-17

This sounds like a strange little story. David had been fighting battles and may have been thirsty, so he asked for a drink of water. But the water he asked for needed to come from a well which was about 40 kilometres away. Three men were willing to go and get this water for David. Getting this water would have been difficult, not only because it was a long walk, but also because they had to walk through the enemies' lands. It would have been a very difficult journey. But these three men made this journey and took the water back to David.

But when they got to David, he refused to drink this water. At first this seems very ungrateful. After these men risked their lives to get this water, David refused to drink it and poured it out. But the Bible tells us that David poured it out to the LORD, so it was not just an aimless, ungrateful pouring out of the water.

David understood the effort these men had gone to. He even called the water their blood. He knew that they were willing to die for him in getting this water. This shows their godly devotion and godly service to their king. These men were delighted to serve the LORD's anointed king.

So, when David poured out the water to the LORD, it was like he was making a sacrifice of thanks to the LORD. The water was too precious to drink. These men had risked their lives for it, so David used it and offered it to the LORD.

This story points ahead to Jesus Christ. He didn't just need to walk forty kilometres through enemy land to save us, but He needed to suffer hellish agony on the cross for us. And He did that for us. What a great King we have—Jesus Christ Himself. How do we serve this King? Are we willing to use each moment of every day to serve Him? Are you willing to make sacrifices to serve this King?

REFLECTION

What are some sacrifices you may need to make to serve this King?

REVELATION 3:5

"He who overcomes shall be clothed in white garments, and I will not blot out his name from the Book of Life."

READ REVELATION 3:1-6

The Lord tells the church at Sardis that even though people say that they are alive, He knows that they are dead. The church was doing lots of great things. It's as if the Lord is telling them, "Yes, I see that your church is full on Sundays, that you pray and read your Bible, that you sing Psalms, that you dress nicely for church, that you go to lots of meetings… but your heart isn't really in your worship."

The same can happen to us. We can do all the right things, but we can be doing them for ourselves and not because we really love the Lord. And so the Lord reminds us in this letter to love Him from the heart. Then the Lord tells us how to do this, how to serve Him from the heart.

First, the Lord tells us to be watchful, or to wake up. Take a look at your life and see how you are serving the Lord. Are you thinking about yourself or the Lord when you do things?

The Lord also tells us to remember what He has done for us in the past. See the blessings of the Lord in your life. Remember what you read in the Bible about the Lord's grace and love and forgiveness. See how greatly the Lord has blessed you in the past.

And then repent. If there are things in your life that need changing, then change them. Do you need to read your Bible more? Then do so. Do you need to be kinder to others? Then do so. Do you need to trust the Lord more? Then do so.

The Lord also gives great promises in this letter. If you keep repenting and keep serving the Lord and keep asking for forgiveness, then you will remain God's special child. Your name will stay in the Book of Life. When judgement day comes, you will not need to worry, as Christ says that you are His because He gave His life for you. Isn't this such a wonderful blessing?

REFLECTION

What are the great promises that God gives in this letter?

REVELATION 4:8

The four living creatures...they do not rest day or night, saying "Holy, holy, holy, Lord God Almighty. Who was and is and is to come!"

READ REVELATION 4

Do you ever think about heaven? Do you wonder what is going on in heaven? Do you think about what God looks like?

In this vision the apostle John is allowed to look into heaven. John is invited to come forward and look through the open door into heaven. And what does John see? He sees God sitting on the throne. God is so majestic that John cannot even describe God with human words. And so, he describes the one sitting on the throne, using the best words he can. He says that God is like some precious stones. God is too majestic, too beautiful to be described with our words.

John sees four living creatures. Again, John cannot describe exactly what they look like, so he says that they look like a lion, a calf, a face of a man and like a flying eagle. These four living creatures have many eyes because they are always looking at God sitting on the throne. They also have many wings because they are always ready to do the work of God. And they are singing praises to God: "Holy, holy, holy, Lord God Almighty."

These four creatures represent everything on earth. They are showing us that all things on earth are working for God. Even though it often does not seem like it, especially when bad things happen, all things are working for the kingdom of God. God is using everything to further His kingdom. The four living creatures are doing the work God wants them to do.

And that is why the twenty-four elders, who John also sees in heaven, bow down in praise whenever the four living creatures give glory to God. They also sing of the greatness of God, the one sitting on the throne.

We are allowed to read about what John sees in heaven, so that we too know that God is working all things for the coming of His kingdom. And then, just like the ones who sit around the throne, we too are called to worship God.

REFLECTION

What is everyone in heaven doing?

REVELATION 5:7

Then He came and took the scroll out of the right hand of Him who sat on the throne.

READ REVELATION 5

While John is being given a look into heaven, he sees God sitting on the throne with a scroll in His right hand. But then John cannot see anyone who can open the scroll so he begins to weep. John is very upset, crying loudly, because no one is found worthy to open the scroll.

Why is John so upset? Why is it so important that the scroll is opened? All the things that were going to happen in the world were written on this scroll. Everything from Christ's ascension into heaven until His return. Someone who could open the scroll and make all these things happen needed to be found. If the scroll could not be opened then it would mean that this world of sin, suffering, death, and judgement would go on forever. An unopened scroll would mean that the new heaven and the new earth would never come. And that is what made John so sad.

But then one of the elders tells John to stop weeping because someone has been found who can open the scroll. This someone was Jesus Christ Himself. He is the Lamb that has been slain. He has paid for all the sin and wickedness in the world, so He is worthy to open the scroll. He can make all the events in the world happen. He will make sure the new heaven and earth come.

When Jesus is found, the twenty-four elders fall down and worship Christ, the Lamb. This means that all the people in the church worship Jesus Christ. Then we read that the angels join in worshipping the Lamb. And while the church and angels are praising God together, all living creatures join together to worship the Lamb. Together, everyone is praising God.

We too must join in praising God. God is working in this world to make everything happen according to His plan. He is working all things so that Christ can return, and we can live with Him in eternal glory. Let us all join in praising God.

REFLECTION

Why did John stop crying?

REVELATION 21:10

...and showed me the great city, the holy Jerusalem, descending out of heaven from God.

READ REVELATION 21:9-21

When you are going to go on a holiday, you think a lot more about where you are going than how you are going to get there.

But do you think very much about the new heaven and the new earth? The Lord tells us some things about eternal life. Often we think about the new life as somewhere up in the clouds, but God tells us that He is going to renew not just the heaven, but also the earth. When God created the earth, He said that it was good. And God is going to use the cities and fields and forests and lakes of this earth and make them completely new. He is going to renew them to be a place without sin.

The earth and heaven will not be two separate places but one place. The dwelling place of man will be the same as the dwelling place of God. We will be living with God in the holy city.

John saw this new city coming down out of heaven. The new Jerusalem is a holy city because Christ has made it holy. John saw it as a very, very large cube. It's a huge city, and its length is the same as its width as well as its height. This won't be the actual size of the city, but what God is showing us here is that it will be very large and holy. You probably remember that the Holy of Holies in the temple was also a cube shape. The Holy of Holies was the place where God lived. It was very special and no one was allowed in there, apart from the high priest once a year. It was God's dwelling place.

The new city is like a massive Holy of Holies. It will be God's holy dwelling place. But then we will be allowed to live in this holy city with God. Isn't this wonderful news? One day we will be living with Him and will be able to worship Him without any sin.

REFLECTION

Do you look forward to living in the new city with God?

PSALM 62:8

*Trust in Him at all times, you people.
Pour out your heart before Him.*

READ PSALM 62

What do you do if you feel troubled, sad, or frightened, or that things are just too hard? Maybe you have a grandparent or friend who is terribly sick. Maybe you have classmates who say nasty things about you. Maybe no one plays with you, and you feel lonely. Maybe you have panic attacks and want them to stop. Maybe your friends are trying to convince you to sin. Or maybe it is something else that is very hard. What do you do at times like this? Where do you go for comfort?

In Psalm 62, David went to God with his hurt and trouble. He says, "Pour out your heart before God." Tell God all about your troubles. Tell Him what is bothering you. Pour out everything to God. Don't hide anything from Him. And then trust God. Trust Him with your troubles. Believe that God is caring for you. Believe that God is your rock and your salvation. Believe that God is helping you and will continue to help you.

You can trust God because of who He is. He is your Father who loves you. Verse 11 tells us that God is all-powerful. God has absolute power over everything. This means that God is in control and He can do anything in your life. If God leaves things in your life that are hard for you, He does this because He loves you, and through these things He is bringing you closer to Him. He is teaching you to trust Him.

It was terribly hard for the Lord Jesus when He knew He was going to die on the cross. And yet Jesus trusted God and went to the cross. Even there, God was in control. Jesus needed to die on the cross so that we can be forgiven and have a loving relationship with the Father. And Jesus rose from the dead so that we can now trust God, knowing that He loves us and will carry us through all the difficulties in life and bring us to eternal life with Him one day.

REFLECTION

Next time something is troubling you, what will you do with your troubles?

2 THESSALONIANS 1:11

Therefore we also pray always for you that our God would count you worthy of this calling...

READ 2 THESSALONIANS 1:11-12

Sometimes we just feel so unworthy, don't we? We've done things we shouldn't have done. We've said things that have hurt others and we wish we could delete these things out of our lives. Or maybe you have had to suffer something very difficult: the death of a loved one, anxiety, or even persecution for your faith. It might feel as though we suffer these things because we are not worthy children of the Lord or that the Lord is just not happy with us.

But Paul tells the Thessalonians that the Lord counts us worthy of our calling. This calling is the heavenly calling to live holy lives in Christ Jesus. It is the calling to be and live as children of God. We are God's children and God says we are worthy of this task. You are worthy to be called God's child and to do the things He wants you to do.

But how are we worthy? Certainly not from ourselves. We all sin and that's why we, from ourselves, are unworthy. But God tells us that because of the suffering and death of Christ Jesus, we are now forgiven and are worthy children of His! Isn't that wonderful? Even though we aren't worthy, God sees us as being worthy, all because of Christ's work for us.

But then we sometimes wonder if we will always keep serving the Lord. Will we always live up to our calling? How can we keep fighting against the same sins every day again? At times it can seem so hard. But again, the Lord assures us here that He will continue to work in us. Through the power of the Holy Spirit, He will help us to keep serving Him till one day we will be glorified. By God's grace we can continue in our calling of serving the Lord in this life, till the day that Christ returns in glory and we can live with Him eternally.

Every day again, pray to God, confessing your sins and thanking Him for making you worthy in Jesus Christ.

REFLECTION

How is the Lord able to call us worthy when we are actually so unworthy?

AMOS 3:6

If a trumpet is blown in a city, will not the people be afraid? If there is calamity in a city, will not the Lord have done it?

READ AMOS 3:1-8

When you face difficult things in your life, what do you do about it? Do they make you scared and worried?

The people who lived in Amos' days were happy with how their life was going. But Amos told them that they had to have a closer look at their life. When the trumpet sounded, they knew that it was time for war, but when other calamities came to them, they had no idea that they came from the Lord. Calamities are very difficult things or disasters. So, when these disasters came, they didn't recognise them as coming from the Lord.

What about when bad things happen in your life or in the world? Do you realise that they are part of God's plan for your life?

So, what should we do when difficult things become a part of our life? What should you do if your grandparent dies or the whole world suffers from a terrible sickness? I'm sure you know that it is the Lord who sends these things. But does that mean that we should just accept it and keep going? Are we allowed to be sad and struggle with these things?

Of course we will struggle during difficult times. Jesus Himself struggled in the garden before His death and asked God to take away the burden if that was possible. But we also need to use these difficult times to look at our own lives. God is using these difficult things to make us grow closer to Him. Maybe the Lord wants us to look closely at our own lives and see if He is the most important one in our lives. Maybe the Lord is reminding us to put all our trust in Him alone and not in our own things. Maybe the Lord is reminding us to focus on serving Him more in our lives.

And the Lord does this because He loves you. He wants you, His precious child, to keep serving Him. That's why the Lord uses everything in your life to help you to serve Him better.

REFLECTION

How can the Lord use difficult things in your life?

"*Be still, and know that I am God*"

PSALM 46:10A

COLOSSIANS 1:16

All things were created through Him and for Him.

READ COLOSSIANS 1:15-17

What do you think when things go so differently from what you expect? When the whole world is struck by a virus, and everybody's lives are changed, is God still in control?

These verses remind us that Christ is and always remains King. Even during the corona virus pandemic God remained King and was in control. He is no less King during hard times than during times when things go well.

Paul says that Christ is the firstborn of all creation. This means that He is above all and in control of all creation. So hardships don't surprise the King. Not at all. Actually, these things are part of His perfect and wise plan for your life and the life of the people throughout the whole world.

Paul says that God created all things. Not just some things, not just most things, but all things. And yes, that means that the corona virus and other sicknesses are also created by Him. We know that these things have come into the world because of the fall into sin, but that doesn't mean that God isn't in control of them.

And this gives us great comfort! Our King, our Saviour, the one who gave up His life for us, the one who loves us, He is the one who is in control of all things. This means that He is busy at work with all these things for our good. We might not be able to see how disasters and terrible things can be used for our good, but they are! Don't ever doubt that! They are being used for our good because Christ the King is in control. *All things were created through Him and for Him.* He is busy using all the things for His good purpose. How? We can't always understand how, but that's because we are people and God is God.

But we *can* trust Him! We can trust our God and King. We don't need to understand everything, but we must just be at peace knowing that He is God, and He is in control of all things, and He will use all things to bring us, His children, closer to Him.

REFLECTION

How does it help you to know that God created all things?

COLOSSIANS 1:21

And you, who once were alienated and enemies in your mind by wicked works, yet now He has reconciled.

READ COLOSSIANS 1:19-23

The people that Paul is writing to didn't always love the Lord. Before they became Christians, they actually hated God. Paul says that they were the enemies of God. Their minds were filled with hatred for the Lord. And this showed in the things that they did and the way that they lived. They did evil things, things that didn't please God.

Do you know, that by nature we are all like this as well? In and of ourselves we would want nothing to do with the Lord and would actually hate Him. That sounds pretty awful, doesn't it? But it's true! If the Holy Spirit wasn't working in our hearts to make us love the Lord, we would actually hate the Lord. We wouldn't want to serve Him.

We know that the Lord doesn't ignore our sins and hatred. Because God is holy, He can't ignore sin. Sin must be paid for. Sin must be punished.

That's why it is so beautiful to read Paul's words, where he tells the Colossians that they have been reconciled. To be reconciled means that God was no longer angry with them because of their sins and that they now loved the Lord. How was this possible? How could God's anger at their sins be gone? Only because Christ died on the cross with His real human body. Instead of punishing the Colossians for their sins, God punished the Lord Jesus instead. Christ took the wrath of God and so the Colossians were now seen by God as holy, without sin.

In the same way, even though we sin every day, when we ask for forgiveness, God does forgive us because of Christ's death. Isn't that amazing? Of ourselves, we hate God. We sin every day and the only punishment God will accept for our sins is for us to be sent to hell. And yet Christ went to hell for us while He was hanging on the cross. He took all of God's anger at sin upon Himself, and now we don't have to be punished. Instead the Lord loves us as His beloved children.

REFLECTION

Does God's gift of forgiveness make you thankful? How should you show this thankfulness?

COLOSSIANS 2:6

As you therefore have received Christ Jesus the Lord, so walk in Him.

READ COLOSSIANS 2:1-9

In the first chapter of Colossians, the apostle Paul reminds the Colossians of how blessed they are in Christ. Yes, he uses lots of difficult words, but in short, Paul tells the Colossians that because of Christ's perfect work on earth, they may belong to God. Well, Christ has done exactly the same for you. His work on earth also means that you belong to Christ.

"Now," Paul says, "walk in Christ." Live in a way that shows that you belong to Christ. If you are walking through a shopping centre, act as though Christ is walking beside you, seeing everything that you do and hearing every word you speak. When you are in your home watching a movie, act as though Christ is sitting next to you watching as well. When you are playing with your friends, act as though Christ is playing with you. Remember that Christ *is* actually there with you all the time. And so Paul tells us to walk, act, talk, sing, and think in such a way that shows that Christ is there with us.

To help you to walk in Christ, you need to be deeply rooted in Him. Just like a tree has roots that go very deep into the earth, so you need to dig deeply into God's Word. You need to take the time to listen when sermons are preached, to ask your parents to help you understand the Bible reading, to concentrate when singing psalms and to pray to God every day.

Remembering all the blessings that you have in Christ should cause you to abound in thanksgiving. Have you ever written a list of things that you are thankful for? It's a great idea to do this if you haven't. Actually, it's a good idea to do it often. And on that list, one of the important things will be that you are thankful for everything you have been given in Christ. You are indeed blessed to belong to Christ. Show your thankfulness for these blessings by walking every day showing that you are His.

REFLECTION

What would be the first five things on your list of things you are thankful for?

COLOSSIANS 2:16

So let no one judge you in food or in drink, or regarding a festival or a new moon or sabbaths.

READ COLOSSIANS 2:16-23

What makes you a Christian? What saves you? Are you a Christian because you read the Bible faithfully every day? Does remembering to pray lots save you? Does wearing your best clothes to church make you a good Christian? Have you got a greater chance of being saved than your friend whose hair is never done nicely or who stumbles with her words a bit when she prays?

Even though these verses are hard to understand, we know that the Holy Spirit is telling us here that these things do not save us. Yes, it is very good and important to pray and read the Bible. Yes, it is very important to prepare properly for church and to listen to the preaching carefully. But just doing all these things is not going to make you want to sin less. It is not going to make you a better person.

There were some false teachers who were telling the Colossian people that they should go back and practice some of the Old Testament laws again. They were saying that this would help them to be better Christians. Others were acting very religious and holy, and making sure everyone knew about all the good things that they did. Paul says that these people were just puffed up and proud.

And so, Paul warns the Colossians here not to worry about these people and what they were teaching. Instead, they needed to be focused on Christ. Christ alone can save us. We need to hold fast to Christ. In Christ we have all that we need to be saved. We need to believe in Jesus Christ, and believe that He came to save us. We need to go to Him for forgiveness when we sin.

And then, out of thankfulness for God's love for you, of course you will want to read the Bible and pray, and of course you will want to prepare well for the Sunday. These things are all very important. But while you are doing these things, always remember Christ and His love and grace for you.

REFLECTION

Can doing all the right things save you?

COLOSSIANS 3:13

Bearing with one another, and forgiving one another...

READ COLOSSIANS 3:12-17

Do you ever think about how Christ acted when He was on earth? Christ was the most gentle, most kind-hearted, most loving, most humble, and most forgiving person who has ever lived. There is no one who has ever been more caring than Christ Jesus. No one has ever been more gentle than Christ Jesus. No one has ever been more forgiving than Christ Jesus.

And now, God tells you that you must be like this as well because you belong to Christ, because you are one of God's elect children. Show that you belong to Christ by being kind and gentle and loving and forgiving.

It's so easy to forget who we are, isn't it? It's easy to forget that we should show that we belong to Christ in every word we speak and everything we do. Yet people should be able to see us and know that Christ is in us, that we are Christians. They should be able to see some of Christ's kindness, gentleness and love in our actions.

One important way to show that you are a Christian is to be forgiving. If someone has said or done something against you, you must be willing to forgive them. You should not stay angry at them for what they have done. If they come to you and ask for forgiveness, they will most likely have already asked God to forgive them. If God has forgiven them, then you must forgive them as well.

Think about how much Christ has forgiven you. He has forgiven all your sins. So, if God has forgiven your sins, you must also forgive others. Imagine you say something nasty to your friend and soon after feel really bad for what you did. You go to your friend and say sorry to them. You would want your friend to forgive you, wouldn't you? And you would also want your friend to continue to be kind and loving toward you. So you must forgive others and continue to show love and kindness to them.

REFLECTION

What are some ways that you can show that you are a Christian?

COLOSSIANS 4:2

Continue earnestly in prayer, being vigilant in it with thanksgiving.

READ COLOSSIANS 4:2-4

Did you know that in some religions people are only allowed to say set prayers? They can't talk to the Lord like we do when we pray to God. We can tell God whatever is on our heart. And that's what the Lord wants us to do. Think of all the prayers that are in the Psalms. The Old Testament believers prayed for many different things. And in the Lord's prayer, Jesus tells us to pray for many things as well. It's a beautiful thing that we can pray to God, talking to Him about all the things in our lives.

In these verses, Paul tells us to "pray, being watchful in it with thanksgiving." When Paul talks about being watchful, he may very well be speaking about watching and waiting for the return of Christ. We know that Christ is going to come back again on the clouds of heaven. We don't know when it will be, but we know with certainty that it will happen one day. So Paul tells us to thank God for something that is still going to come. We are to give thanks because the day of Christ's return will be wonderful. It will mean the end of sin, the end of death, the end of tears, the end of arguments, the end of sickness. It will be a time of great joy. It will be the beginning of eternal life, when we will live forever with God. So thank God for allowing you to look forward to that great day.

Paul also tells the Colossians to pray for him and for Timothy. They are mission workers. They are preaching the gospel to many people. And they need the prayers of the Colossians. They need to be able to speak clearly and make the gospel easy to understand for the people. And so they need the prayers of the believers.

REFLECTION

Do you remember to pray for Christ's return? Do you remember to pray for missionaries? Can you name the missionaries that your church supports?

DANIEL 2:35

And the stone that struck the image became a great mountain and filled the whole earth.

READ DANIEL 2:31-35, 44

Do you ever wonder if the LORD is actually in control of all things? Sometimes really bad things happen in the world. We hear of mass shootings and wars. We hear of sinful lifestyles. We hear of terrible accidents, and we may wonder if the LORD is actually in control.

Daniel may have been thinking the same in the days that he lived. He was stuck in Babylon, far away from his own people, and he had to live and train with the ungodly wise men. He may have wondered where God was in all of this and if God was really in control.

Well, God gives a dream, not to Daniel, but to King Nebuchadnezzar, to show to all the world that God is in control. God's kingdom will one day destroy all other kingdoms and rule over the whole world.

In this dream the King saw a great image which had a head of gold, a chest and arms of silver, the belly and thighs of clay, the legs of iron and the feet of iron and clay. This was the meaning of the image: After the kingdom of Babylon there would be other great kingdoms - maybe the Medes and Persians, Alexander the Great, and the Roman Empire. But that's not the important part. The important part is what happens next. A small stone comes and knocks down the image and then grows into a big mountain filling the whole earth.

This stone that fills the whole earth was pointing ahead to Jesus Christ. He has come and He has destroyed all the other great kingdoms. He is in control of the whole world. Now, it doesn't always look like that. But that's because Christ hasn't returned yet. For now, God still allows the rulers of this world to do their sinful things, but we know that one day all the world will be totally destroyed, and sin will be destroyed with it. On that day, God's kingdom will be the only kingdom, and we will be allowed to live with God in His kingdom. We are His sons and daughters and so we will reign with Him. Oh, what a glorious future we can look forward to.

REFLECTION

How can knowing that Christ is going to return comfort you when scary things happen in the world?

DANIEL 3:17

Our God whom we serve is able to deliver us from the burning fiery furnace.

READ DANIEL 3:13-18

Do you ever think about persecution? Do you wonder if you would be strong enough to stand up for the Lord? Do you ever think that if you were one of Daniel's three friends, you might have been too scared and bowed down to the statue of Nebuchadnezzar?

Well, Daniel's three friends, Shadrach, Meshach, and Abednego, were no different than you. But they gave the king a very bold answer. The king tells them that he will give them one more chance to bow down to the statue. If they don't, then they will be thrown into the fire, "where," Nebuchadnezzar said, "no god will be able to save you." And they answer by saying, "We actually don't have to answer you, O King, but we want you to know that our God is certainly able to save us from the fire. We don't know if He will choose to save us, but we know that He is able to."

They have total faith in God's ability to save them. They know that He is all-powerful, and totally able to save them. And even though they don't know whether God will actually save them, they are okay with that.

How can they have such faith and calmness when being faced with the possibility of being thrown into the fire? It is because God is with them. God gives them this faith in Him. God gives them this confidence to trust in Him.

So how can you have this same faith and confidence when you are faced with uncertainty or possible persecution? Would you be as brave as these three friends? Yes! Because God is at work in you as well. He will give you the strength and grace you need when you face hard things.

Know that God is with you each and every day, and He is giving you all you need to serve Him, each and every day!

REFLECTION

Would you be able to stand up for the Lord, in a difficult situation? How?

DANIEL 4:34

...and I blessed the Most High and praised and honoured Him who lives forever.

READ DANIEL 4:1-3, 34-37

Nebuchadnezzar was a very mighty king. He had achieved many things during his life. He had built the great city of Babylon and made huge hanging gardens. He had won many battles and ruled over the known world of his days. All these things made Nebuchadnezzar a very proud man. He thought that he had achieved all these things, and he didn't acknowledge the LORD as the one who gave him all things.

So the LORD warned Nebuchadnezzar in a dream. If he continued to be a proud man then the LORD was going to bring him down completely, just like the tree in his dream was chopped down.

The LORD gave Nebuchadnezzar a whole year to listen to this warning. But Nebuchadnezzar didn't listen, so a year later he was brought down completely and he became like an animal. After his time as a beast, Nebuchadnezzar finally humbled himself and acknowledged God as the Most High.

Here is a warning for all of us as well. Do you think you are a proud person? Maybe you don't think you are, but do you get angry when someone says things that you don't like? Do you sometimes think that you are better than others, or are you proud of your sporting ability? We all have pride in our hearts. We all think that we are very important. So often we don't realise that we are being proud, but whenever we say something bad about others, or boast about our things, we are making ourselves out to be important. We are praising ourselves instead of God.

To be truly humble means to stop looking at ourselves and instead look up to God. He is the one who gives us our clothes, food, and abilities at school or in sport. He gives us everything we have. Ask God to make you humble, and with His Spirit He will help take your eyes off yourself and focus on Christ and the wonderful gifts He has given you. Then you can praise God with your gifts.

REFLECTION

List some things that you sometimes say that can be prideful.

DANIEL 5:27

You have been weighed in the balance and found wanting

READ DANIEL 5:24-30

It would have been scary for King Belshazzar to see a hand, writing on the wall. But the meaning of the words should have made him even more scared. He had been weighed and found wanting or sinful. His kingdom was going to be divided and given to the Medes and Persians. The writing on the wall told of the great fall of Babylon.

And that is exactly what happened that very night. King Belshazzar was killed, and the Babylonian kingdom was taken over by the Medes and Persians.

These words were not only a warning to King Belshazzar, but also to God's people in Babylon and to us today. The people of Israel had gone into exile because they had been weighed and found wanting. This means that they had turned their backs on the Lord and refused to repent of their sins.

But we too have been weighed by God. God looks at us too and sees that we are found wanting. Of ourselves we are totally wicked and sinful. Unless we repent from our sins, we will also face punishment.

But thanks be to God, Jesus Christ has come to take our punishment and to be righteous in our place. So now when God weighs us, when He looks at us to judge us, we are not found wanting, but we are found worthy. We are found worthy because of Christ's worthiness.

The book of Revelation also talks about the fall of Babylon. In Revelation, Babylon refers to all things sinful. Revelation talks about people who share in the sins of Babylon, people who do not repent from their sins and are destroyed. But it also speaks about those who are saved, those who have come out of Babylon. God will destroy sin and everything that is sinful. God will destroy everyone who does not repent but continues to live in sin. But those who know their sin and turn to the Lord Jesus Christ will not be destroyed but will be saved. They will have everlasting life through Jesus Christ. Thank the Lord that Jesus came to save you!

REFLECTION

How come God looks at us, His children, and sees us as worthy and not sinful?

DANIEL 6:22

My God sent His angel and shut the lions' mouths, so that they have not hurt me.

READ DANIEL 6:10-23

Can you imagine how Daniel must have felt when he was thrown into the den with hungry lions even though he had done nothing wrong? But we don't read about Daniel being scared. Instead we just read about how the Lord shut the mouth of the lions so that Daniel remained safe. The Lord saved Daniel from death, just like He had saved Daniel's three friends when they were thrown into the fire.

We see here God's love for His people in saving them. He sent His angel to protect Daniel from the mouth of the lions. Did you know that the Lord also sends angels to us as well? Even today the angels are protecting us. That doesn't mean that difficult things will never happen to us. Sometimes the Lord knows that hard things are actually good for us. We might never understand that, but we do need to trust that.

But this story about Daniel being sent into the lion's den is also a picture of something much better. It points to us being saved from eternal death. Because of our sins, we deserve to be punished eternally in hell, and that's a lot worse than being thrown to the lions. But the Lord is going to save us from eternal death, just like He saved Daniel from the lions. God declared that Daniel was innocent, that he had done the right thing by continuing to pray to Him, and so the Lord saved him. And because the Lord Jesus died and was punished because of our sins, now the Lord also says that we are innocent. He says that we are beautiful and perfect and holy. We know that so often we aren't like Daniel; so often we don't stand up for the Lord, or we sin in some other ways, and yet because of Jesus' payment for our sins, the Lord says that we are without sin and so saves us from eternal hell. So, believe in the Lord Jesus and you will live with the Lord for eternity!

REFLECTION

What is Daniel being saved from the lion's den a picture of?

DANIEL 9:5

*"We have sinned and committed iniquity,
we have done wickedly and rebelled..."*

READ DANIEL 9:3-9

God had punished the children of Judah for their disobedience by sending them to the land of Babylon for seventy years. When Daniel prays this prayer, it is at the end of these seventy years. Daniel knows from the prophecies of Jeremiah that after seventy years, if the people repented, they would be allowed to return to Jerusalem again.

Daniel knows that God always keeps His promises. And that is why he can pray this prayer of repentance with hope. God had said that they would return to Jerusalem after seventy years if they repented of their sins.

In this prayer, Daniel humbles himself before the Lord, confessing his sins and the sins of the people. Daniel prays in a very reverent way. He doesn't try and play down their sins, or just ask God to forget about their sins. Instead, he tells God how terribly they have all sinned. He says, "We have done wickedly and have rebelled. We did not listen to Your prophets or kings. We have not obeyed Your laws."

Do you know that we can use Daniel's prayer to pray our prayers? Tell the Lord that you have sinned wickedly. Tell God that you are sorry for disobeying your parents, for having anger in your heart, for being nasty to your brother, for not loving God with all your heart. Point out to God that He is faithful and righteous.

If you pray this kind of prayer, where you confess your sinfulness to the Lord, then you will be given hope and peace. Then God will show you that He is faithful and that He does forgive your sins.

It is very hard to pray this way, but ask the Lord to show you your sins and He will help you. Ask for forgiveness, and God, who is always faithful, will forgive you and draw you close to Himself. He will love you and help you to keep loving Him.

REFLECTION

Why is it so important to confess our sins to God?

Your word is a lamp to my feet and a light to my path

PSALM 119:105

ESTHER 1:2

In those days when King Ahasuerus sat on the throne of his kingdom...

READ ESTHER 1:1-12

King Ahasuerus was a mighty king. He was a rich man who ruled over one of the most powerful empires at that time. He wanted all the people in his kingdom and beyond to see how mighty and powerful he was, and so he had a feast that lasted for 180 days. That's a six-month long party. Can you imagine having a party for that long?

During this party the king asked his wife, Queen Vashti, to go in front of all the men to show off her beauty. He didn't ask this because he loved the queen and because this would be nice for her. He did this because he wanted to use the queen as another way to show how great and powerful he was.

Queen Vashti refused to listen to the king, which in turn made the king very angry so he didn't allow her to be queen any longer.

You may wonder why the Lord included the book of Esther in the Bible. Even though the book of Esther doesn't include God's name, it sure teaches us a lot about the Lord and how He cares for His people. It's a Bible book in which we see the antithesis, the fight, between the kingdom of Satan and his followers, and the kingdom of God and His children.

King Ahasuerus was part of Satan's kingdom. His pride, anger, and selfishness all show Satan at work. The Jewish people, who were still living in Persia at that time, would have found it hard to serve the Lord there. But the Lord hadn't forgotten His people living in this wicked kingdom. And when Queen Vashti refused to listen to the king, the Lord was at work in her, working to make Esther queen instead of her so that the Jewish people could be saved. The people at that time wouldn't have seen how the Lord was working, but He was. And so the Lord is working in our lives as well. We don't always understand what the Lord does, but we do know He is busy and we can trust Him.

REFLECTION

How is God working in your life?

ESTHER 2:17

The king loved Esther...and made her queen instead of Vashti.

READ ESTHER 2:12-18

It had been about three years since King Ahasuerus had divorced Vashti his queen. The king was lonely and wished for the company of his wife again. The king's rulers quickly thought of a plan to keep the king happy. They suggested that he should find himself another wife.

God used the king's loneliness to make sure His plans would happen. The Lord was caring for His covenant people. Yes, He had sent them into exile to punish them, but because of His covenantal love for His people, He cared for them even in exile. God is always working on His plan of salvation, and that can be seen in this chapter as well.

Satan was also busy. He probably thought that if he could convince the king to take Esther as queen, this Jewish girl would join in with the culture of the Persians and serve their gods. He was probably very happy when the king chose Esther as queen. He also began to form his plan to use Haman to destroy all the Jews.

But God is always ahead of the devil. Though Satan may think that he is winning, God is always protecting and caring for His covenant people. God is always at work, even when we don't see it. Esther may very well have been frightened about being chosen as queen for this heathen king, and may have wondered where God was, but we know the whole story and know that God was indeed busy. God made sure that Esther became queen because He was going to use her to save His people.

That is also why God made sure Mordecai was in the king's court and heard about the plot to kill the king. God made sure this event was recorded in the king's books because God was also going to use this later in His plan to save His people.

REFLECTION

Do you think Esther and Mordecai knew how the Lord was going to use them?

ESTHER 3:9

If it pleases the king, let a decree be written that they be destroyed.

READ ESTHER 3

What do you think is really happening in this chapter of Esther? Is it just an interesting story or more than that?

We see in this passage the antithesis, the struggle, between God and Satan, between God's people and Satan's people. When Mordecai didn't bow down to Haman, it wasn't because he was a proud man, nor was it because God had commanded them not to bow to other people.

The reason Mordecai didn't bow down to Haman, was because Haman was an Agagite, which means that he was an Amalekite. You may remember that it was the Amalekites who fought against the Israelites when they were in the wilderness. That was the time when Moses had to hold up his hands in prayer to keep the Israelites winning. God had cursed the Amalekites and declared war against them. King Saul was supposed to destroy them all completely. Haman was a descendant of these people who were cursed by God. And that's why Mordecai didn't bow down to him.

This made Haman very angry. He wanted to kill Mordecai and all his people. Behind Haman's anger, we see Satan's anger. He hates the people of God and he wants to destroy them completely. And so, he used Haman to come up with this plan to get rid of all God's people. He wanted to destroy them all because he knew that Jesus was going to be born from one of the Jews. And so, he thought that if he destroyed all the Jews, then Jesus couldn't be born. That was his aim! Satan didn't want Jesus to come to save us.

But God was at work here also. He made sure that the lot Haman cast fell on the month Adar. This was eleven months away. God gave this time so that He could work in Esther and Mordecai to go to the king to come up with a way to save His people. He was not going to let His plan of salvation stop. He was going to send Jesus to save His people!

REFLECTION

How can you see the struggle between God and Satan in this chapter?

ESTHER 4:14

Yet who knows whether you have come to the kingdom for such a time as this?

READ ESTHER 4

In the palace, Queen Esther had no idea about the decree that had been sent out to destroy all the Jews. But her cousin Mordecai had heard all about it and he tore his clothes to show his distress and sadness. When Esther heard that Mordecai was sitting at the gate in sackcloth and ashes, she sent for him, but he refused to come.

So, Esther sent a servant to Mordecai to find out what the problem was. Mordecai told the servant to tell the queen all about the plot to kill the Jews and commanded Esther to go to the king to beg to have the Jews spared.

Esther sent a message back to Mordecai telling him that she didn't dare to go to the king, because if anyone went to the king without permission, they would be killed, unless the king held out his golden sceptre. Mordecai told her that if she didn't try to save all her people, she would be killed anyway when all the other Jews were destroyed, so she should at least try to save her people. Mordecai said, "Maybe the LORD made you queen for this very reason." Mordecai believed that God was going to save His people, either through Esther or another way.

And so we see that the LORD continued to work to save His people. God was not going to allow Satan to win and destroy the Jews. Because God loved His covenant people, He moved Esther's heart so she was willing to obey Mordecai. Esther obeyed even though she had no idea if she would be allowed to speak to the king or if she would die. She had no idea if God was going to use her for this or not. She had to act in faith, trusting God.

We now know that God used Esther to save the Jews, so that Christ could be born. God worked His plan of salvation using Mordecai and Esther. God is always working, also in your life, for the salvation of His children.

REFLECTION

Can you always see how the LORD is working in your life?

ESTHER 5:14

And the thing pleased Haman; so he had the gallows made.

READ ESTHER 5

Esther had come up with a plan to invite the king and Haman to a feast that she had prepared for them. We may wonder why she didn't ask the king straight away for the Jews to be spared and just leave the outcome to the Lord. The Lord has given His people the ability to be able to think, and He wants us to act wisely in all that we do. If you are sick you would use the medicine the doctor gives you. You wouldn't just say, "I'm not going to take any medicine because I will leave it up to the Lord to decide if I get better." In the same way Esther could come up with a plan to try and save her people, instead of doing nothing and leaving it to God. And God used Esther's courage and plan. He was at work through her.

And so, when Esther went before the king and was accepted by him, she asked him and Haman to come to a feast that she had prepared. She does this twice.

Wicked Haman was very happy to have been invited with the king to Esther's feast. He walked out of the palace very proud and joyful. He felt like an important man. But then when he saw Mordecai at the gate and Mordecai didn't bow down to him, proud Haman was filled with rage and anger. Trying to control his anger, he invited his friends and wife to come to him. He told them that he was angry because Mordecai didn't bow down to him, even though he was very rich and important.

His wife suggested that Haman build gallows that could be used to hang Mordecai. Haman liked this suggestion and had the gallows built.

So again in this chapter we see the antithesis, the fight between God and His children, and Satan and his children. We see Esther acting wisely in trying to save her people, and Haman acting foolishly in trying to destroy God's people. But God was behind all these events, saving His people so that Christ could be born.

REFLECTION

Who is fighting in this chapter?

ESTHER 6:6

So Haman came in, and the king asked him, "What shall be done for the man whom the king delights to honour?"

READ ESTHER 6

Do you know what God's providence is? God's providence means that He is in control of everything that happens in life. The Bible tells us that God knows exactly how many hairs are on your head. That means that if a hair falls from your head, it is because God caused it to fall.

In Esther 6 we see God's providence very clearly. Everything in this story happened in exactly the way God wanted it to happen. The king could not sleep. It was God who made sure the king couldn't sleep, because He was going to work through the king. It was also God who made the king decide to have the book of the records read to him. God made sure the king heard the record of Mordecai saving his life four years earlier. It was also God who had made sure that Mordecai wasn't rewarded for this at that time.

As you keep reading this chapter, you continue to see God's providence. The king decided that he wanted to reward Mordecai, and then Haman walked in. Haman was just about to ask the king if he could hang Mordecai on the gallows. These things didn't just happen by accident. It was God who made all these things happen at exactly the right time.

And we continue to see God's providence in the rest of the chapter, as Haman is made to honour the very man he wanted to hang on the gallows. God continued to work to protect His people so that Christ could be born. No matter how crafty Haman was, God was still in control.

And so, you too can trust in God's providence. There is not a single thing that happens in your life that is not in God's control. You will certainly not always understand why God allows things to happen in your life, but you can trust that He is working in every single thing, and because of His love for you, He is working all things for your eternal good.

REFLECTION

What are some things in your life in which you can see God's providence at work?

ESTHER 7:10

*So they hanged Haman on
the gallows that he had prepared
for Mordecai.*

READ ESTHER 7

The day finally came for the feast in which Esther was going to tell the king that her people were going to be destroyed. The feast must have gone on for a while because we are told that on the second day of the feast, the king again asked Esther what she wanted.

Esther could have just accused the king and said something like, "You and Haman have agreed to kill me and all of my people." But if she had accused the king like that, he might have become angry at her. Instead she wisely told the king that her people had been sold and would be destroyed. She didn't blame the king at all, even though he had agreed to this decree.

When the king found out that Esther was a Jew and learned about what Haman had done, he became really angry. He was probably angry because he realised that he had also played a part in the problem. He had agreed to let Haman make that rule, so he was involved too. This wouldn't make the king look very good.

And so, when he found Haman on the same couch as Esther, begging to have his life spared, the king used this to accuse Haman of attacking the queen. He demanded that Haman be hanged on the gallows that he had made for Mordecai.

God was at work here as well. He was the one using the king and queen to destroy Haman. God showed that He is always faithful to His covenant promises. Satan was using Haman to try and destroy all of God's people. Satan didn't want Jesus to be born. But God never leaves His children alone or forgets His promises. He had promised in Genesis already that He would send a Saviour to save His people, and so God made sure that happened. He destroyed wicked Haman, the seed of the devil. And through Jesus Christ, God has destroyed all our enemies: Satan, the world, and our own sinful flesh.

REFLECTION

How can you see God working in this chapter?

ESTHER 8:8

'You yourselves write a decree concerning the Jews, as you please, in the king's name, and seal it with the king's signet ring.'

READ ESTHER 8:7-14

Haman was dead, but there was still the decree that said that all the Jews would be killed. When a decree had been written and signed by the king, it could not be ignored or changed. It appeared that nothing could be done to save the Jews.

But we see here that God hadn't finished His work. He continued to use Esther and Mordecai to save His people. Even though the decree couldn't be changed, God could work a way to save His people, and that's exactly what He did.

Mordecai went to the king and was given permission to write a new decree. The old one still existed, but this new decree allowed the Jews to gather together and defend themselves on that day when they were going to be destroyed. They were allowed to use weapons and destroy anybody who tried to kill them. They weren't allowed to just kill anybody, but they were allowed to kill those who tried to kill them.

This new decree was translated into many languages and handed out throughout the land. Everyone heard about this new decree and knew that if they tried killing the Jews on the appointed day, the Jews were allowed to defend themselves. Many people became scared and even became Jews themselves so that they wouldn't be killed on that day.

So we see again how God was working to protect the Jews. This pointed ahead to something even greater. God has saved us from something much bigger. God has saved us from eternal punishment. We deserve to be punished eternally in hell, not because of a decree from a wicked Haman, but because of a decree from holy God. But in His great love for us, God has made a way for us to escape this punishment. Instead of punishment, we have eternal life through the work of Jesus Christ. We can live forever with the Lord. We can rejoice and give thanks to God for His grace in saving us and giving us life with Him forever.

REFLECTION

How does this chapter point to our salvation?

ESTHER 9:1

Now in the twelfth month, that is, the month of Adar, on the thirteenth day, the time came for the king's command and his decree to be executed.

READ ESTHER 9:1–17

The day had arrived—thirteen Adar. It was the day for both decrees to be carried out—the decree of Haman to kill the Jews, and the decree that the Jews could defend themselves.

There were many great fights that day. The seed of Satan fought against the seed of the woman. Again we see this battle, this fight between God's people and the followers of Satan. Satan tried to destroy all the Jews so that Jesus Christ couldn't be born, but God didn't allow this to happen. Instead, the victory on this great day went to the people of God. Many enemies of the Jews were killed. We read that seventy-five thousand died.

God was the one who saved the Jews from the hands of their enemies. He was the one who put fear into the hearts of the enemies so that they would lose this fight. God gave the victory.

God also gives us victory today. We are also fighting a battle. But our battle isn't fought with swords and spears. We don't need to kill people. We are fighting against sin in our lives. Our hearts are sinful and we often do the wrong thing. Satan and the world around us try hard to make us sin. Every day we need to fight in this battle. We need to fight against our sins.

And just as the Lord was with the Jews in Esther's day and gave them victory over their enemies, God will give us victory as well. Actually, God has already given that victory in Jesus Christ. Jesus has already won the battle against sin. This doesn't mean that we no longer sin. While we are still on this earth, we need to fight against our sins every day. But we know that Christ has already overcome Satan so one day our sins will not send us to hell, but instead our forgiveness in Jesus Christ will allow us to live eternally with the Lord. Thank the Lord for giving us this victory.

REFLECTION

What battle are you fighting today?

ESTHER 9:26

*So they called these days Purim,
after the name Pur.*

READ ESTHER 9:18-31

What a great victory the Jews had been given. Their enemies had been destroyed and they had great reason to rejoice. Their salvation was so great that it needed to be celebrated, not just for one day but for two. How much joy there must have been.

The people knew that they were sinful and that they might slowly forget the work of the Lord in their lives, even though it seemed impossible to forget at the time. We can sometimes be a bit like that. It's so easy for us to forget things that have happened, even if they were very special at the time. Maybe that's why we have birthdays and other anniversaries so that we don't forget special events and blessings in our lives.

In the same way, the Jewish people always wanted to remember their salvation from the enemies at the time of Esther. And they wanted the future generations to remember it as well. So they established this feast of Purim. Purim comes from the word *Pur*, which means "lot." They wanted to remember the lot that Haman cast, by which God chose the day that the Jewish people would be saved.

Queen Esther added her part to the celebrations. She said that fasting and lamenting were to be added to the celebration. Fasting was a way to show humility, a way of acknowledging that it was not the Jews who had saved themselves, but God who had saved them.

What about us? Do we need feasts to celebrate and remember God's work in saving us? We have been saved from eternal death in hell. We have been saved from our sins. And that certainly needs celebrating. That's why every Sunday we can get together and sing praises to the Lord and listen to the preaching of His Word. That's why we have the Bible, a whole book which calls us to remember God's salvation. That's also why we can celebrate the Lord's Supper together. Our salvation is something to be remembered and celebrated.

REFLECTION

Why did the Jewish people celebrate the feast of Purim?

PHILIPPIANS 4:6

Be anxious for nothing, but in everything by prayer and supplication, with thanksgiving, let your requests be made known to God.

READ PHILIPPIANS 4:1-9

Do you ever worry? Everyone does from time to time. Maybe you're worried about your parents who are away for a few days. Maybe you have a test coming up that worries you. Maybe you're worried that you will miss the bus.

Do you know what Paul says about worrying? He says, "Stop it. Just stop it. Stop worrying about everything."

Paul had many things that he could have worried about. He came very close to death a number of times. He was put in prison, he was beaten, he was hungry. And yet he still tells us not to worry.

Paul says that instead of worrying about things, you need to pray about everything. Tell the Lord your concerns. Through prayer, God will give you His peace.

When you pray, you are telling the Lord about your concerns; you are laying your concerns before the Lord. Now, of course the Lord already knows what worries you. But the LORD wants you to tell Him about it anyway. Because when you tell the Lord, you are learning to trust in the Lord. You are handing your worry over to the Lord.

The LORD is in complete control of your life. He cares for you. You are His precious child because Christ died for you. And so you need to remember that the Lord is working everything in your life to help you serve Him better. God is with you, so things are going to be okay! This doesn't mean you will never have troubles in life. You will, but the Lord will carry you through these hard times. Pray to Him, and ask Him to carry you, to care for you and to give you peace. Ask the Lord to help you to leave your worries with Him, and to move forward, knowing that He cares for you. God is caring for your parents who are away. He will be with you during the test, even if it is hard. He will be with you even if you miss the bus. Trust Him instead of worrying.

REFLECTION

When you are worried, how does prayer help?

PROVERBS 3:7

Do not be wise in your own eyes; Fear the Lord and depart from evil.

READ PROVERBS 3:1-8

Often things are repeated so that we learn them. To learn a psalm, you sing it many times. Your parents have told you often to say, "Please" and "Thank you." Your teachers have told you the same spelling rules over and over again. By hearing things many times, we learn them and hopefully put them into practice.

In Proverbs, the Lord also repeats Himself. What He tells us is important and He wants us to learn it and always remember it. In verse 7 God says, "Do not be wise in your own understanding," and just two verses before that He says, "Lean not on your own understanding."

The Lord doesn't want us to think that we know everything and can do everything ourselves. Sometimes we would like to be able to control the world, to make things happen how we would like. But that is exactly what Adam and Eve tried to do in Paradise and that's what led to all the sin in the world.

Instead of trying to control the world and the events of our lives, we must fear the Lord and depart from evil. That is what the rest of verse 7 says. To fear the Lord doesn't mean to be scared of Him, like you might be scared that you will get caught after you have done something wrong. Those who reject the Lord and don't love Him will be afraid of the Lord in this way.

But for believers, to fear the Lord means to truly know the Lord and to trust Him, to know that He is in control of our lives. It is to believe that God is who He says He is. He is holy, righteous, loving, just, merciful, and faithful. He is the one who sent Christ to die on the cross for our sins.

To fear God means to trust Him and to pray to Him. It means to ask God to guide you, to show you your sins and to change you. It means to know that you are forgiven through Jesus Christ.

REFLECTION

What does it mean to fear God?

PROVERBS 4:23

Keep your heart with all diligence, for out of it spring the issues of life.

READ PROVERBS 4:20-27

When the Bible talks about your heart it is talking about something different than that organ that pumps blood around your body. Your heart is the centre of your life. Your heart is your inner feelings of joy and sadness. Your heart is your thinking and your mind.

Because your heart is the centre of your life, you need to keep, or guard, your heart. This means you need to protect it, to look after it. You need to protect it from sin and Satan. You need to make sure you use your whole life, your whole heart, to serve the Lord.

So how do you guard your heart? How do you make sure your heart is always focused on serving the Lord? Verse 24 says we must put away deceitful mouths and perverse lips. And verse 25 adds that we must keep our eyes looking straight ahead. So if you know there are things that are going to make your heart want to do what is wrong, keep those things far away from you. If there are programs you watch on TV or things you look at on the internet that the Lord is not pleased with, don't watch or look at those things. If going somewhere with certain friends is going to make you do the wrong thing, don't go there.

All of us have evil hearts, all of our hearts are full of sin, and the Lord knows that and that's why He tells us to flee from sin. Whatever we read or look at will affect our hearts. So make sure you always read and look at godly things. Spend more time reading the Bible.

And keep your eyes focused ahead on the Lord. Remember that you are heading towards eternal life with the Lord. Keep thinking and focusing on that. Sin wants us to go to the right or to the left, to get distracted from serving the Lord. But the Lord says we must remain focused on Him, looking straight ahead where God is on His throne.

REFLECTION

How can you guard your heart?

PROVERBS 15:15

All the days of the afflicted are evil, but he who is of a merry heart has a continual feast.

READ PROVERBS 15:12-15

If tomorrow you were to have only the things that you are thankful for today, would you have much? Are you a thankful person? Do you remember to thank the Lord for His blessings?

In this proverb the Lord teaches us to have our hearts focused on the right things. This proverb is not a command, but Solomon is telling us what he sees around him.

Solomon sees that there is so much trouble in the world. Many miserable and horrible things happen. There is a lot of suffering. How are we as children of God to see this? What does all this suffering teach us?

We need to know that this suffering is because of sin in the world. If Adam had not fallen into sin, there would be none of these bad things: no sickness, no death, no crying, no pain. But Adam did fall into sin, so now we live in this sinful world. And there is nothing that we can do about it. We cannot make things right. We cannot take away the suffering. We cannot make ourselves right with God.

But God sent His Son into this world to take away our sins and suffering. Jesus Christ came to pay for our sins and to make us have a covenant relationship with the Lord again. How wonderful is that?

Jesus is the only way that we can have a merry or happy heart. We can always have joy, even when we need to go through hard things. This does not mean that we can't be sad and cry. Of course we can. But even while we are sad, we can still have joy. We can have joy because we belong to God. Jesus is our real Saviour. God is our real Father who loves us deeply. The Holy Spirit really lives in our hearts.

And we have a very real feast to look forward to: The marriage feast of the Lamb! On the new earth we will live with God forever. Oh, what joy that will be!

REFLECTION

How can you have joy even when things are hard for you?

PROVERBS 27:5

Open rebuke is better than love carefully concealed.

READ PROVERBS 27:1-6

Do you like it when a friend tells you that you are doing the wrong thing? It hurts, doesn't it? No one likes it when someone tells them that they shouldn't have said or done something. Yet this verse tells us that a rebuke—a telling off—is good. Actually, as Christians it is our duty to rebuke our friends when we see them doing the wrong thing.

We read of rebuking in the Bible. The prophet Nathan had to rebuke David after he sinned by killing Uriah. We also read of Jesus rebuking His beloved disciples when they argued about who was the greatest. The LORD Himself says to the church in Laodicea, "As many as I love, I rebuke" (Rev. 3:19). Because we are all sinful, we all need to be rebuked sometimes.

So how do you react when a friend rebukes you? If your friend tells you that you shouldn't have told that dirty joke or that you shouldn't go to that place, how do you respond? Often we want to turn our back on that person and walk away. We don't like being told off. We prefer to be friends with people who ignore it when we do the wrong thing. But God tells us that these rebukes of a faithful friend are exactly what we need. Yes, they will hurt. Verse 6 even calls them wounds; that's how much they will hurt. But it is important that we listen to the rebukes and that we then change our ways. The LORD is using those friends to help us serve Him better.

But what about when you need to rebuke others? When you need to tell someone that they are acting in an ungodly way, you must do so in love. You can only rebuke someone if you love them and actually want to help them. If you are angry at them or want to get them in trouble, then you are not rebuking in love. So before you rebuke someone, think about why and how you are going to speak to them, and think about what you are going to say, and make sure you rebuke them in love.

REFLECTION

How can you be a good friend to others?

*Let everything that has breath praise the L*ORD

PSALM 150:6A

EZEKIEL 33:7

"So you, son of man: I have made you a watchman for the house of Israel."

READ EZEKIEL 33:1-9

In the Old Testament, watchmen had a very important task to do. They would sit in a high tower on the wall of the city and keep watch. If they saw enemies anywhere on the horizon, they would immediately need to inform the people in the city so that they could be ready to defend themselves. If the watchmen fell asleep or were busy talking to someone else and didn't see the enemies coming, the city could be attacked and destroyed.

Ezekiel was appointed by God to be a watchman as well. But he didn't have to watch for physical enemies like the Assyrians or Amorites. Rather, he had to watch out for the spiritual enemies. He had to make sure that the people were serving God correctly, and he had to discipline them, reminding them to keep their hearts focused on the Lord.

Today the Lord gives the church watchmen as well. These watchmen are the ministers and elders in our church. They are God's gift to keep the people of the church safe from the enemies.

Our enemies today are Satan, our own sinful flesh and the world around us. Every day these three enemies are trying to attack us. They are trying to make us sin against God. They are trying to make us love the things of the world instead of God. They are tempting us to be lazy, to not bother to read the Bible, to be greedy, to be nasty and say unkind things, to become addicted to things, including computer games. These enemies are working hard to take our attention away from God.

And so the office bearers, the elders, have to watch for these enemies and warn us when they see us being tempted, or when we take our focus off God and focus instead on ourselves or things in the world. So, when the elders of the church come and visit you in your homes, listen to what they have to say. They are important watchmen given to you by the Lord.

REFLECTION

How are the elders like watchmen?

HEBREWS 10:25

Not forsaking the assembling of ourselves together, as is the manner of some.

READ HEBREWS 10:19-25

Do you love your church—not only going to church, but also the people in your church? Do you love being a part of the church community?

Some of the Hebrews that Paul wrote to, were a bit discouraged and sad. And so Paul reminds them to love each other and help each other in serving the Lord. It is important to come together to worship the Lord so that we can help and encourage each other.

You don't go to church just for yourself. Church isn't just about you and your relationship with the Lord. Oh yes, that is very important, and you must go to church to grow in your love for the Lord and to praise God. But being a part of the church is also important so that we can learn together, pray together and help each other. After church you can talk with your friends about the sermon. But you can also show love and concern in other ways. Ask your friends how they are doing, instead of always talking about yourself. If they are sad, speak to them about it. Encourage them that God is caring for them. If they are happy, be thankful with them for the blessings that the Lord gives to them. And if someone reminds you that something you are about to do is wrong, listen, and remember that the Lord is using others to help you serve Him.

The Lord knows that if we didn't have a church to belong to and tried to serve the Lord just by ourselves or in our own families, we could soon lose joy in Christ, and we might forget about praying and reading the Bible. That's why God wants us to be part of a church, to belong to the communion of saints, so that we can help each other to serve the Lord.

We know that Christ will return soon, and so we must use the days that the Lord gives us to serve Him. It is such a wonderful blessing that we can gather together in church twice a Sunday, and love and help our brothers and sisters in Christ.

REFLECTION

Why is it so important to belong to the church?

HEBREWS 11:1

Now faith is the substance of things hoped for, the evidence of things not seen.

READ HEBREWS 11:1–11

As you read through this list of people who lived by faith, what do you think? Does it make you think that they must have been holy people who hardly ever sinned? The Lord did not write this list of people to make us feel like we could never have faith like these holy people. Not at all. The people listed here were just as sinful as you and me. The Bible even lists some of their sins.

One of the things the Lord teaches us with this list is what it looks like to live by faith. You can say that you love the Lord, but loving the Lord must also show in your life, in how you live. As you live your life, you must not be focused on the things around you, but you must be focused on serving God and on eternal life with the Lord. We haven't seen that eternal life yet, but we know God has promised it to us. So, living by faith means believing that we have a great future with the Lord even though we haven't seen it.

Look at some of these people and how they lived, serving the Lord even though they hadn't seen the things that were to come. Noah spent years building the ark in obedience to the Lord even though he couldn't see the coming flood.

Abram left a great country where he lived well to go to Canaan in obedience to the Lord even though he never saw the land of Canaan belonging to the Israelites. He left his house and family and lived in tents away from his family, in obedience to the Lord.

And so, we must also live by faith. Of course, we need to be busy working in this life, but as we do so we must always think about the Lord and how we can serve Him, and we must think about the eternal life that He promises us. Always keep your eyes focused on Christ and His love for you.

REFLECTION

What can you learn from this list of people who lived by faith?

ISAIAH 44:3

I will pour My Spirit on your descendants, And My blessing on your offspring.

READ ISAIAH 44:1-5

Do you ever wonder if Jesus died for *you*; if *you* are actually forgiven? This is something that many people struggle with. Even God's people in Jesus' day didn't believe. It wasn't until the Holy Spirit was poured out at Pentecost that they believed. That was fifty days after Christ rose from the dead. They had all those days to think about Christ Jesus' death, but they didn't believe that He had died to save them until after they received the Holy Spirit.

In the Old Testament, the prophet Isaiah prophesied about the coming of the Holy Spirit: "I will pour My Spirit on your descendants." The Lord knew that the Israelites would keep wanting to be like the nations around them. And so the Lord promised them that He would send His Spirit to help them. With the Holy Spirit they would be able to fight against sin.

You have the Holy Spirit as well. The Holy Spirit lives in your heart too. You have been baptised, and at your baptism the Holy Spirit promised to sanctify you. This means that He promised to help you fight against all those sins in your life and to live a life that is holy and pleasing to the Lord.

People should see by the way you speak and by the way you act that you are different from the people around you who do not believe in Jesus. And that difference is because you have the Holy Spirit in you. With the Holy Spirit working in you, you are able to serve the Lord. Of course you will still fall into sin. But the Spirit's work in you causes you to feel sorry for your sins and makes you want to fight against them. You ask the Lord for forgiveness, and you continue to serve the Lord.

So you don't need to wonder whether you are actually forgiven. Of course you are! God promised that at your baptism, and the Holy Spirit helps you to live close to the Lord. Thank the Lord for this promise, and continue to live as God's child.

REFLECTION

What should you do if you doubt that you are forgiven?

JOHN 2:11

This beginning of signs Jesus did in Cana of Galilee, and manifested His glory, and His disciples believed in Him.

READ JOHN 2:1-11

Signs always tell us something. They may tell us what direction we need to go, or the name of a shop. When Jesus performed signs, they always pointed to something as well. John told us that he recorded the signs that Jesus did so that we may believe.

What can we learn about Jesus from His first miracle of changing water into wine? Firstly, Jesus performed this miracle in Cana in Galilee. John tells us this twice so it must be important. Galilee was to the north and was influenced by the nations around it. The people there weren't serving the Lord; they were living in darkness. And this is exactly where Jesus began His work. It is there, where the people were most in need of the Gospel, that Christ did His first miracle.

This is great news for us, as we also have great need for the Gospel. We are so sinful, so unworthy to be called God's children. It's to people like us, people who need the Gospel, who sin daily, that Christ comes.

At this wedding feast in Cana, Christ changed water into wine. Wine in the Old Testament showed God's presence and blessings. When the prophets talked about the wine being returned to the people of Israel it meant that God was returning to the people with His blessings. He was restoring the people to Him. When they repented of their sins, God returned His love and care to them.

In a similar way, when Christ changed the water into wine, He was showing the people living in darkness that He had come to restore them. He had come to bring salvation. Joy could be restored because salvation had come in Christ.

The water in the pots was meant to be used for washing, but that washing could only remove dirt from the body. Christ changed it into wine to show that He was going to do something much greater: He was going to remove our sins, to bring salvation. And that's exactly what Christ has done! Believe in Him.

REFLECTION

What can you learn from Jesus' first miracle?

JOHN 2:16

And He said to those who sold doves, "Take these things away! Do not make My Father's house a house of merchandise."

READ JOHN 2:13–22 (PART 1)

It was nearly the time of the Passover in Jerusalem. There would have been a lot of people travelling and a lot of excitement and activities. It is during this time that Jesus goes to the temple. When Jesus sees all the buying and selling that is happening, He takes a whip and drives out all the people who were buying and selling in the outer court. And while He is doing this, He says, "Do not make my Father's house a house of merchandise."

Notice how Jesus calls the temple His Father's house. This is where His Father lived among His people. God dwelt in the temple. We know this from the Old Testament. The glory of the Lord was in the temple. And God was only able to dwell in the temple because of the sacrifices that were made every day. God is too holy to live among sinful people. And so, God had told the Israelites to offer sacrifices. These sacrifices pointed to the taking away of the sins of the people so that they could go to the temple where God was.

In the outer court of the temple, the people should have been repenting from their sins and offering sacrifices so that they could enjoy the glory of the Lord—a relationship with the Lord. That's what the temple and the sacrifices pointed to. And that is what should have been happening at this time before Passover.

But the Lord Jesus didn't see people who were sad because of their sins and who were seeking to be reconciled to God; He saw people trying to make money and do business. And so Jesus drove away all these things that were stopping the people from seeing what the temple was really for.

Are there things in your life that are stopping you from serving the Lord correctly? These need to be driven out of your life so that you can have a beautiful relationship with the Lord. And that is what Christ Himself came to do—to cleanse us from our sins.

REFLECTION

What would Christ Jesus whip out of your heart and home?

JOHN 2:19

Jesus answered and said to them, "Take these things away! Do not make My Father's house a house of merchandise!"

READ JOHN 2:13-22 (PART 2)

The words that Jesus Christ spoke to the people after He cleansed the temple made them very confused. He said that He was going to build the temple again in three days. The people laughed at Him because they knew that it had taken forty-six years to build it. How could the Lord Jesus build it in three days?

But the Lord Jesus was talking about Himself and not the actual temple. We've seen how God dwelt among His people in the temple. He could do this because of the sacrifices that were offered. These sacrifices all pointed to Jesus Christ Himself. And now He had come to fulfil all these sacrifices.

The temple wasn't about buying and selling, but it was all about repentance from sins, sacrifices, and the people being restored to God. And that is exactly what the Lord Jesus does for us. Every day He drives out our sins and forgives us. Every day He replaces our sins with His perfect obedience. Just like He cleared out the temple so that the sacrifices could be brought again, so He clears out our hearts with His sacrifice on the cross.

That is why the curtain in the temple was torn in two when Christ died on the cross. It showed that Christ's death was the payment for our sins that was needed for us to be forgiven. Christ's sacrifice was the one that bore all of God's wrath. He was punished in our place. Now we can have a relationship with the Lord again.

In the Old Testament they needed to offer sacrifices before they could go into the temple where God dwelt, but now we are the temples of the Holy Spirit. And because of Christ's sacrifice, God is dwelling in us. He actually lives in our hearts. God talks to us in the Bible and we can pray to Him. He loves us and cares for us always. And so we can live our lives in such a way that the glory of God shines in us.

REFLECTION

What does it mean that you are the temple of the Holy Spirit?

JOHN 4:50

Jesus said to him, "Go your way; your son lives." So the man believed the word that Jesus spoke to him, and he went his way.

READ JOHN 4:46-53

Why do you believe in Jesus? Why do you live a Christian life? What do you want most from God? These might seem like funny questions, but if you think about your prayers, you can probably work out what you want the most from God. What do you ask God for the most? Do you want Jesus to fix all your problems—do you want a *fix-it* Jesus, or do you want a Jesus that gives you salvation—a salvation Jesus.

The Jews in Jesus' days just wanted a *fix-it* Jesus. They welcomed Jesus because of all the signs and miracles that He did. They wanted Him to heal them and perform miracles. Jesus says when He responds to the nobleman, "You (by which He means all the Jews) only believe in my signs and wonders. You don't believe in me, but just want me to perform miracles for you."

But then we read about the nobleman who believes the words that Jesus speaks to him. The Spirit works faith in this man, and he believes without even seeing. Along his way home, the nobleman is told that his son had been healed at the exact time that Jesus had said that his son lives. We are told again that the nobleman believes. He doesn't just believe that Jesus can heal, but he believes that Jesus is the Saviour of the world. He believes what the sign points to. Jesus performed these miracles to show that He has come to be our Saviour. We were dead in sin and He makes us alive in Him.

And that's the Saviour that we need. We don't need a *fix-it* Jesus, but a *Saviour* Jesus. We need Him to forgive our sins and restore us to our God. Of course, we can still pray to God to ask Him to help us in our difficulties. God wants us to do that. But even in these difficulties, and no matter how God answers our prayers, we know that we are safe with our *Saviour* Jesus.

REFLECTION

What do you want most from God?

JOHN 5:46-47

"For if you believed Moses, you would believe Me; for he wrote about Me. But if you do not believe his writings, how will you believe My words?"

READ JOHN 5:1-14, 46-47

Jesus had just performed a great miracle, but the Jews who were watching weren't even that impressed with it. Can you imagine knowing a man who had been unable to walk for 38 years and then seeing him suddenly being able to use his legs? That would be amazing.

But instead of being amazed at what Jesus had done and about who Jesus really was, the Jews tried to persecute and kill Jesus because He had done it on the Sabbath day. They were also upset that He called God His Father. Jesus answered them by telling them that His miracles alone were proof that He is the Son of God, and He told them that they were refusing to believe that.

Jesus said, "If you believed Moses, you would believe me." This is interesting because the Jews knew the words of Moses and the whole Old Testament very well. And they even thought that they believed Moses. But Jesus pointed out to them that they didn't believe Moses. The whole Old Testament pointed to Jesus. Just think about the last plague when Moses went to Pharaoh. The reason that the oldest child of each of the Israelite families was saved, was because they put blood on their door posts. This blood pointed to the blood of Jesus Christ. Or even think about the lists of names of the people returning from exile. These lists show that God gives His grace to individual people who belong to Him, because God saved them through the blood of Jesus who was still to come.

The whole Old Testament pointed to Jesus, but the Jews didn't want to believe that. They didn't have a love for the Lord. If they loved the Lord, they would have believed Jesus. They would have been amazed that Jesus healed the lame man, and they would have seen that He was the Son of God.

REFLECTION

Do you believe the words of Moses and do you believe Jesus? Are you amazed at the miracles of Jesus, especially the miracle of saving us from our sins? Always read and study the Bible and ask the Spirit to help you see Jesus on every page and to believe!

JOHN 9:3

Jesus answered, "Neither this man nor his parents sinned, but that the works of God should be revealed in him."

READ JOHN 9:1-12

When something terrible happens in your life, you may wonder why. You may have been told that your suffering will be for your good because God has promised that. This is very true and is a great comfort to us when we are suffering.

But in this text, God teaches us that suffering has an even greater purpose. Suffering isn't just about us, but it is about God and bringing glory to Him. Jesus says that about the blind man. He was born blind so that the works of God should be revealed in him.

This can seem a bit unfair, can't it? Is it really fair that this man was blind for many years just so God could get glory? You suffer, so that God can receive the glory—is that fair?

When we ask this question, we must remember two things. Because of our sin and disobedience to God, we all deserve to suffer greatly. We deserve to suffer in hell, so we really can't complain if the Lord makes us suffer in this life for a while. The other thing that we need to remember is that we have been born to give glory to God. That's what God created us to do.

You may wonder how your suffering gives God glory. We might not always know how, but there are often many ways in which this happens. When the doctors and nurses see families praying together around the bed of their sick family member, they can marvel at this and this gives God glory. When you praise God for helping you through something very tough, that gives glory to God.

So, when you suffer, don't focus on yourself and how this will be good for you. Oh yes, God has promised that it will be good for you, and that can be your comfort. You might not know how, but you can trust God. It will be good for you. But instead focus on how you can use this suffering to give God glory! How is God going to use this suffering to His glory?

REFLECTION

Can you think of something that you have suffered and how it could have given glory to God?

JOHN 15:16

"You did not choose Me, but I chose you and appointed you that you should go and bear fruit."

READ JOHN 15:9-17

Imagine sitting in a room with a crowd of people. You are the only one in the room who belongs to the Lord. Why did the Lord choose you to belong to Him? Was it because the Lord knew that you were going to serve Him better than all the others? Not at all. You are no better than anyone else in the room. You did not decide to serve the Lord by yourself. No, the only reason that you belong to the Lord is because He chose you first. The Lord could have chosen anyone in that room, but He decided that He would choose you.

Jesus tells us that we belong to Him because we have been chosen by the Lord. Just like a branch is part of a vine, so we belong to Christ. We are part of Christ. The Lord wants to abide in you. And He has done this because Christ died on the cross.

But why did God choose you? Jesus tells us that God chose us so that we can go and bear fruit. Just like a branch of a vine will bear fruit, so we must bear fruit. He wants us to live a life that shows that Christ lives in us. People around you should be able to see that you belong to Christ. The fruits that we must show are not apples and oranges, but love, peace, kindness, gentleness. We must produce the fruit of the Spirit. Those who belong to Christ must show obedience to Him.

And Christ also promises us that those who are chosen by God will get whatever they ask Him for. This does not mean that if you ask for a new book you will get it. "Whatever" means whatever we need to serve the Lord. We should be asking for the things that God has promised. In our prayers, we should ask God for what we need to obey the Lord and show the fruit of the Spirit. If we pray for these things, the Lord promises us that He will give them to us.

REFLECTION

Why has God chosen you to belong to Him?

JOHN 19:26

When Jesus therefore saw His mother, and the disciple whom He loved standing by, He said to His mother, "Woman, behold your son!"

READ JOHN 19:17-30

Do you ever ignore your sins? Maybe you think that because your brothers and sisters always wait a while before listening when Mum asks them to do the dishes, you can wait a while as well. Or maybe you don't mind that you *thought* nasty things about your brother, because you didn't actually *say* anything mean.

It's so easy to ignore or downplay our sins. But did you know that God never ignores any of our sins? Every single sin that we do makes us unworthy of God's love. Every single sin that we do needs to be punished!

And that's exactly why Jesus went to the cross. He died on the cross as a payment for our sins. He was punished by the Father instead of us! That lie you told was paid for on the cross. That wrong thought you had was paid for on the cross. *Your* sins sent Jesus to the cross. He died for *you*! You need to take your sins seriously, realising that they cost Jesus His life.

We see in these verses that even while Jesus was dying on the cross, He showed His love and forgiveness for His people. He showed that He will forgive sins. You may remember that at the time that Jesus was captured, all His disciples ran away. This included John, the disciple whom Jesus loved. He escaped with all the other disciples. And here, on the cross, Jesus doesn't tell him off for running away, but in love and grace, He forgives John and asks him to care for His (Jesus') mother. John may continue to be a disciple of the Lord Jesus. He is forgiven!

Christ shows that same grace and love to you. No sin is too big or too small for God to forgive. Christ Jesus paid for them all. When you tell God that you are sorry for your sins, and when you ask for forgiveness, then you will be forgiven! So don't ignore your sins, but turn to God, asking for forgiveness.

REFLECTION

Did Christ die for *all* of your sins?

JOHN 20:29

"Blessed are those who have not seen and yet have believed."

READ JOHN 20:24-29

Jesus had risen from the dead, and the twelve apostles found it hard to believe. Even though Jesus had told them that He was going to rise, they didn't believe it. When Jesus appeared to them on the Sunday morning, they had to believe. But Thomas was not with the other disciples at that time, so he didn't see Jesus. When the other disciples told Thomas that Jesus had risen and that they had seen Him, Thomas refused to believe. Thomas didn't just doubt it, but he refused to believe it. He said, "It can't be true. I won't believe it unless I actually see Him with my own eyes and feel the holes in His hands. No, I do not believe you."

Thomas' unbelief is a picture of what we are all like in and of ourselves. If it wasn't for God's work in us, we also would refuse to believe in Jesus and that He died and rose again. That's what our sinful hearts are like.

But Jesus appeared to Thomas a week later. The following Sunday morning when all the disciples were together again, including Thomas, Jesus entered the room. He spoke directly to Thomas telling him to feel the holes in His hand and to believe.

When Thomas saw Jesus and heard His words, He did indeed believe. He then realised that Christ had risen and that, by doing so, He had forgiven Thomas' sins. Jesus had overcome death. Thomas confessed, "My Lord and My God." He understood that Jesus was actually the Lord. He could put all his hope in Him.

There will be many people who will believe through the working of the Holy Spirit without seeing. Jesus said, "Blessed are those who have not seen and yet have believed." Who are these people? It's us that Jesus is talking about. You have not seen Jesus and yet you believe. You are blessed! Jesus said that Himself. To be blessed means that God loves you and looks down on you with special care and love, knowing everything about you. You are blessed to believe in Jesus.

REFLECTION

Why did Jesus call you blessed?

My help comes from the Lord

PSALM 121:2A

MALACHI 1:7

"You offer defiled food on My altar."

READ MALACHI 1:6-14

The priests in the days of Malachi appeared to be doing all the right things. They were making all the sacrifices they needed to make and doing their other tasks. And yet the Lord told them that they have defiled the altar. In other words, God was telling them that He was not pleased with their sacrifices.

But the priests asked, "What have we done wrong? How have we defiled You?" The problem was that the priests had been offering sacrifices that weren't perfect; rather, they were sick or lame. Why was it so important for them to offer only perfectly healthy animals? The sacrifices pointed forward to the fulfilment of the wonderful promise from God, that one day He would send His Son to die on the cross to forgive their sins. Of course you know that Jesus had to be perfect. It is only because He was perfect, without any sin, that He could pay for all of our sins. So if the priests were offering sick animals they were showing that they didn't understand what a great promise God was giving them. They didn't think they needed a perfect Saviour.

What about you? The Lord wants you to give your whole life as a sacrifice to Him. This means you need to serve the Lord in everything you do. And the Lord wants you to be perfect in your service as well. He wants wholehearted love from you. But can you do that? No, you can't. None of us can, and yet that is still what God requires from us.

But the beautiful Gospel message is that God made a way in which we can offer our life perfectly to Him. Jesus, the perfect sacrifice, was offered for us. And with His perfect sacrifice He covers all of our imperfect service to God.

So, yes, we must wholeheartedly serve the Lord our whole life, just like the priest had to offer perfect sacrifices. But we can also thank God for His love in sending Christ to cover our sins with His perfect obedience. What a loving God we have!

REFLECTION

Why did the animals that were offered have to be perfect?

MALACHI 3:16

So a book of remembrance was written before Him for those who fear the Lord and who meditate on His name.

READ MALACHI 3:16-18

Even though most of the people in Malachi's days weren't serving the Lord properly, God made sure that there were still some who faithfully served Him. The Lord always keeps a remnant (a small group) of true believers. God promised those faithful believers that their names are written in the book of remembrance. They are the Lord's own people, as precious as jewels to Him. And the Lord tells you the same. As God's beloved child, your name is also in the book of remembrance. You are also precious to the Lord, and the Lord will keep you close to Him.

Verse 16 tells us that these faithful believers really feared the Lord. This means they loved the Lord, believed in Him, and worshipped Him. They praised the Lord for His greatness and awe. They marvelled at His work in their lives and in creation around them.

Malachi says that they meditated on the Name of God. To meditate means that they spent time thinking about God and His attributes. This means that they thought about the great things they knew about God. They would have thought about things like His power, His love, His care and His forgiveness. Then they would have praised God for it.

These believers also spoke together about the Lord and His marvellous acts. Do you spend time together with your friends talking about the Lord? Instead of talking about sport or a movie or your new clothes, it would be a good idea to talk about the things the Lord is doing in your life.

And what about meditating on the work of the Lord? Do you do that? Maybe you can try that as you walk to school or relax in the evenings. Think about the fact that God is eternal, that He has no beginning and will never end. Think about God's love in sending His beloved Son to die on the cross. Think about God's wonderful power in creating the whole world. Meditate on God's wonderful acts.

REFLECTION

What does it mean that your name is in the book of remembrance?

MALACHI 4:2

But to you who fear My name, the Sun of Righteousness shall arise with healing in His wings.

READ MALACHI 4:1-3

Malachi teaches us that the day of the Lord is coming. It is a day when the wicked will be completely destroyed, but the children of the Lord will receive full salvation.

Firstly, Malachi speaks about the wicked. They will be completely destroyed on that day. They will be burnt up, just like stubble is burnt. Nothing will be left of them.

Malachi says that there won't even be a root or a branch left. You know that the root of a plant is where it gets its life from. If you want to get rid of a plant while you are weeding the garden, you will need to take out its roots, otherwise it may grow back. But if you remove the roots there is no chance of it growing back. It is this picture that is used to show what will happen to those who don't repent. They will be completely destroyed. There will be no chance for them to come back.

Does this message about God destroying the wicked make you scared? If you love your sins and want to keep on sinning, and don't love the Lord, then you should be scared. But if you love the Lord and are sorry for your sins and want to live in thankfulness to the Lord, then you don't need to be scared at all.

Then the Day of the Lord is a day of great rejoicing. Just like a calf that has been cramped in a small stall for many days will leap with joy when it is let out of the stall, so we will rejoice on the Day of the Lord. On that day, when the wicked are destroyed, we will receive full salvation. On that day all our sin will be totally destroyed and God Himself will give us new life with Him. We will be free of our sins and will be able to serve and praise God continually.

REFLECTION

Why don't you need to be scared of the Day of the Lord?

MARK 5:15

Then they came to Jesus, and saw the one who had been demon-possessed and had the legion, sitting and clothed and in his right mind.

READ MARK 5:1-20

In this story we see a rather horrible scene. Jesus crosses over to the other side of the sea to a graveyard where a fierce, naked, uncontrollable man lives. Why does Jesus go to this man?

You will remember that after the fall into sin in Paradise, God said that there would always be an antithesis between God and Satan. This means that there is a struggle, a fight going on between God's children and Satan's demons. Satan does everything he can to get people to follow him. But we know that God, through Jesus, has overcome Satan.

This Bible passage shows us something of that fight, that antithesis, between God and Satan. This uncontrollable man who stands before Jesus is demon-possessed. He lives among the tombs, the place of the dead. He has the powers of Satan at work in him.

When he sees Jesus, he immediately cries out to Him. Satan wants to attack Christ, but Jesus shows His power over the devil. This demon-possessed man stops in his tracks and falls down on his knees in front of Jesus. And then Christ removes the demons from this man. Christ totally changes this man from someone who is naked and uncontrollable, into someone who is well-dressed and who sits peacefully at Jesus' feet, listening carefully to His teachings. And so we see the power of Christ over Satan. Christ has total power over the devil.

We see this same fight in our own lives as well. Sometimes it is just so hard to do the right thing. Sometimes sinning really looks like the most fun thing to do. This is all part of that struggle. But know that Christ has won the victory over Satan. He is all-powerful and totally able to destroy the attacks of Satan in your life. Turn to Christ and ask Him to help you fight against Satan in your life.

REFLECTION

What does it mean that there is an antithesis between God and Satan?

MARK 12:44

"For they all put in out of their abundance, but she out of her poverty put in all that she had."

READ MARK 12:41-44

As Jesus was sitting in the temple, He saw and heard people putting their money in the treasury. Some were putting in large amounts of money. But Jesus saw something that others didn't see. He saw a poor widow putting in two little coins. It wasn't very much money at all, but Jesus said that it was more than what everyone else put in. Not that it was actually more than others put in, but it was everything that this widow had. The little bit of money she had, she gave. The rich people had put in lots of money, but they still had a lot more; however, this widow had no money left after giving those two coins. She gave from her heart. She gave in faith, trusting in the Lord to look after her. She gave the kind of sacrifice that pleases God.

In a way, she pointed to Jesus Christ Himself. Jesus gave up everything. He made the biggest sacrifice ever by giving up His life for us. Even though Christ had the glory of heaven, He gave that all up to come down to earth. And then at the end of His life on earth, He made the ultimate sacrifice by dying on the cross! He did that for us so that we can have salvation. He was the great High Priest.

We know from the Bible that we too are to be priests. We share in Christ's anointing as priests. And so, God calls us to respond to His love and grace shown in Jesus' sacrifice by giving our whole life to Him. Jesus could see into the heart of that widow and knew that she gave from the heart. Her gift was precious and beautiful to God because she gave it out of love for the Lord. In the same way we have to serve the Lord with our hearts. We have to use our time, our money and our talents to worship God. God wants our hearts to be hearts that truly love and worship Him.

REFLECTION

Why did Jesus say that the widow gave more than everyone else?

NUMBERS 6:24-25

"The Lord bless you and keep you; The Lord make His face shine upon you."

READ NUMBERS 6:22-27

Just imagine for a moment that God were here with you. Of course, God is always with us, but imagine that He were standing in front of you. Imagine the glorified Lord Jesus, still with His human face and human body, were standing in front of you. How would He be looking at you? What expression would the Lord have on His face? Remember that He knows all your thoughts, words, and actions. What look would be on His face?

Let me tell you that God would have His face turned towards you and He would be looking at you with love and tenderness. There would be no anger in His eyes or disappointment on His face. He would not be scowling at you. Rather He would be smiling at you with a look of total love and grace.

This is because God sees you through Jesus Christ. When He looks at you, He sees you as being without any sin. He sees you as His child, who has kept all His commandments perfectly. And so God would be looking at you with tenderness, love, and grace.

We are reminded of this every Sunday when we leave church and hear these words of blessing from the Lord: "The Lord bless you and keep you. The Lord make His face shine upon you and be gracious to you. The Lord lift up His countenance upon you and give you peace."

Just before you leave the church building you receive the blessing of the Lord. This means that the Lord looks on you with favour and love. The Lord is going to help you to serve Him. He is going to keep you close to Himself. He is going to help you fight against sin and evil.

And God will never turn His face away from His children. Even if you are going through hard things, God will continue to care for you and love you and keep you close to Himself. He will always look at you through Jesus Christ and so make His face shine upon you!

REFLECTION

How does the Lord look at you?

NUMBERS 9:2

"Let the children of Israel keep the Passover at its appointed time."

READ NUMBERS 9:1-14

In Numbers 9, Moses tells the people of Israel to celebrate the Passover. It had been a year since the children had been led out of Egypt. I'm sure you remember the story of the Israelites painting blood on their doorposts so that the angel of the LORD would pass over their house when he killed the firstborn son from each family. At that time, the LORD had given them instructions to have a Passover meal before they left. They had to do it in exactly the way the LORD wanted. They had to kill a specific lamb, make bread that wouldn't rise, and use the correct herbs.

Now Moses is telling the people that they need to celebrate it again in exactly the way the LORD told them. However, there were some people who had touched a dead body (maybe a relative had died), so they couldn't celebrate the Passover. God had commanded that unclean people—people who had touched a dead body—couldn't celebrate the Passover. This was a problem. They wanted to obey God and celebrate the Passover, but they couldn't because another command of God said that unclean people couldn't celebrate it.

So what did they do? Well, they didn't just say, "Who cares? We're unclean, so let's just forget about celebrating the Passover." No, they really wanted to obey the LORD. They wanted to do His will, so they asked God what to do. God didn't answer them by saying, "Just celebrate Passover anyway. It doesn't matter how you do it." No, God wanted them to obey all His commands. And so God, in His love, gave them a special instruction to celebrate the Passover a month later.

Do you really want to serve the LORD in the way that He requires? Is it important to you to obey the LORD? Then listen carefully when your parents teach you, and pay attention when you are being taught about the Bible. Serve God in the way He teaches you.

REFLECTION

Think of some ways in which you can serve the LORD how He wants.

NUMBERS 9:16

So it was always, the cloud covered it by day, and the appearance of fire by night.

READ NUMBERS 9:15–23

Have you ever had a time when you were frightened because of something new that you had to do? Maybe it was your first day at school. Maybe it was meeting some people for the first time. At times like this it is nice to have someone you know with you, isn't it?

The Israelites may very well have been frightened too when they went into the wilderness. They wouldn't have known where they would get their food from or what enemies might attack them. But they didn't have to go alone. The Lord went with them in the cloud. It was as if God was saying through the cloud, "I am going with you. You will never be alone."

The Lord used this cloud to teach the Israelites to trust Him. If they couldn't sleep at night because they were worried about what enemies might attack them the next day, then they would see the cloud above the tabernacle, reminding them that God was with them. He was looking after them.

The cloud also taught the Israelites to depend on the Lord. Many times they would not have known where their water was going to come from. There certainly isn't much water in the desert, but they had to trust that God would provide for them. He would lead them to the places where there was water.

The cloud also taught the Israelites to obey the Lord. Sometimes God would keep the cloud in the same place for a few days, and at other times for only one day. They had to learn that when God stopped, they had to stop, and when God moved, they had to move.

God is with us today as well. No, we don't have the cloud of the Lord leading us every day, but we do have God's Word and His Spirit with us every day. Through His Word and Spirit, God is with us always. We can trust Him, knowing that He is leading us. He never leaves us.

REFLECTION

How is the Lord leading you today?

NUMBERS 11:1

Now when the people complained, it displeased the Lord, for the Lord heard it.

READ NUMBERS 11:1-15, 31-35

Do you ever grumble and complain? I think we all do from time to time. But do you know that God hates grumbling?

When you are complaining, you are thinking about yourself and what you want. You are making yourself the most important person. The children of Israel did this. They wanted better food. The Lord was supplying them with manna every day, but they wanted meat. They even said that the food was better in Egypt. Did they forget about the baby boys that were killed in the river, or about their slavery?

When the people complained to Moses, Moses went and complained to the Lord. Through his complaining he too showed that he was only thinking about himself and what he wanted. He said things like this: "Did *I* make these people? Why are the people angry at *me*? How am *I* supposed to get them meat? *I* can't bear these people on my own." He forgot that the Lord was with him and that the Lord would supply him with everything that he needed.

That's what we are doing when we complain as well. We're focused on ourselves and our wants: *I don't want the food the* Lord *gives me. I don't want to play with the person the* Lord *put in my class. I am annoyed at the sister God gave me.* Yes, when we're grumbling, we're actually making an idol of ourselves.

God did give the complaining Israelites meat, but this meat was a punishment for them at the same time. Verse 33 tells us that they died while the meat was still in their mouths. This shows us how deeply God hates grumbling! When we're grumbling we're not trusting in God enough, we're not thankful enough for what He gives us.

Moses, as the mediator of the people, failed because he grumbled as well. But know that Christ our Mediator never grumbled. Rather He went to the cross for our sins. So when you realise you are complaining, go to Him, confess your sins and ask God to help you to be thankful.

REFLECTION

Why is God so angry at our grumbling?

NUMBERS 12:5

Then the Lord came down in the pillar of cloud and stood in the door of the tabernacle, and called Aaron and Miriam.

READ NUMBERS 12

Do you ever envy other people? Envy means wanting to do what others do or wanting to have what others have. If you see that someone is good at something, then you want to be able to do that too. You see the attention they get, and you want that for yourself. It's being jealous of what other people have or what others can do.

In this passage, God teaches us that He hates envy. In front of all the people, God tells Miriam and Aaron that they are not to be envious or jealous of Moses, but instead they must listen to Moses as he is God's servant and God has chosen to speak through him.

Why does God hate envy so much? Well, when you are jealous of the things others have or can do, then that means that you are not happy with the gifts that God has given you. You are not acknowledging that God made everyone different and gave everyone different talents. So, instead of being jealous of what others can do, thank the Lord for the talents He has given you and use them to praise Him.

In this passage God is teaching Miriam, Aaron and the children of Israel not to be envious of their leader, Moses. God is using Moses to lead them to the Promised Land. Sometimes we are envious or jealous of the people God has set in authority over us as well. We might not like the way that a teacher does things. We may be angry at our parents because of the Bible study they expect us to do. But then we are forgetting that the Lord is using these people to lead us to the Promised Land—our eternal home with God. So don't become upset at your leaders, but thank God for using them to lead you.

This is really hard to do, isn't it? So how can you stop being envious or jealous of other people? Pray, pray and pray! Ask the Spirit to help you, and thank the Lord for the gifts He has given to you and the gifts He has given to others.

REFLECTION

What is the best way to stop being envious of others?

NUMBERS 14:8

"If the Lord delights in us, then He will bring us into this land and give it to us."

READ NUMBERS 13:32-33, 14:6-9

Twelve spies were sent to check out the land of Canaan before the people of Israel were about to enter it. All twelve came back with this information: the land and the food were very good. They even took some of the fruit back from the land to show Moses. And they also told Moses about the big people that lived in the land—there were giants in the land.

However, the spies didn't agree on everything. They gave two different reports to Moses and the people. Ten of the spies reported that the giants were much too big and there was no way that they would be able to fight against them. "We are like grasshoppers next to those giants," they said. They thought that it was impossible for the Israelites to go into that land and take it over.

But two spies, Caleb and Joshua, said, "Even though the giants are big, we can easily conquer the land because the Lord is with us. We don't need to be afraid, but we just need to trust in the Lord. He will give us the land." These two spies trusted in the promises of the Lord. God had promised them the land, and so they were certain that the Lord would help them to fight against the giants in the land. They were willing to obey the commands of the Lord.

This is exactly how you must live too. You must trust God's promises and have faith in Him. If you want to enter eternal life with Him, then you must obey God's commandments, trusting that God will be with you in everything.

You must realise that you are walking on the path to eternal life every single day. Just like the Israelites were on their way to the Promised Land, you are on your way to eternal life with God. God has promised that He will be with you on the way. Even if things get hard, He will care for you. Remember this and trust in the Lord to look after you.

REFLECTION

Do you remember to trust in the Lord's promises to you?

NUMBERS 14:20

Then the Lord said: "I have pardoned, according to your word."

READ NUMBERS 14:11–25

After the ten spies gave their bad report about the land of Canaan, the people of Israel cried out and wept. They all became scared and didn't want to go into Canaan. Because they didn't trust in God's promises, they didn't believe that He would help them fight against the giants, and so they were scared. God had promised to give them the land, but they didn't believe it anymore.

Because of their unbelief, the Lord punished them. They were not allowed to enter the Promised Land but had to go back to the wilderness for another forty years. This is a warning for us. If we don't trust God's promises, if we don't have faith in the Lord, then we will not enter eternal rest with the Lord either.

But we also read that Moses begged the Lord not to destroy the people, but to be merciful to them. He asked the Lord to forgive their sins.

The Lord listened to Moses and He did forgive them. Yes, the people who didn't trust God were still punished and needed to return to the wilderness for forty years and die there. But the nation of Israel, as a whole, would not be destroyed. In forty years, the people who were left would be able to enter the Promised Land. They were able to do this because Moses pleaded for them before the Lord and the Lord forgave them.

And we know that God forgives our sins as well. No, Moses is not pleading with the Lord to forgive us, but the Lord Jesus Christ Himself is pleading for us. And the Father will certainly hear the Lord Jesus because He died on the cross for us. So if you confess your sins, you have the Lord Jesus Christ pleading for you, asking God to forgive you and to allow you into eternal rest with Him. God will certainly hear the pleas of Jesus—so you have eternal life with the Lord to look forward to!

REFLECTION

Who is pleading for your forgiveness?

NUMBERS 14:44

But they presumed to go up to the mountaintop. Nevertheless, neither the ark of the covenant of the Lord nor Moses departed from the camp.

READ NUMBERS 14:39-45

The people had been given the chance to obey the Lord and go into the Promised Land. However, they had refused to trust in the Lord. But when they heard the punishment of the Lord for this refusal, they mourned and cried. And the next morning some of them got up early and told Moses that they were now willing to go into the Promised Land.

This may seem like a good thing. The people have turned around. They hadn't been willing to obey the Lord before, but now they were. But were they really sorry for not listening to the Lord earlier? No, they weren't. If they had been truly sorry, they wouldn't have woken up early in the morning and gone off to Canaan without their God-appointed leaders and the ark of the Lord. Instead it would have been better if they had put on sackcloth and ashes and gone to the tabernacle in true repentance. They should have confessed their sins to God and asked for forgiveness.

So what happened to them? Because they went off without the Lord's blessing, they were all destroyed by the enemy. They thought that because God had promised them the land, they could still claim it. They thought they could conquer the land on their own, even though they didn't listen to the Lord. But God showed them that it was now too late. They should have obeyed the Lord in the first place. They couldn't just receive God's promises without obeying Him.

We, too, can't expect to receive God's promises without obeying Him. The Lord gives you many times in which you can obey Him. Do you do this? Do you obey God and the parents He has given you? And when you do sin, do you repent and ask God for forgiveness?

When you do truly repent from your sins, God is full of grace and will forgive you. Even though the children of Israel were not allowed into the Promised Land, they were allowed into eternal life. So when we repent, God forgives us and we are allowed into eternal life too.

REFLECTION

Why were the Israelites destroyed when they went to Canaan?

NUMBERS 15:20

"You shall offer up a cake of the first of your ground meal as a heave offering"

READ NUMBERS 15:1-10, 17-21

As you read these verses from Numbers 15, you may think, *Why is it so important to read about all these offerings and sacrifices as we don't need to make sacrifices today anymore?* But do you know that we can still learn a lot about how the Lord wants us to serve Him from these verses?

Moses had to tell the people that when they entered the Promised Land, these sacrifices were to be a part of their lives. These offerings showed their love and thankfulness to the Lord. God was to be the focus of their worship and praise. Everything was to be centred on God.

We see that the people were told that when they made a loaf of bread, they were to give the first of that bread to the Lord. We know from Leviticus that this was given to the priests. But the point is that they had to *first* give some to the Lord to show their thankfulness and to acknowledge that it was God who gave it to them. It was an everyday reminder to them that everything belonged to the Lord. It also reminded them that they had to depend on the Lord to receive all their blessings.

So what about you? When you open a loaf of bread, do you need to give the first slice to the Lord? When you open a bag of apples, do you need to give the first apple to the Lord? No you don't, but you do need to remember that it is the Lord who gives you all these blessings, and so you need to thank Him for them. And when you're old enough to earn money, always remember to give some to the Lord first, before you use it for yourself.

If you want to live close to the Lord, then you need to show your love for the Lord, you need to trust in the Lord in everything, and you need to thank Him for His many blessings.

REFLECTION

How do you remember that everything you have comes from God?

NUMBERS 15:25

"So the priest shall make atonement for the whole congregation of the children of Israel, and it shall be forgiven them.

READ NUMBERS 15:22-31

Because the LORD was preparing the people for their entrance into the Promised Land, He told Moses to tell the people that they had to remember that God is a holy God. But the people of Israel were sinful. How could sinful people live with a holy God? That's why the LORD told Moses how they had to deal with their sins.

It was possible for the people to sin unintentionally. But even if the sin was an accident, our holy God was angered by that and so they had to make sacrifices for these sins.

Sometimes the people sinned, but afterwards they were sorry for their sins. Also then they could make sacrifices, and God would forgive them. Think of King David who sinned by killing Uriah. That sin wasn't an accident at all. But David was very sorry for that sin and so he could make sacrifices for that sin, and his holy God forgave him.

But there were also sins that the people did on purpose. They knew that they were sinning, but they didn't care, and they just kept on sinning. They weren't sorry for these sins. The LORD said that these people couldn't continue to live in the Promised Land with Him. His holiness is too great to live in the midst of sin. And so such people needed to be cut off from the rest.

What about us? How can we continue to live as God's covenant children? Every day we sin. And God is just as holy today as He was in Moses' days. And He hates sin just as much today as He did then.

It's only because of Jesus' death on the cross that we can live with God. Forgiveness through Jesus allows us to continue to live as God's children. So don't ignore your sins. Don't think that your sins don't matter. They matter very much. Holy God hates your sins. But the LORD also offers you His love and forgiveness in Jesus Christ. Tell the LORD how sorry you are for your sins and He will forgive you. And you may continue to live in covenant love with Him.

REFLECTION

How can we as sinful people live with a holy God?

NUMBERS 15:38

"Tell them to make tassels on the corners of their garments throughout their generations, and to put a blue thread in the tassels of the corners."

READ NUMBERS 15:37-41

The children of Israel received many commands about how they were to live in the Promised Land. One of those commands was that they needed to put tassels on all of their clothes. They had to put blue thread in these tassels.

Do you know what tassels are? They are bits of thread or wool bundled together and hung at the bottom of clothes. This might seem like a strange command, but the Lord tells us why they had to do this. These tassels were a daily reminder to the people that they had to obey the commandments of the Lord. As they were walking along during the day, the people would look down to see where they were putting their feet. When they looked down, they would see these blue tassels hanging on the bottom of their clothing. And when they saw them, it would remind them that they were God's special people and they had to obey God's commandments.

They had to include a blue thread because the colour blue was used to show God's presence. The veil that lead into the Holy Place in the tabernacle was blue to show that God was there. And so the blue in the tassel reminded them of God as well.

You can imagine the children in those days might have asked their dads and mums why they had to wear these tassels. And their parents could tell them it was to remind them to always obey the Lord.

Even though we don't wear tassels on our clothes today, we must remember that the Lord always wants us to obey His commandments as well. We should not just do our own thing and ignore what God wants us to do. We have to be careful to obey the Lord. We can't say, "as long as I love the Lord, as long as my heart is in the right place, it doesn't matter what I do." It matters very much what we do. God wants us to obey and follow Him.

REFLECTION

How can you show that you love and obey the Lord in the clothes you wear, the language you use, the games you play, and in everything you do?

There is therefore now no condemnation to those who are in Christ Jesus

ROMANS 8:1A

MATTHEW 5:3-4

"Blessed are the poor in spirit, for theirs is the kingdom of heaven. Blessed are those who mourn, for they shall be comforted."

READ MATTHEW 5:1-10

What does it mean to be blessed? To be blessed by God means that you have the favour of God. It means that you experience joy and peace in God. In these verses, Jesus tells us how we can be blessed, and how we will be happy in the Lord. He's not telling us how to become a Christian. We are already children of God. But He is telling us how we must live as Christians.

As God's children, we should know that we are poor in spirit. A poor person has nothing: no money, no goods—nothing. Jesus uses this word 'poor' and tells us we must be poor in spirit. This means we know that we have nothing in our own hearts with which to serve God. From ourselves we can't go about our day acting in a Christian way. If we know this, then we are blessed by God, because then we will ask God to help us serve Him in this life, as we live in God's kingdom.

But as children of God's kingdom, we still sin all the time. Jesus tells us that we are blessed if we see these sins and if they really make us sad. We must hate the sins that we do every day. They must really upset us, knowing that we are sinning against God. If you say, "Ah, it doesn't matter if I lie a bit, everyone else does," or, "It doesn't matter if I don't work hard at school because the teachers won't notice," then you are not mourning over your sins, but you are making excuses. Or if you are more worried about being caught for the things you've done wrong, rather than thinking about how your sins anger God, then you are also not truly sorry for your sins. But Jesus says that when you truly mourn over your sins, then you will be blessed and comforted because then you will know that you are forgiven in Christ.

May you indeed know how wicked you are, repent of your sins and turn to God for forgiveness. Then you will be blessed.

REFLECTION

How must you live as a child of God?

MATTHEW 5:6

"Blessed are those who hunger and thirst for righteousness, for they shall be filled."

READ MATTHEW 5:2-10

Have you ever felt really hungry? You may not have eaten for quite some time and your stomach told you that it needed some food. Without food you can't live, can you? That's why your body gets hungry when it hasn't had food for a long time. You need that food to stay alive. In the same way you also need water to stay alive. If you don't drink, you get really thirsty.

When Jesus told His disciples that they must hunger and thirst for righteousness, He was telling them that they must really want righteousness, and must seek it always, because God's people cannot live without righteousness. Righteousness is essential for life. We need righteousness to live.

What is this righteousness that we must desire? We must long to be free from sin. We must hunger for the forgiveness of sins. We must desire to live close to the Lord. We must want God's grace and love to fill our lives. We must hunger and thirst for God Himself. We must long to live a life in which we obey God.

Jesus promises us that if we hunger and thirst for these things, then we will be filled. We will receive God's love and forgiveness, His grace and care. God always fills His hungry children. But you must also keep hungering, keep wanting, keep asking for more of God's love and grace. And He will keep filling you with His love, grace and forgiveness. Just like a fountain keeps pouring water into a stream, so God will continue to fill you.

It sounds strange, doesn't it? We need to keep being hungry, while at the same time the Lord will keep filling us. How can we be hungry at the same time as we are being filled? It's a little bit like a box of chocolates. You eat one and you keep wanting more and more. And yet the one chocolate you did have tasted great. So, while the chocolate satisfies you, you continue to want more and more. In the same way, although God continuously fills us, we should never stop seeking righteousness.

REFLECTION

What must we be hungry and thirsty for?

MATTHEW 5:7-9

"Blessed are the merciful... blessed are the pure in heart... blessed are the peacemakers"

READ MATTHEW 5:1-10

Are you merciful? Are you pure in heart, a peacemaker? What does it even mean to be these things? Jesus tells us that as His forgiven children we should be these things.

To be merciful means to be forgiving of others, to be caring and kind. So, when you are angry at your friend who has just said something very nasty to you, don't respond in anger, but remember how many times you have said the wrong thing to others. Remember that you are forgiven by God. Remember that God is willing to forgive your friend, and so you must be willing to forgive your friend as well. You can't do this in your own strength. In and of yourself, you would just want to remain angry, but through the power of God working in you, God will give you the mercy you need to show this love and forgiveness.

Being pure in heart means you want to serve God completely—with your whole life. Happiness isn't the most important thing for you, but God is. So, don't try and find happiness in toys, videos, friends, games or sport. Don't try and be the most popular person, but focus on serving the Lord. If you are focused on serving the Lord and finding your happiness in Him, you can wake up in the morning as a joyful person. God has cleansed your heart and will help you serve Him throughout the day. Begin your day by reading from the Bible. Listen to God's words to you. Pray to the Lord and ask Him to give you a pure heart, and then go about your day.

As a peacemaker you will not try to argue with people but will be willing to make peace. You will pray for those who do wrong things to you. You will want to sort through arguments with others and forgive each other.

As children of God's kingdom, He will help you live in this way.

REFLECTION

What does it mean to be pure in heart?

MATTHEW 5:13

You are the salt of the earth, but if the salt loses its flavour, how shall it be seasoned?

READ MATTHEW 5:13-16

In these verses, Jesus is talking to the children of His kingdom. He is talking to His disciples, the New Testament church. He is talking to His covenant children.

Jesus tells them that they are the salt of the earth and the light of the world. Notice that Jesus doesn't tell them that they have to be the salt and the light, but that they already are the salt and light. Jesus has made them the new Israel; they are His special covenant people. Jesus has made them part of His kingdom. And just like Adam, Noah and Abram were God's special people, set apart to be a light in the dark world, so the New Testament people are lights in this world.

Through us, God's people, God wants the world to be able to see His work and His kingdom. Through the church, God makes sure that people can see His work in this dark world.

God isn't telling us here that He wants us to talk to others about the Lord and by doing that we will become the salt and the light. God has already made us salt and light. That's who we are. He has taken us out of this dark world and made us His light.

Now that we are salt and light, we have to live as salt and light. Salt that isn't salty is useless and can be thrown away, and light that is hidden is also useless. It can't light up a room if it is hidden. Jesus explains in the rest of the Sermon on the Mount how we can live as this salt and light.

But here already He wants us to know that we are the salt and light of this world. In the things we do, in how we speak and in what we play, we must show that we belong to the light, the King of the earth. It must be seen in the way that we act that we are Jesus Christ's salt and light. This will then give glory to God.

REFLECTION

What does it mean that you are the salt and light of the earth?

MATTHEW 5:17

"Do not think that I came to destroy the Law or the Prophets. I did not come to destroy but to fulfil."

READ MATTHEW 5:17-20

Have you ever filled a glass with water right to the brim? It was so full that you couldn't fit another drop of water into it. This is what the word fulfil means: to make completely full.

Jesus tells the disciples that He came not to destroy the law but to fulfil it. He doesn't want His disciples to think that he is getting rid of all the Old Testament laws.

Jesus says, "Don't think that at all. I haven't come to destroy the law and prophets, but to fulfil them." The prophets all preached about the coming of a Saviour. They talked about a suffering servant who would be punished for the sins of His people. The laws and sacrifices all pointed to blood needing to be shed so that the people could be saved.

And now Jesus says, "I am the one who has come to fill all these promises." If Christ hadn't come, then these Old Testament promises would still be empty. But Jesus has filled them. And now Jesus wants us to focus on Him and the work He is doing. If a jar is filled to the brim with gold, you will focus on the gold and not the jar. And so, we must focus on Christ and His work.

But there are still more promises in the Bible that haven't been fulfilled yet. God promises us a new heaven and a new earth, when there will be no more death or pain or crying. Jesus tells us that every single promise will be fulfilled. Christ is still working in heaven for us. That's what Jesus means by jot or tittle. A jot and a tittle were the tiniest dots of the Greek alphabet. So, Jesus is saying that even the smallest promises will not be forgotten. Every single promise of God will be fulfilled in Christ!

REFLECTION

What does it mean that Jesus fulfilled the law and prophets?

MATTHEW 5:22

"But I say to you that whoever is angry with his brother without a cause shall be in danger of the judgment."

READ MATTHEW 5:21-26

Why do you think God hates murder or killing? Do you think it is just because we need to be nice people? Of course we do need to be nice, but God hates murder because He is the God of life. God has created people to have a special relationship with Him. People have been created in the image of God. This means that we are God's representatives here on earth. A representative is someone who does things in the place of someone else. For example, the king has representatives in different countries to carry out the work that he wants done. So, God created us as His image bearers, as His representatives, so that we can look after the earth as He wants us to.

That is why God says we may not murder. Murdering is killing God's representative, killing God's image bearer. But murder is even more than that. It starts in our hearts. Hating someone is the beginning of murder.

Even being angry at someone else is murder in your heart and deserves punishment, Jesus says. We all get angry at others from time to time, don't we? But when we are angry, it is usually selfish on our part. We're angry because they took the book we wanted. We're angry because they didn't do what we wanted them to do. But then we are angry at God's image bearer, the person God created to represent Him on earth.

Jesus says that we may not call our brothers or sisters "Raca" or "fool." To say "Raca" to someone is like calling them an idiot. It's like saying that they have no brains, that they are stupid. Again, then we are attacking God who gives people brains.

Christ Jesus never murdered anyone and was never wrongly angry at others. He obeyed this commandment perfectly. And because of His obedience we are forgiven when we do sin against this commandment. Christ has also changed our hearts and will help us as we try not to get angry, hate others, or call people names.

REFLECTION

Why is anger and name calling bad?

MATTHEW 5:37

"But let your 'Yes' be 'Yes' and your 'No', 'No.'"

READ MATTHEW 5:33-37

Is everything that you say true? Do you always do what you say that you will do? Do you sometimes lie? Maybe just a little lie?

Jesus teaches us that we should always tell the truth. Everything that we say should be truthful. Even a little lie is still a lie, and not the truth.

Jesus speaks about swearing, or oaths. An oath is a strong promise. The purpose of an oath is to call on someone greater than yourself to say that your words are the truth. God Himself made oaths sometimes and that was to assure His people that He really would do what He had promised. After Abraham had been about to offer up Isaac, God made an oath to Abraham. He said, "By myself I have sworn." This was to make sure Abraham knew that God would certainly keep His promises, because God Himself is true. So, oaths were used to make sure the truth was always told. The people also made oaths sometimes in the Old Testament. This meant that they would certainly do what they had promised, that they would only speak the truth.

During Jesus' days the leaders of the people were using oaths, not to tell the truth, but to tell lies. For example, they would swear by the gold of the temple, but since it wasn't really the temple or God Himself, they didn't keep the promise. So, in these verses Jesus told them that everything actually belongs to the Lord, so if they made an oath by the temple, or by Jerusalem, or by their hair, it made no difference because everything belongs to the Lord anyway.

Instead, Jesus told them, that they should always tell the truth. Whenever they promised to do something, they should intend to do what they said they would do. They should never tell lies.

And we should do the same. We belong to Christ, who always told the truth. And so, we must always tell the truth as well. People should know that Christians are truthful people.

REFLECTION

Why is it important to always tell the truth?

MATTHEW 5:44

"But I say to you, love your enemies."

READ MATTHEW 5:43-48

In the Old Testament, God had chosen His people Israel. They were God's covenant children. And the Lord had instructed the Israelites to destroy all their enemies. To keep their covenant relationship with the Lord, they needed to destroy all the people who went against them.

In these verses Jesus tells the disciples that now that His kingdom has come, this battle has become a spiritual battle. We no longer need to destroy our enemies as the Old Testament people did, but now Jesus teaches us to deal with our enemies differently. We must love our enemies. Love here means to serve the other person and to try and help them.

Yes, there are still enemies of God today. Many people don't believe in the Lord and some people even persecute Christians. Maybe you've had people say nasty things to you because you are a Christian. Jesus tells us to be loving to these people and to pray for them. Show kindness and pray that they too will come to faith in God.

Why do we need to love our enemies in this way? Jesus says, "Because you are sons and daughters of your Father in heaven." Through the work of Jesus Christ, you now belong to this kingdom. By grace you are God's adopted child. Now show that you are God's child by showing the same love to others as He shows to them. The Lord is very patient with the unbelievers. He keeps sending them sunshine and rain to give them time to repent and turn to Him. So we too must be kind and patient with the enemies of God.

This will not always be easy. It certainly wasn't easy for people who were persecuted when thrown to lions or burnt at the stake. And yet some of them prayed for their persecutors as they were dying. And it may not always be easy for you. But you are God's child, so He will help you to love your enemies and pray for them.

REFLECTION

What does it mean to love your enemies?

MATTHEW 6:5

"And when you pray, you shall not be like the hypocrites."

READ MATTHEW 6:5-9

What are your prayers like? How should you pray? When Jesus was preaching the Sermon on the Mount, He told His listeners some things about praying. The first thing Jesus said was, "When you pray, do not be like the hypocrites." They prayed so that they could impress others. They wanted all the people around them to see how good they were and how great their prayers sounded. They were not really praying to God.

Jesus tells us not to be like that. God does not need to be impressed by you. God does not want your prayers to look good to others, but He simply wants you to speak to Him from the heart. Tell God what you are thinking, without trying to impress others.

Jesus then also warns us not to use vain repetitions as the heathens do. This means that God does not want us to think that we must have long prayers with lots of fancy words. Again, God is not interested in lots of fancy words, but He is interested in what is in your heart. He wants to have a loving relationship with you and so wants to hear what you are thinking.

Just like a little child will crawl up onto his dad's lap and talk to him, so God wants us to come close to Him and talk to Him. God loves us. He sent His Son, the Lord Jesus Christ, to die on the cross so that He could be our Father.

What a blessing it is that we can call God our Father. He is not a Father to everyone. He is Father for His children only. And you are His child. You belong to Him because Jesus Christ died on the cross for you. Jesus tells us that He is the only way to the Father. So if you believe in Jesus Christ as your Lord and Saviour, then God is your Father.

Then when you pray, pray to your Father not with lots of fancy-sounding words and long prayers, but from deep within your heart speak to your loving Father.

REFLECTION

What is important when you pray?

MATTHEW 6:21

"For where your treasure is, there your heart will be also."

READ MATTHEW 6:19-24

Do you have any treasures? Treasures are things that are very precious to you, things that you love and wouldn't like to lose. In these verses, Jesus tells us to lay up for ourselves treasures in heaven and not on earth. What does He mean? How can we lay up treasures in heaven?

There are two types of treasures that we can have. Earthly treasures are things like money, stuff, toys, food, friends, health, and freedom. All of these things are here for a little while, but they all disappear. Jesus says that moth and rust destroy these things. Your clothes grow old and need to be thrown out. Your money gets used up. Your friends can change. Earthly treasures keep changing and we can't keep any of them forever.

But heavenly treasures are things that don't change. They always stay the same. These treasures are things like God Himself, being God's child, having forgiveness of sins, and calling God our Father.

To get treasures on earth we have to work hard. Gaining money and clothes and friends is all hard work. But laying up treasures in heaven is not hard work. It is a gift from God. It is God's grace. He gives you heavenly treasures. He gives you His Word, the Bible. He gives you His love and righteousness. He forgives your sins. These treasures are already yours as a child of God.

Jesus tells us to focus our eyes on these treasures. Just like the headlights of a car show the way it's going, our eyes show the direction we are headed. If we are focused on and looking at earthly things, then our life is nothing more than these things which will disappear.

But if your eyes are focused on the heavenly treasures that God has already given you—His love, His forgiveness, His grace—then you are traveling with God already today. As you go about your day, doing schoolwork or playing with your friends, always remember God's love for you.

REFLECTION

What things are important to you?

MATTHEW 6:34

"Therefore do not worry about tomorrow."

READ MATTHEW 6:25-34

Do you ever have times when you struggle with your faith? You might have times when you aren't sure if the Lord listens to you. You might sometimes struggle with your sins and feel like you can't really be forgiven. Maybe you sometimes wonder, "Did Jesus really die for me?"

Over the years, many people have asked the same question. If you think these things sometimes, you are not alone. There is even an article in our confessions that says believers have times of doubt and questions.

Here in Matthew 6, Jesus Christ calls His disciples "people of little faith." Even the disciples who lived and worked with Jesus doubted sometimes. So just because you sometimes struggle to believe that God is listening to you, don't think that you are not His child.

But what should you do when you feel this way? You need to keep reading and studying the Bible, including this passage in Matthew. Jesus reminds us that God is in control of our whole life. Even when we don't feel it, God is still there caring for us. He is our heavenly Father. He loves you and will always care for you. If He cares for the birds and the flowers, He will care for you, His child. He is working through everything in your life even if it doesn't feel like it.

Jesus said, "Don't worry about tomorrow." Christ wants you to trust the Father. He knows what you need today, and He will give you His grace for everything that you need today. Tomorrow He will help you again, so leave tomorrow in the Lord's hands. Instead focus on today and serving the Lord today. Seek His kingdom. Walk by faith, and God your loving, heavenly Father will be with you. He never grows weary or tired, but always looks after His children.

So, when you start struggling with your faith and doubting God, read His Word. See in there all His promises to care for you His child and to forgive you for Jesus' sake.

REFLECTION

What should you do if you start doubting God's love for you?

MATTHEW 7:15

"Beware of false prophets, who come to you in sheep's clothing."

READ MATTHEW 7:15-20

In these verses, Jesus gives a strong warning, and it is important that we listen to His warning. Jesus doesn't want to scare us, but He wants us to be warned about false prophets. Jesus tells us that there are false prophets and that they can be difficult to see. Just like you might be tricked into thinking that a thistle is a fig tree when you see it from a distance, so false prophets are hard to recognise.

So how can we tell the difference between a false prophet, (especially when they use some of the Bible in their preaching) and someone who is actually preaching God's Word? A true preacher will preach that Jesus Christ is the only way to salvation. Jesus Christ will be the centre of all that they are teaching. False preachers may tell you to work harder, to have more faith and then you will be saved. But the only way to be saved is through Jesus Christ. And a true preacher will preach that message.

A true preacher will also teach us that true peace and happiness can only be found in Jesus Christ. Because of Jesus' perfect obedience and death on the cross, we can now be God's children again. He loves us because of Jesus' work. And that's the only thing that can give us true peace and happiness. False prophets may tell us that we can find peace in ourselves. They may tell us to look at the good in ourselves, but that message is a lie. Only when we know that our sins are forgiven in Jesus Christ can we be truly at peace.

Jesus also tells us that a preacher will be known by his fruit. Can you see a love for God, patience, kindness, mercy, and other godly fruits in the life of the preacher and those who listen to him?

Listen carefully to this warning that Jesus gives to us. Always read the Bible and study it closely. And always turn to Jesus alone for your salvation and happiness.

REFLECTION

Why does Jesus warn us against false prophets?

MATTHEW 7:21

"Not everyone who says to Me, 'Lord, Lord' shall enter the kingdom of heaven."

READ MATTHEW 7:21-23

In these verses Jesus is speaking to the Jews, the members of the church of that day. Jesus says that some of them would hear these words from Him on the final judgement day: "I never knew you." Does reading this make you a bit worried?

But Jesus doesn't want to scare us here. He wants to welcome us into heaven. And that's why He gives us a warning in these verses. Many of Jesus' listeners thought that because they were great grandchildren of Abraham they would be saved. They even did a lot of good things in Jesus' name. They thought that these things would surely save them. It would be the same as us believing that just because we are members of the church or because our parents believe we will be saved.

But Jesus tells us that we all need to have a living faith. We can't just say to Jesus, "I sang praises to you in church, and I gave collection money. Surely that will be enough to save me." Jesus says that we have to do the will of our heavenly Father. We have to truly love the Lord.

So how do you know if you have a living faith? Do you truly love the Lord? Do you want to talk to Him in prayer? Do you ask the Lord to be with you, and do you thank the Lord for His love for you? Is God important in your life? Are you truly sorry for your sins and do you ask the Lord to forgive you? Do you want to obey the Lord? Do you want God to be glorified by the things that you do? Do you realise that you are a sinner and can only be saved because of Christ's work?

If you love the Lord and go to Him with your sins, if you know that Jesus alone can save you and you ask Him to do this, then you can know that you are safe in the arms of Jesus. Then He will welcome you into heaven with Him.

REFLECTION

Why is saying, "Lord, Lord," not enough to save us?

MATTHEW 13:44

"Again, the kingdom of heaven is like treasure hidden in a field, which a man found and hid; and for joy over it he goes and sells all that he has and buys that field."

READ MATTHEW 13:44-52

What is God's kingdom? When someone speaks about the kingdom of heaven, or when you pray, "Your kingdom come," what does it actually mean? Do you belong to the kingdom of heaven? Jesus says that the kingdom of heaven is like a treasure that a man found and hid in a field. The man sold everything that he had so that he could buy the field that the treasure was hidden in.

This can all sound a bit confusing, so it is important to understand what the kingdom of heaven is. God's kingdom is wherever God is reigning. It is the place where God is King. It is where God's will is being obeyed.

God's kingdom is already here. You are part of that kingdom if Christ is ruling your heart. You and your family and others in your church who love the Lord are all part of this kingdom.

It is something very special, very precious, to belong to God's kingdom. Not everybody is part of that kingdom, but only those who are God's special covenant people. The man in the parable found a treasure. A treasure is something very precious and very special. This man knew that he had found something special, and that is why he sold everything that he had so that he could buy the field that the treasure was in. His house and his clothes and his business would probably all have been very important to this man. But now that he found this treasure, all those other things weren't that important anymore. He could get rid of all of them, just so he could have the treasure.

And that's exactly how precious God's kingdom must be to us. Nothing is more important than God's kingdom. Your clothes, your friends, your family, your toys, your home—none of these should be as important to you as the kingdom of heaven. This means that if there are things that are too important to you, or sins in your life that you enjoy, you must get rid of them so you can focus on your treasure—on serving the Lord.

REFLECTION

Are you part of the kingdom of heaven?

MATTHEW 18:3

"Unless you are converted and become as little children," you will by no means enter the kingdom of heaven.

READ MATTHEW 18:1-5

When the disciples were arguing about who was the greatest in the kingdom of heaven, Jesus took a little child to Himself and said, "Unless you become as little children, you will not enter the kingdom of heaven." Does Jesus mean that children don't sin much and so we must all be like innocent children to be part of God's kingdom? I'm sure you know that you actually sin a lot, so that can't be true.

So what does Jesus mean? Children are really the littlest of people. Children are dependent on their parents. You can't make the big decisions in your family, but your parents do. And you need to trust them and others in authority over you. You need to trust that they will do what is best for you, even if it doesn't always feel like it is good.

In the same way we don't become a part of God's kingdom because we are important and deserve to be part of God's kingdom. We must be humble, or the littlest people, to be part of God's kingdom. We can only be part of God's kingdom if we depend on God for everything. We need God's forgiveness, mercy and grace. That's how we are part of God's kingdom. It's all God's grace and love. He has chosen us to be one of His children. Now out of thankfulness for this grace of God, we need to be humble by being the least.

This is very hard for us to do. So often we want to be the most important person, or the person who is first or gets the best marks. But that is not how we should act as God's children. We are already part of God's kingdom, so we must show love and kindness to others remembering that we are nothing more than dust held together by God. If it wasn't for God's love for us, we wouldn't even be one of His children. So always remember to show love to the people around you.

REFLECTION

Why did Jesus say that we need to be like children?

MATTHEW 21:12

Then Jesus went into the temple of God and drove out all those who bought and sold in the temple.

READ MATTHEW 21:12-14

The day after Jesus had ridden a colt through the streets of Jerusalem and all the people had called out, "Hosanna to the Son of David," He went into the temple. And what did Jesus see in the temple? He saw lots of tables and animals and money. The outer court of the temple was being used to sell animals for the sacrifices in the temple.

According to the Old Testament, the people who had to make a long trip to Jerusalem were allowed to buy animals for their sacrifices in Jerusalem. But this should have happened outside the temple somewhere, and not in the outer court. The outer court was supposed to be a place where the Gentiles could come to pray to God. This was an area that the Lord had put aside so that people who were not Jews could still come and pray to God.

And when Jesus walked in there, He saw many people buying and selling. And they were also selling the animals for a very high price. They were charging far too much for the animals. When Jesus saw this, He was very angry. How could the Gentiles come and pray in this marketplace? And so, Jesus went around the outer court and turned over all the tables, throwing all the money on the ground. This would have taken a while to do because it was a large area. Yet no one stopped the Lord Jesus. He had great authority that no one was able to stop.

Jesus said to the people, "It is written, My house shall be called a house of prayer, but you have made it a den of thieves." Jesus wanted to make this area a place of prayer again. Jesus was about to go to the cross. He was about to make a sacrifice for all His people, from every nation. Jesus was about to restore our relationship with God. And that's what Jesus showed by clearing out the temple's outer court so that the Gentiles could also have a place of prayer.

REFLECTION

Why did Jesus clear out the outer court of the temple?

MATTHEW 25:13

"Watch therefore, for you know neither the day nor the hour in which the Son of Man is coming."

READ MATTHEW 25:1-13

The parable of the five wise and five foolish virgin ladies is very well known. But what is the Lord teaching us in this parable? The Lord Jesus is telling us that we don't know when He will return a second time, and so we must always be ready for that great day.

Are you ready to meet the Lord? What does it mean to be ready for Christ's return? That's what Jesus tells us in this parable. We must always be ready for Christ's return, just like the five ladies who were well prepared, even though they knew it could take a long time for the bridegroom to come. This means that every day you must serve the Lord. Read your Bible and pray every day. Love the Lord and serve Him in all you do.

This parable is not meant to frighten you. It is not meant to make you wonder whether the Lord will close the door of heaven to you on the day He returns. Sometimes you may even think about that and be a bit frightened. But then remember God's promises to you. You are His covenant child. He has promised you forgiveness of sins. He has promised you eternal life with Him. All these promises are in the Bible, so never doubt them.

Because of God's love for you, He looks at the work Jesus has done for you, and even though you aren't good enough in and of yourself, He opens the door of heaven for you. If you love the Lord with all your heart and really want to serve Him, then you are ready for Christ's return. If you trust in Christ to forgive your sins every day, then you are ready for this wonderful day.

And what a great day it will be. On that day, we will be changed in the twinkling of an eye to receive our glorious body, and from then on we will live eternally with the Lord. We will be without sin, and perfectly happy.

REFLECTION

How are you ready for Christ's return?

MATTHEW 26:67

Then they spat in His face and beat Him.

READ MATTHEW 26:57-68

Just before Jesus was crucified, He stood in front of the Jewish leaders. Because the Jewish leaders had studied the Old Testament well, they should have known all about Christ and the saving work He had come to do. But instead they were Christ's enemies. They were trying to accuse Christ of doing something wrong so that they could kill Him by crucifying Him on a cross. They decided that Jesus deserved to be killed because they believed He had blasphemed. They all spat on Jesus and beat Him. They struck Him with the palms of their hands.

These actions of Jesus' enemies show what was actually living in their hearts. They hated Jesus Christ. They didn't believe that He was the Christ. They didn't believe that God had sent Him, and that He was God Himself. They didn't believe that He had power over all things. They didn't believe that He had authority and that they should have been listening to Him and obeying Him. Instead of obeying, they spat on Him and hit Him.

Their actions also point to what actually lives in our hearts. Our hearts are also filled with sin. If it wasn't for the working of the Holy Spirit in our lives, we would hate Jesus in just the same way. Actually when you choose to sin on purpose, it is as if you are spitting into Jesus' face. When you decide not to obey your parents as God told you to, then it is as if you are beating Jesus.

And Jesus took all of this abuse without saying anything. He didn't deserve to be beaten, because He never did anything wrong. It is actually we who deserve to be punished. We deserve to be punished by God in a much harder way. We deserve hell. And yet the wonderful news is that we don't have to be punished, we don't have to go to hell, because Christ was punished in our place. He went to the cross with all of our sins, so that we will never have to be punished.

REFLECTION

Why do we not need to be punished anymore?

TITUS 3:5

Not by works of righteousness which we have done, but according to His mercy He saved us.

READ TITUS 3:3-8

You serve the Lord, don't you? That means that you believe the Bible, and you love the Lord. You believe that Jesus died on the cross for you, and you want to live for the Lord every day. But how can you know that you will always serve the Lord? Do you sometimes wonder if you will still be serving the Lord when you are an adult? Do you sometimes doubt whether Christ died for you?

The new believers that Paul writes to in this letter to Titus would have had the same thoughts. They too may have wondered how they could keep serving the Lord and not go back to their sinful lifestyles.

But God tells us in these verses that we can be sure of our salvation because our love for the Lord doesn't come from ourselves. We serve the Lord because God has chosen us, and Christ has come and worked in us. The Holy Spirit has been poured out and is working in your heart. It is only because of Christ's work and death and the working of the Holy Spirit that you belong to the Lord. You serve the Lord because He chose you and made you love Him. This is a miracle, but it is true.

If you look at your own life and see your sins and your doubts, and then wonder if you are good enough to belong to God, the answer is this: no, you are not good enough. Verse 5 says that our works can't save us. But thankfully we are saved because of God's work in us. That is exactly why Christ had to come to earth. He came to save us because we can't save ourselves.

So whenever you have doubts, or wonder if you are saved, go to God's Word and read about God's love for sinners like you. Know that your works can't save you, but God's work in you is what makes you love and serve Him. God will never, ever let go of His own children!

REFLECTION

How can you be sure that you are saved?

INDEX

OLD TESTAMENT

Genesis 3:9-15	72	Joshua 2:8-15	116
Genesis 4:3-8	73	Joshua 3:1-6	117
Genesis 4:16-26	74	Joshua 3:7-9	118
Genesis 6:11-22	75	Joshua 3:9-13	119
Genesis 7:11-16	76	Joshua 4:1–7	120
Genesis 12:1-9	77	Joshua 5:1-9	121
Genesis 12:10–20	78	Joshua 5:13-15	122
Genesis 14:17–24	79	Joshua 6:15-18	123
Genesis 15:1–6	80	Joshua 6:26-27	40
Genesis 15:7–21	81	Joshua 23:1-8	124
Genesis 16:1-13	82	Judges 2:1-5	126
Genesis 17:15-22	83	Judges 2:7-10	127
Genesis 18:1-15	84	Judges 2:11-19	128
Genesis 27:18-29	85	Judges 3:7-11	129
Genesis 37:23-28	86	Judges 4:1-3, 17-22	130
Exodus 2:23-25	2	Judges 6:1-10	131
Exodus 3:7-12	3	Judges 6:11-16	132
Exodus 3:13-17	4	Judges 6:17-24	133
Exodus 4:10-17	5	Judges 6:25-32	134
Exodus 7:8-12	6	Judges 6:36-40	135
Exodus 13:3-10	7	Judges 7:1-8	136
Exodus 14:21–26	8	Judges 7:22-8:3	137
Leviticus 1:3-9	154	Judges 7:22-8:3	138
Numbers 6:22-27	218	1 Samuel 16:6-13.	90
Numbers 9:1-14	219	2 Samuel 9:1-13	159
Numbers 9:15-23	220	2 Samuel 18:9-15	160
Numbers 11:1-15, 31-35	221	2 Samuel 23:13-17	161
Numbers 12	222	1 Kings 3:5-9	39
Numbers 13:32-33, 14:6-9	223	1 Kings 16:34	40
Numbers 14:11-25	224	2 Chronicles 7:12-15	108
Numbers 14:39–45	225	2 Chronicles 33:10-13	109
Numbers 15:1–10, 17–21	226	Esther 1:1-12	183
Numbers 15:22-31	227	Esther 2:12-18	184
Numbers 15:37–41	228	Esther 3	185
Deuteronomy 6:4-9	27	Esther 4	186
Deuteronomy 11:8-12	28	Esther 5	187
Joshua 1:1-4	114	Esther 6	188
Joshua 1:5-9	115	Esther 7	189

Esther 8:7-14	190	Jonah 1:10-16	95
Esther 9:1-17	191	Jonah 1:17	96
Esther 9:18-31	192	Jonah 2:1-9.	97
Job 19:25-29	41	Jonah 3	98
Job 28:20-28	42	Jonah 4:1-4	99
Job 38:1-11	43	Malachi 3:16-18	214
Psalm 1	9	Malachi 4:1-3	215
Psalm 2	10		
Psalm 27:1-6	26		
Psalm 32	63		
Psalm 37:1-11	64		
Psalm 46	111		
Psalm 50:7-15	112		
Psalm 57	156		
Psalm 62	166		
Psalm 63:1-8	140		
Psalm 73:1-17	147		
Psalm 73:18-28	148		
Psalm 116:1-14	157		
Psalm 139:1-12	35		
Psalm 139:13-16	36		
Psalm 145	88		
Psalm 146	89		
Psalm 147:12-20	1		
Proverbs 3:1-8	194		
Proverbs 4:20-27	195		
Proverbs 15:12-15	196		
Proverbs 27:1-6	197		
Isaiah 44:1-5	202		
Lamentations 5:15-22	152		
Lamentations 5:15-22	153		
Ezekiel 33:1-9	199		
Daniel 2:31–35, 44	176		
Daniel 3:13-18	177		
Daniel 4:1-3, 34-37	178		
Daniel 5:24-30	179		
Daniel 6:10-23	180		
Daniel 9:3-9	181		
Amos 3:1-8	168		
Jonah 1:1-9	94		

NEW TESTAMENT

Matthew 5:1-10	230	John 4:46-53	206
Matthew 5:1-10	232	John 5:1-14, 46-47	207
Matthew 5:2-10	231	John 6:1-14, 51	101
Matthew 5:13-16	233	John 8:1-12	102
Matthew 5:17-20	234	John 9:1-12	208
Matthew 5:21-26	235	John 10:7-10	103
Matthew 5:33-37	236	John 10:10-14	104
Matthew 5:43-48	237	John 11:17-26	105
Matthew 6:5-9	238	John 14: 1-6	106
Matthew 6:19-24	239	John 15:1-8	107
Matthew 6:25–34	240	John 15:9-17	209
Matthew 7:15-20	241	John 19:17-30	210
Matthew 7:21-23	242	John 20:24–29	211
Matthew 12:38-41	96	Acts 1:9-11	91
Matthew 13:44-52	243	Acts 4:8-12	92
Matthew 18:1-5	244	Acts 16:25-34	93
Matthew 21:12-14	245	Romans 4:22-25	141
Matthew 25:1-13	246	Romans 5:19-21, 6:23	143
Matthew 26:57-68	247	Romans 6:1-11	142
Mark 5:1-20	216	Romans 7:14-25	144
Mark 12:41-44	217	Romans 8:18-27	145
Luke 1:5-17	45	Romans 13:11-14	146
Luke 2:25-35	46	1 Corinthians 1:4-9	11
Luke 2:41-52	47	1 Corinthians 10:23-33	12
Luke 5:1-11	48	1 Corinthians 15:56-58	13
Luke 5:12-16	49	2 Corinthians 9:6-15	110
Luke 5:33-39	50	Ephesians 1:1-6	14
Luke 6:1-5	51	Ephesians 2:1-10	16
Luke 9:28-36	52	Ephesians 2:19-22	17
Luke 12:22-34	53	Ephesians 3:14-21	18
Luke 14:16-24	54	Ephesians 4:7-16	19
Luke 14:16-24	55	Ephesians 4:7-16	20
Luke 15:11-32	56	Ephesians 4:25-32	21
Luke 17:5-10	57	Ephesians 5:7-14	22
Luke 17:11-19	58	Ephesians 5:15-21	23
Luke 19:1-10	59	Ephesians 5:19-21	24
Luke 23:13-25	60	Ephesians 6:10-18	25
Luke 24:28-35	61	Philippians 4:1-9	193
John 2:1-11	203	Colossians 1:15-17	170
John 2:13-22	204	Colossians 1:19-23	171

Colossians 2:1-9	172
Colossians 2:16-23	173
Colossians 3:12-17	174
Colossians 4:2-4	175
1 Thessalonians 1:1-4	149
1 Thessalonians 1:2-6	150
2 Thessalonians 1:11-12	167
1 Timothy 6:1-10	151
Titus 3:3–8	248
Hebrews 10:19-25	200
Hebrews 11:1-11	201
James 1:2-8	30
James 1:5-8	31
James 4:13-17	32
James 5:7-8	33
James 5:9–11	34
1 Peter 1:1-9	65
1 Peter 1:13-16	66
1 Peter 1:22-2:3	67
1 Peter 2: 4-8	69
1 Peter 2:4-8	68
1 Peter 5:5-10	70
2 Peter 3:1-9	158
1 John 1:5-7	37
1 John 1:8-10	38
Revelation 3:1-6	162
Revelation 4	163
Revelation 5	164
Revelation 21:9-21	165

www.ingramcontent.com/pod-product-compliance
Lightning Source LLC
Chambersburg PA
CBHW061745070526
44585CB00025B/2803